D1605635

Exchange Rate Regimes

Exchange Rate Regimes

Choices and Consequences

Atish R. Ghosh
Anne-Marie Gulde
Holger C. Wolf

The MIT Press
Cambridge, Massachusetts
London, England

This book was set in Palatino on 3B2 by Asco Typesetters, Hong Kong. Printed and bound in the United States of America.

Library of Congress Cataloging-in-Publication Data

Ghosh, Atish R.
 Exchange rate regimes : choices and consequences / Atish R. Ghosh, Anne-Marie Gulde, Holger C. Wolf.
     p. cm.
 Includes bibliographical references and index.
 ISBN 0-262-07240-8 (alk. paper)
 1. Foreign exchange rates. 2. International finance. I. Gulde, Anne-Marie. II. Wolf, Holger C. III. Title.
HG3851 .G47   2003
332.4′5—dc21   2002026333

To Rudi
In Appreciation

Contents

1   Introduction

Does the choice of exchange rate regime matter? Few questions in international economics have sparked as much debate and yielded as little consensus.

Up until the early 1970s, the issue was, in any case, moot: Countries were not individually free to choose their exchange rate regime, being circumscribed by the prevailing norms of the international monetary order—whether that was the gold standard or the Bretton Woods system. Over the thirty years since the breakdown of Bretton Woods, however, countries have adopted a wide variety of regimes, ranging from dollarization and currency boards to simple pegs and basket pegs, crawling pegs, and target zones to clean and dirty floats. This very proliferation of exchange rate regimes suggests that they must matter for *something*—but exactly what remains an open question. In this book, we try to answer that question.

Our approach is unabashedly empirical. Theory certainly offers many insights—too many, in fact. Such an abundance of possible linkages exists between the exchange rate regime and macroeconomic performance—some offsetting, others reinforcing—that, at a theoretical level, it is difficult to establish any unambiguous relationships at all. Accordingly, in this book, we draw on the experience of some 150 member countries of the International Monetary Fund (IMF) over the past thirty years to address some simple questions. For example, does pegging the exchange rate lead to lower inflation? Are floating exchange rates associated with faster output growth? Are pegged regimes particularly prone to crisis? These (and other) questions must first be answered before one can even hope to tackle the more ambitious question of what is the "optimal" exchange rate regime.

We have written *Exchange Rate Regimes: Choices and Consequences* in the hope that it will appeal to policymakers, professional economists, and academics alike.

We begin with an overview of the evolution of exchange rate regimes and the international monetary system, placing current debates in historical context. In chapter 3, we turn to theory. The literature on exchange rate regimes is vast, but much of it can be organized around a few central themes that constitute the main trade-offs in the choice of exchange rate regime. In the latter half of the chapter, we draw these themes together in a formal model. This part of the chapter may be skipped without losing the gist of the argument. In chapter 4, we ask the (deceptively) simple question of what exactly is meant by a "fixed" (or "pegged") versus a "floating" exchange rate regime, and how one might go about classifying countries.

Chapters 5 and 6 present our main empirical results, relating the exchange rate regime to macroeconomic performance, especially inflation and output growth. These results pertain to long-run economic performance under alternative exchange rate regimes. However, there is also a venerable—and often controversial—tradition of using the exchange rate as a tool for short-term objectives, in particular for achieving disinflation. Whether such exchange rate–based disinflation programs are indeed a magic bullet in the war against inflation—or, as some would contend, a recipe for disaster—is taken up in chapter 7. In the second half of the chapter, we depart from the broad cross-sectional evidence and present three case studies of recent exchange rate–based stabilizations—one of which is generally considered a success, while the other two ended in spectacular collapses. This brings us to the thorny issue of exits and crises.

Whether it is Mexico, Russia, or the East Asian countries, the only time exchange rates seem to make headlines is when a peg collapses and the country is forced to let the exchange rate float. Actually, most transitions between regimes do not take place in the context of a crisis. Nonetheless, one may ask whether some regimes are more prone to crisis, a question we take up in chapter 8. Finally, chapter 9 offers some brief concluding remarks.

This book draws on research we have undertaken over a number of years.[1] Our pursuit of this line of research originated in a suggestion by Jeffrey Frankel to consider the economic impact of publicly known versus secret basket weights.

From this rather narrow question, the project took on a life of its own. Our motivation to pursue the research in this book owes much to the support and encouragement of Rudi Dornbusch. He has been an inspiration to us all. We dedicate this book to his memory.

Over the years that we have worked on these issues, we have presented papers at various conferences and seminars and have received useful comments from many friends and colleagues, too numerous to all be named here. In acknowledging our thanks, we hope that it goes without saying that the views presented in this book are our own, and do not necessarily reflect those of our friends who were kind enough to provide comments (or, indeed, of the institutions to which we are affiliated). Carlo Cottarelli, Menzie Chinn, Sebastian Edwards, Charles Engel, Stanley Fischer, Swati Ghosh, Javier Hamann, Graciela Kaminsky, Peter Kenen, Carmen Reinhart, John Rogers, and Shang-Jin Wei provided incisive comments on earlier research. We are grateful to Siba Das, who helped us assemble the database used in this book, and to Elizabeth Murry, Jane Macdonald, Kathleen Caruso, and Hans Rempel for supporting this endeavor in a manner more forgiving than can rightfully be expected even of an editor. Holger Wolf partly wrote this book while at George Washington University and gratefully acknowledges the support and the spirited discussions with colleagues and students.

We would like to thank Natalie Baumer for carefully reading the entire book, and to Peter Winkler both for his cheerful support and for weighing in against some of our more egregious econ-linguistic excesses. Last but not least, we would like to thank our families, in particular young Lars-Henryk for insisting that his parents (and his "uncle") "stop wasting time, and come and play."

2   A Short History of the International Monetary System

What is past is prologue.

—William Shakespeare, *The Tempest*

"International monetary system" is a term that evokes images of sage deliberation and conscious construction. The best known of those images, the Bretton Woods Agreement, indeed initially shone as an icon of reason and vision. Guided by some of the best intellects in the business—John Maynard Keynes and Harry Dexter White—delegates from forty-five countries set out to craft a postwar order that would banish the monetary chaos that had plagued the interwar period.

Yet Bretton Woods was an exception. Historically, chance played a significant role in the emergence of new international monetary arrangements. Even the venerable classic gold standard reigning between 1880 and the outbreak of World War I might never have come into existence without a simple miscalculation by Sir Isaac Newton, the timely discovery of gold deposits, and Prussia's 1870 defeat of France.

This chapter provides an overview of the various constraints and considerations that influenced the evolution of monetary arrangements among nations. While a historical review soon reveals that the choice of regime has always depended on more than narrowly rational cost-benefit analyses, many of the considerations that were relevant one hundred years ago remain equally valid today. A brief history of the international monetary system thus provides a useful context.[1]

2.1   The Gold Standard: 1880–1914

Mr. Bagehot, than whom there is no higher authority on such a matter, says that there never was, since the world began, so high and massive a brain-power applied to any one question as is applied to financial problems in England.
—Alfred Marshall, Evidence before the Indian Currency Commission (1899)

While no single date marks the emergence of the modern international monetary system, the widespread shift from bimetallic standards to gold in the 1870s and 1880s provides a convenient starting point.[2]

The deflationary pressures generated by the demonetization of silver (and thus, the contraction of world monetary reserves) sparked strong political opposition, perhaps best illustrated by Bryan's refusal to be "crucified upon a cross of gold" during the 1896 U.S. presidential campaign.[3] Eloquence, however, proved no match for economic forces. The gold standard, once entrenched, proved hard to dislodge. Its survival may be attributed to four factors. First, trading nations were discovering the benefits of global standards, whether it was defining the prime meridian or measuring the meter. Setting a standard for trade and payments was a natural complement of those conventions.[4] Second, the fortuitous discovery of the Klondike gold fields in 1896, coupled with advances in mining technology, augmented world gold stocks, easing the deflationary pressures.

Third, downward flexibility of wages and prices (figures 2.1 and 2.2) reduced the costs of the deflationary pressures. Finally, there was no serious challenger to the gold standard: Stabilizing output or reducing unemployment were not yet considered proper policy objectives. This consensus gave the regime much greater credibility than any modern exchange rate peg—with its competing and conflicting objectives—can hope to enjoy.

Textbooks at times depict the classic gold standard as a system of symmetrical adjustment between surplus and deficit countries where central banks, playing by "the rules of the game," would allow gold flows to regulate the money supply, thus enabling the Humeian adjustment mechanism to work its magic.

The practice of monetary policy under the gold standard differed rather starkly from this idealized depiction.[5] Indeed, beyond the

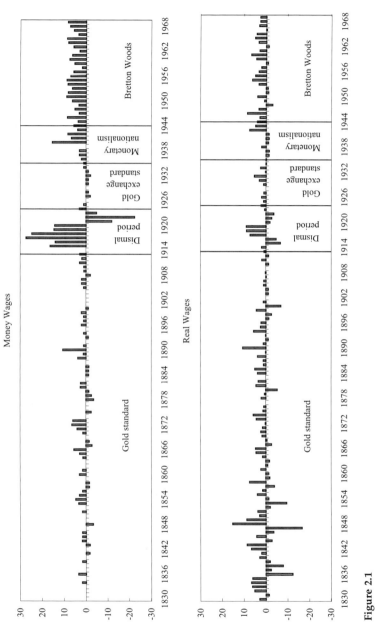

Figure 2.1
Great Britain: money wages and real wages, 1830–1969 (percent change per year)
Source: Mitchell (1991).

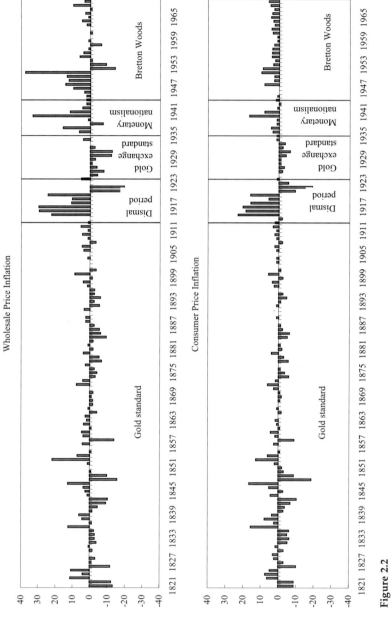

Figure 2.2
Great Britain: Wholesale and consumer prices (percent change per year) 1820–1969
Source: Mitchell (1991).

central focus on maintaining convertibility,[6] there were no established rules of the game (the very term, in fact, dates to the 1920s, long after the demise of the regime).

Central banks were seldom prepared to accept the full consequences of unfettered gold flows. As Arthur Bloomfield (1959) documented in his classic study, it was common practice for central banks to sterilize balance of payments surpluses, while providing additional liquidity during times of financial distress.

It would thus be misleading to portray the classic gold standard as a historical example of establishing credibility through a hard peg to gold. While the gold link conveyed a strong signal, credibility ultimately derived from the absence of any policy objective rivaling the defense of the fixed exchange rate. Freedom from any perceived policy trade-off, in turn, allowed central banks, at least in the core countries, some policy flexibility without risking a loss of credibility.[7]

The three decades of the gold standard were a period of exchange rate stability and rapidly expanding trade and financial linkages. The performance was greatly helped by the stabilizing role played by Great Britain, particularly her readiness to recycle surpluses into foreign loans and investments rather than hoarding gold (Hobson 1914). Sterling assumed an increasingly pivotal role in international transactions, both private and between central banks.[8] Monetary policy in Great Britain thus took on a leadership role, allowing the Bank of England to function as the "invisible conductor" of the system.

Not everything was golden, however. Both real and financial volatility was pronounced. Booms and busts plagued the periphery countries, which suffered frequent shifts in their terms of trade. Figure 2.3, which graphs the growth rate of industrial production and the unemployment rate in Great Britain, illustrates that even the largest and most diversified economy of the day was not immune to pronounced swings. The industrial and financial crises typically did not last long, however. Sharp recessions tended to be followed by dramatic booms. The British unemployment rate, though fluctuating wildly between 2 and 8 percent over most of the gold standard period, was not, on average, especially high. From the perspective of persistent malaise of the 1920s, nostalgia no doubt cast a golden afterglow on the prewar period.

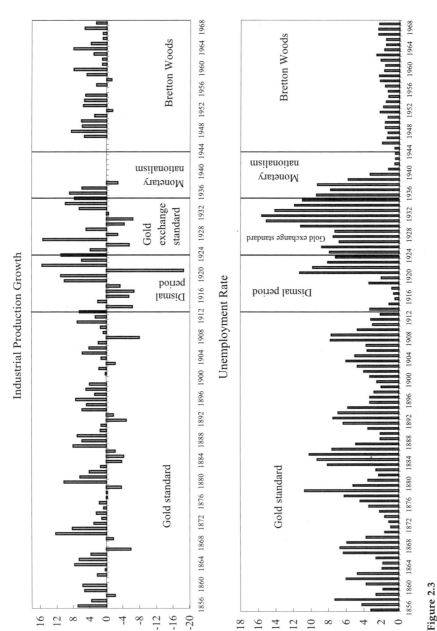

Figure 2.3
Great Britain: industrial production (percent change per year) and unemployment (in percent) 1855–1969
Source: Mitchell (1991).

2.2   The Dismal Period: 1919–1925

Since there's no money, let's make it then.

—Goethe, *Faust*

With the outbreak of hostilities, gold convertibility was immediately restricted through both legal prohibitions and patriotic appeals. Temporary suspensions (albeit not on a systemic scale) were nothing new (Bordo and Schwartz 1994), and there was every expectation that this time, too, the suspension would soon be followed by a return to convertibility at unchanged parities.

The United States, a late entrant to the conflict, incurred fairly minor economic costs and indeed experienced little difficulty in returning to the gold standard at the prewar parity. However, her experience was the exception. The war, lasting far longer than initially expected, forced most European governments to resort to the printing presses for revenue, shifting their monetary systems to de facto paper standards.[9]

The process was extreme in many central European countries, including Germany, where monetization of the deficit culminated in hyperinflation, a trauma coloring German inflation preferences to this day. Hyperinflations were eventually ended by orthodox stabilizations, combining fiscal austerity measures with a return to the gold standard (Dornbusch, Sturzenegger, and Wolf 1990). In central Europe, the return to fixed exchange rates was thus largely influenced by the need to impose discipline and engender confidence— presaging the modern credibility arguments for fixed exchange rates.

France and Great Britain found themselves between the extremes defined by the United States and Germany. Wartime inflation in France had been sufficiently high to rule out a return to the prewar parity. As fiscal stabilization and the accumulation of gold reserves proved elusive, France remained on floating rates for seven unhappy years of rapid credit expansion, high and volatile inflation, and trend depreciation before stabilizing in 1926 at an undervalued exchange rate (Dulles 1929). The experience left a lasting impression on French attitudes that would soon play a role in France's response to gold inflows and later in her reluctance to use expansionary monetary policy to escape the grasp of deflation.[10]

For Great Britain, the cumulative inflation differential vis-à-vis the United States since the beginning of the war made a return to the previous parity difficult, but not impossible. A spirited debate soon arose between advocates of deflation and proponents of devaluation. Champions of returning to gold at the prewar rate argued that devaluation would undermine credibility and harm those on fixed incomes. Establishing the prewar parity was "the decent thing to do."

Advocates of devaluation, among them Keynes in *A Tract on Monetary Reform*, challenged this view. In his famous attack on the "barbarous relic of the past," he emphasized that the success of the classic system had rested on the prevailing political and economic circumstances, notably the acceptance of the exchange rate target as the overriding policy concern. That priority, he argued, was no longer appropriate. "All of us, from the Governor of the Bank of England downwards, are now primarily interested in preserving the stability of business, prices, and employment, and are not likely, when the choice is forced on us, deliberately to sacrifice these to the outworn dogma, which had its value once, of £ 3: 17: 10.5 per ounce. Advocates of the ancient standard do not observe how remote it is from the spirit and the requirement of the age" (Keynes [1923, 173]).

Keynes's arguments did not prevail. Great Britain embarked on a painful attempt to eliminate the wartime inflation differential through deflationary policies. The challenge was made all the more difficult by the early postwar fall of prices in the United States, and later, her reluctance to accept the inflationary consequences of sustained gold inflows. At the cost of high unemployment and labor unrest, the deflation succeeded in reducing wages and prices (figures 2.1 and 2.2), allowing Great Britain to reestablish convertibility in 1925 at the old nominal parity, albeit at a level that still implied a slightly overvalued real exchange rate.

2.3   The Gold Exchange Standard 1925/27–1931/36

The time of purely national currencies is over.

—Charles Rist, *Die Deflation*

By 1927, a modified gold standard had been reestablished. World output, however, had grown relative to the global supply of monetary gold since the Klondike discoveries, placing a premium on retaining gold in central bank coffers. This was reflected both in high thresholds on convertibility,[11] and an increasing willingness on the part of most central banks to hold interest bearing foreign exchange (notably sterling) securities as an alternative to gold (hence the name "gold exchange standard").

The increased use of foreign exchange reserves conserved on the use of gold, helping to avoid some of the deflationary pressures that had occasionally buffeted the classic gold standard. However, it also made the gold exchange standard (much like the dollar exchange standard some thirty years later under the Bretton Woods system) vulnerable to potentially destabilizing forces whenever a confidence crisis triggered attempts to test the convertibility commitment.

From its inception, the gold exchange standard faced uncertain prospects. The relative stability of prewar bilateral balances had given way to pronounced instabilities reflecting rising trade barriers, payments for war reparations, and the misalignment of both sterling and the French franc. A return to equilibrium real exchange rates was impeded by the reluctance of the surplus countries—the United States and later France—to accept the inflationary consequences of inflows. The adjustment burden was thus effectively shifted to the deficit countries (Nurkse 1944).

Great Britain, following a brief respite, soon slipped back into recession (figure 2.3). While wages and prices were still flexible (figures 2.1 and 2.2), the political costs of adjustment through deflation had risen greatly. Labor movements had gained prominence and were naturally less concerned with the niceties of the international monetary system than with reducing unemployment. Looking back on this period, Keynes (1930, 2: 338) lamented "the economic losses, second only to those of a great war, which it (the gold standard) has brought upon the world," a view prominently influencing his positions in the discussions leading up to the Bretton Woods Agreement.

Loans from the United States allowed Great Britain to finance persistent current account deficits, albeit at the cost of making her more vulnerable to a reversal of capital flows. That reversal eventually came in 1928, following a tightening of U.S. monetary policies, motivated by domestic concerns. Perhaps the gold exchange standard could have survived the diminution of New York as a source of international capital. That shock, however, proved minor compared to the stock market collapses in 1929 (itself not unrelated to the monetary tightening), followed two years later by the contagious financial crisis emanating from Austria.

The Austrian exit from the gold standard heralded the arrival of domestic objectives as a serious challenger to the primacy of the exchange rate anchor in monetary policy. The insolvency of the country's largest bank presented the Austrian government with a difficult choice between salvaging the domestic financial system or remaining on the gold standard.[12] The government opted for financial stability, engaging in sizeable lender-of-last-resort functions that sharply reduced the gold coverage ratio.

The situation was not unprecedented. Temporary monetary loosening in times of crisis had not been uncommon during the classic gold standard. This time, however, the government lacked the luxury of credibility. In the midst of global recession, the combination of worsening fiscal balances and expectations of further banking problems eroded the confidence in the convertibility promise. Faced with a bank run as depositors attempted to convert balances into gold or foreign currencies, the government again came down on the side of maintaining financial stability, effectively abandoning the gold standard by imposing exchange controls.

In a cascade of developments not dissimilar to the crises of the European Monetary System (EMS) and the East Asian countries some sixty years later, Austria's exit highlighted the vulnerabilities of countries perceived to be similarly exposed. The crisis initially spilled over to neighboring Germany, which soon followed the Austrian example, leaving the gold standard by imposing exchange controls. Germany's exit eroded confidence in the convertibility promises of the remaining gold standard countries, triggering conversions of foreign exchange reserves into gold that finally stretched the system to its breaking point.

In September 1931, Great Britain, whose political commitment to the gold standard had come under increasing doubt, suspended convertibility. Just as the experience of the early 1920s helped shape French and German attitudes toward floating exchange rates, Britain's economic stagnation and vulnerability to attacks under fixed rates (reinforced in 1947, 1967, and 1992) influenced popular views on the merits of fixed rates.

Great Britain's decision raised the pressure on the remaining countries, eventually leading to a wave of devaluations including the United States in 1933 and the French gold block in 1936. It is hard to say whether the collapse of the gold exchange standard was inevitable (Bordo and Eichengreen 1997). Arguably, had France and Great Britain adopted parities more consistent with balance of payments equilibrium, the system might have proved more resilient. Yet, even with more reasonable par values, the fundamental difference between the classic and the interwar system would have remained: Whereas in the classic system, monetary policy could focus exclusively on maintaining the fixed exchange rate regime, it now had to contend with achieving "internal balance" as well. More than a decade later, the new rivalry between internal and external objectives was to play a decisive role in the negotiations leading up to the Bretton Woods standards.

2.4 Monetary Nationalism 1936–1946

Although many contemporaneous observers had decried the gold exchange standard,[13] there was little consensus on a better alternative.[14] Reflecting a pervasive disenchantment with free floating—based largely on the French experience—managed floats and de jure pegs protected by extensive capital controls became the norm. A last ditch attempt to resuscitate a (nearly) global standard with the 1937 tripartite agreement between France, Great Britain, and the United States came to naught. By the early 1940s, even current account convertibility was the exception rather than the rule. In little more than four decades, the world had gone from highly integrated goods and financial markets at the zenith of the classic gold standard[15] to a system of bilateral barter with inconvertible paper monies.[16]

2.5 The Bretton Woods System 1947–1969/1973

The world consciously took control of the international monetary system.

—Louis Rasminsky, Governor of Bank of Canada

If there is anything that interwar experience has clearly demonstrated, it is that paper currency exchanges cannot be left free to fluctuate from day to day under the influence of market supply and demand.

—Ragnar Nurkse, *International Currency Experience*

The interwar experience provided a telling illustration not only of the importance of stable international monetary arrangements, but also of the dangers of leaving their creation to a serendipitous coincidence of national preferences.

The experience after World War I was not to be repeated: Anglo-American discussions about the postwar international monetary system, spearheaded by John Maynard Keynes and Harry Dexter White, began in the early 1940s. They culminated in the 1944 Bretton Woods Agreement, perhaps the closest the world has come to formalizing the "rules of the game" in international monetary affairs.[17]

The agreement was a compromise between the American and British views. In terms of the central question—fixed or floating—disagreements were of degree rather than of principle. Keynes mirrored the somewhat ambivalent stance of most Europeans (Nurkse 1944),[18] combining skepticism of flexible rates as an adjustment tool with a reluctance to reinstate the exchange rate peg to the primacy it had enjoyed under the classic gold standard. The United States, enjoying a strong external position, looked more favorably upon hard pegs but, as the major potential creditor, was reluctant to meet European demands for open-ended balance of payments financing. The compromise was a system of pegged but adjustable parities built around a new institution, the IMF, charged with providing financing in the face of temporary shocks and with supervising adjustment—including devaluation—in the face of fundamental disequilibria (a term never formally defined).[19]

To ensure that countries would only have to devalue as a last resort, Keynes wanted substantial resources for the IMF—some $35 billion—while White proposed a rather more modest $5 billion. In addition, Keynes proposed delinking the provision of world reserves from gold by creating an artificial reserve asset—the "bancor"—as well as an explicit system for penalizing surplus countries.

The eventual compromise—$8.8 billion for the IMF, no bancor (at least until its arrival twenty years later in the guise of the Special Drawing Right) and a never invoked "scarce currency" clause in the IMF's Articles of Agreement—reflected the shift of bargaining power from the Old to the New World in the postwar era.

While gold retained its position as an anchor, the decline in the global gold coverage ratio and the unequal distribution of reserves rendered direct gold convertibility infeasible. Again a compromise was struck. The United States reestablished gold convertibility (albeit only for transactions between central banks), while other countries pegged their currencies to the dollar. The dollar thus became the de facto dominant reserve currency, allowing the United States, in Jacques Rueff's memorable words, to run "a deficit without tears."

Convertibility restrictions were a key element of the postwar era. In the clash among the "impossible trinity" of fixed exchange rates, capital mobility, and monetary autonomy, capital mobility (in the eyes of many a prime culprit in the collapse of the interwar regime) was considered the most expendable. For current account transactions, by contrast, there was widespread agreement on the need to reestablish convertibility—the only question being when the war-torn economies of Europe would be in a position to do so.

Liberal use of the printing presses to finance expenditures, coupled with extensive price controls, had generated sizable monetary overhangs in most European countries (Dornbusch and Wolf 2001). Even after the resolution of the overhangs through the reestablishment of internal convertibility—the German currency reform of 1949 being perhaps the best-known example—considerable doubt remained about the efficacy of real exchange rate movements in restoring external balances.

European faith in the power of markets had been badly shaken by the interwar experience. It was widely believed that the dollar shortage was a structural phenomenon, due to a low price elasticity of demand for European exports, that could not be easily remedied by devaluations.[20] The short-lived and disastrous convertibility episode in Great Britain in the summer of 1947 reinforced these views (somewhat unfairly)[21], leaving the continued use of current account restrictions as the sole remaining tool for maintaining external balance.[22] These temporary restrictions, organized within the framework of the European Payments Union (EPU), proved to be quite durable: Most European countries did not introduce current account convertibility until the demise of the EPU in 1958.[23]

For all the brilliance of its designers, the Bretton Woods system suffered from two fundamental flaws. The use of U.S. dollars as a reserve asset avoided some of the deflation that a return to universal gold backing would have implied. But it also meant that growth of world reserves—required to finance increasing world trade and income—depended upon U.S. balance of payments deficits.[24] Yet, nothing in the system tied U.S. policy to world monetary needs. Furthermore, as Triffin (1960) noted, even if the U.S. external balance were to reflect the global need for reserves, the increased supply of dollars relative to the unchanged U.S. gold stock reduced the dollar's gold coverage, thereby undermining confidence in the system's key reserve asset. It also soon became clear that, except during crises, there was little effective pressure for deficit countries to adjust policies. For surplus countries there was none at all. The interwar problem of delayed and asymmetric adjustment had returned.

In 1969, the Triffin dilemma was finally resolved through the First Amendment to the IMF's Articles of Agreement, establishing the Special Drawing Right (in effect, Keynes's bancor) as an alternative reserve asset, thereby severing the link between the U.S. balance of payments and world liquidity growth. By this time, however, the system was already buckling under severe pressures.

The political consensus for subordinating domestic policies to the imperative of fixed rates had largely vanished. The reluctance to alter par values in a timely fashion generated one-sided bets triggering speculative attacks, increasingly so as borders became more porous to capital flows. These outflows, far from disciplining policies, were often viewed by policymakers as an affront and vigorously combatted with an intensification of controls. Adjustments, when they finally came, usually took place under duress,[25] with attendant credibility losses. In the face of these mounting problems, the alternative of moving to more flexible exchange rates—originally proposed by Haberler (1937) and Friedman (1953)—gained academic adherents but remained an anathema in official circles.[26]

The ultimate demise of the Bretton Woods arrangement came as the United States substantially relaxed policies in the late 1960s, swelling the dollar glut.[27] Attempts to salvage the system by engineering a revaluation of the surplus countries failed amid disagreements on how the adjustment was to be apportioned.[28] As the need for an eventual resolution of the dollar overvaluation became more apparent, hard currency countries, such as Germany, received capital inflows exceeding their capacity to sterilize.

The resulting conflict between price stability and the fixed exchange rate was again resolved in favor of the domestic objective. On May 5, 1971, after receiving inflows exceeding $1 billion in the first hour of trading, the Bundesbank suspended large-scale dollar purchases and allowed the Deutsche mark (DM) to float; several other Europeans currencies followed soon thereafter. Three months later, on August 15, 1971, President Nixon slammed shut the gold window, effectively ending the Bretton Woods era.

Not unlike the collapse of the gold exchange standard forty years earlier, the Bretton Woods system was thus brought down by a clash between the external peg and domestic priorities—fiscal constraints in the United States, inflation concerns in Germany.[29]

Before we leave the Bretton Woods period, it is worth noting that, whatever its underlying flaws, the system was in many respects remarkably successful. As Bordo (1993) points out, economic performance under the Bretton Woods system, viewed over its entire lifespan, was superior to both the classic gold standard and the interwar period (figure 2.4). Although these years of recovery and reconstruction were probably unique, there is good reason to believe that at least part of the explanation for the explosive growth in world trade, income, and investment over this period lies in the relative stability of nominal and real exchange rates that the Bretton Woods Agreement afforded.

2.6 The Post–Bretton Woods Period

It is not easy to design a smoothly functioning international monetary system by the collective wisdom of a committee.

—Robert Mundell, "Concluding Remarks," *The New International Monetary System*

The end of the Bretton Woods system—or, more exactly, the collapse of the Smithsonian Agreement two years later—marked the beginning of a "brave new world" in which countries were free to choose their exchange rate regime. The United States, Japan, Europe, and the developing and emerging market economies embarked on different courses.[30]

The United States embraced floating exchange rates, grudgingly at first, wholeheartedly later as free-floating became identified with free-market policies. It required substantial misalignments—such as the sharp appreciation of the dollar between 1982 and 1985 (reflecting the tight monetary policy of the Volcker disinflation, and the expansionary fiscal policy of the Reagan administration), or the threat of a hard landing in 1987—for the United States to intervene in the foreign exchange markets.[31]

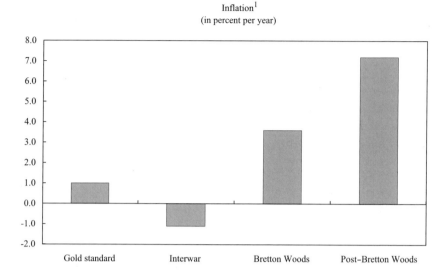

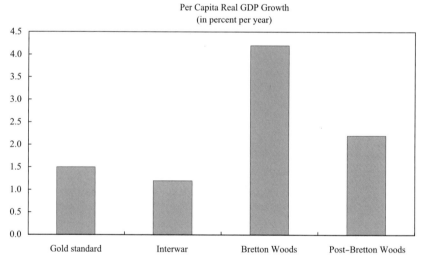

Figure 2.4
Macroeconomic performance of the G7 countries
Source: Bordo (1993). Gold standard (1881–1913); Interwar (1919–1938); Bretton Woods (1946–1970); Post–Bretton Woods (1974–1989).
[1] GNP deflator.

Concerned about competitiveness, Japan's preoccupation after the breakdown of Bretton Woods was to avoid a trend appreciation of the yen. While Japan was philosophically more inclined toward a role for the government in exchange rate determination, given the attitude of the United States, she lacked a natural partner for co-coordinated exchange rate stabilization.

In sharp contrast to the hands-off approach of the United States, there was little disagreement in continental Europe about the desirability of a return to fixed exchange rates. Such stability was viewed as essential to fostering greater cross-border trade and investment, themselves stepping-stones to eventual economic and monetary union.

Initial attempts at salvaging even a modicum of exchange rate stability failed in the face of sharply divergent monetary policy responses to the 1973 oil crisis. But the growing recognition that it was not possible to inflate out of supply-side shocks crystallized support for the 1979 creation of the EMS of pegged, but adjustable rates, with (at least in theory) symmetrical adjustment and intervention obligations for deficit and surplus countries.

The EMS encountered its first serious challenge in 1981–1983 when France used expansionary monetary policy to stimulate output, triggering repeated attacks on the French franc. The episode presented French policymakers with a stark choice between retaining monetary autonomy and maintaining exchange rate stability. The French government ultimately choose the latter, marking the beginning of the "hard EMS" period during which the higher-inflation EMS member countries tried to achieve disinflation by "importing" the Bundesbank's credibility.

The hard EMS period came to an abrupt end with the crises of 1992–1993. The collapse reflected the asymmetric interests of post-unification Germany and the other EMS members. The crises refocused attention on the hegemon problem and on the intrinsic fragility of fixed exchange rate systems in a world of high capital mobility. Partly reflecting the dynamics set into motion by the Maastricht treaty, the crises ironically also provided the final impetus for completing the move to full European monetary union[32] culminating with the introduction of the euro in January 2002, and thus, at least for Europe, completing the circle of the twentieth century.[33]

Among developing and emerging market countries, adjustable pegs, protected by capital controls, remained the regime of choice in the early post–Bretton Woods years. Pegged regimes also proved popular in attempts to achieve disinflation after years of high inflation or hyperinflation. Chile, Mexico, Israel, Argentina, and Brazil, among others, undertook exchange rate–based stabilizations in an attempt to import credibility. The success of these attempts is a matter of some contention. Although inflation typically fell sharply, it often remained above the rate in the anchor country, leading to an appreciation of the real exchange rate. Not infrequently, the stabilization attempts ended in balance of payments crises.

In the late 1990s, another group of emerging market countries, widely viewed as immune to Latin-style upheavals, experienced currency crashes. The East Asian crisis countries did not fit the mold of chronically poor performance; on the contrary, inflation had been low, growth had been strong, and the de jure or de facto pegs against the U.S. dollar had been maintained for many years. Rather, the main roots of the crisis lay in stock imbalances—mostly unhedged (short-term) foreign currency liabilities of the banking and corporate sectors—creating disproportionate contractions once the pegs collapsed.

In response to these new fragilities, developing and emerging market countries have pursued two sharply different strategies: either seeking to enhance credibility by adopting hard pegs (such as full dollarization or currency boards), or else trying to remove the target for speculative attacks by eschewing pegs in favor of de jure floats, albeit with extensive intervention.

Both industrialized and developing countries have thus pursued a wide variety of exchange rate policies in the post–Bretton Woods period. In the remainder of the book, we explore how they fared.

3   The Theory of Exchange Rate Regimes

The theoretical literature on the choice and consequences of the exchange rate regime is vast.[1] Choices and consequences are in a sense flip sides of the same coin: a rational choice of the exchange rate regime presumably reflects the properties that the regime promises. While historically countries enjoyed limited choices—being circumscribed by prevailing norms of the international monetary system[2]—the adoption of the Second Amendment of the IMF's Articles of Agreement meant that the exchange rate regime became a matter of each country's individual preferences.[3]

At its crux, the choice between "pegged" and "floating" exchange rates comes down to the trade-off between reducing exchange rate volatility and foregoing an independent monetary policy. How this trade-off is manifested, and what precisely are the costs and benefits, is the subject of a wide-ranging and ever growing literature.

At the risk of oversimplification, the literature on the properties of exchange rate regimes can be divided into three broad categories. The first strand focuses on the insulating properties of regimes. Influential papers by Marcus Fleming (1962) and Robert Mundell (1963) showed that, if capital is highly mobile, fixed and floating exchange rates have starkly different implications for the conduct of stabilization policy. Reinterpreting monetary and fiscal policies as nominal and real shocks respectively, fixed exchange rates provide greater insulation of output (or, under full employment, of prices) in the face of nominal shocks, while floating exchange rates are better at absorbing real shocks.

The second strand, originating in postwar Europe, examines how different exchange rate regimes might foster economic integration. Central to this debate are two questions. First, do fixed exchange rates reduce uncertainty and transactions costs, thereby encouraging greater cross-border trade and investment? Second, given the degree of integration, does it make sense for a group of countries to forego national monetary policies in favor of rigidly fixed nominal exchange rates (perhaps culminating in full monetary union)?

The third strand, motivated by the high-inflation experiences of the late 1960s and 1970s, emphasizes the credibility aspects of monetary (and exchange rate) regimes. In these models, the central bank faces a credibility problem reflecting its incentive to reduce unemployment (or erode the value of nominal debt) by generating surprise inflation. As workers factor this incentive into wage demands, the result is higher inflation, but unchanged employment. In the closed economy, the problem can be mitigated by appointing an ultraconservative central banker or, if reputational effects are sufficiently strong, by earning credibility through tight monetary policies. In an open economy, pegged exchange rates may provide an alternative precommitment device, as long as the political (or other) costs of breaking the peg are sufficiently large.

In contrast to the large body of literature on exchange rate regimes and inflation, few papers directly address the link between the exchange rate regime and output growth. Nonetheless, various strands of the literature touch upon the issue obliquely, in particular through the implications for trade and investment.

In the remainder of this chapter, we review each of these strands of the literature in greater detail before presenting a formal framework that draws together some of their key elements.

3.1   Insulating Properties of Exchange Rate Regimes

During the late 1960s, increasing strains on the Bretton Woods system (as well as periodic balance of payments crises in individual countries) prompted a number of economists—drawing on earlier work by Milton Friedman (1953)—to argue the merits of flexible exchange rates. The rationale was straightforward: The automatic adjustment of the nominal exchange rate to trade imbalances would obviate the need for the large, delayed, and often traumatic devaluations that had come to characterize the Bretton Woods system.

In the event, the move to floating exchange rates turned out to be neither the panacea that its more avid supporters had promised, nor the unmitigated disaster that some of its critics had predicted.[4] Among the major industrialized countries, floating exchange rates appeared to be driven more by capital flows than by underlying trade imbalances (Mussa 1986). At the same time, most countries seemed to cope reasonably well with the higher volatility of nominal and real exchange rates.

During the 1960s and early 1970s significant advances occurred in understanding how various regimes would operate under conditions of high capital mobility. Two seminal papers by Fleming (1962) and Mundell (1963)—following earlier work by James Meade—showed that fixed and floating exchange rates had starkly different implications for the conduct of stabilization policy.

Under fixed exchange rates, a monetary expansion lowers interest rates, which leads to capital outflows; the resulting loss in reserves shrinks the money supply. In the limiting case of perfect capital mobility, the offset is one-for-one and monetary policy is completely ineffective in stabilizing output. In contrast, under a floating regime, the outflow depreciates the exchange rate, thus stimulating output.

The results are reversed for fiscal expansions. Under floating exchange rates, a fiscal expansion raises the domestic interest rate and causes a capital inflow, thus appreciating the exchange rate and deteriorating the trade balance. In the limiting case of perfect capital mobility, the crowding out is complete, and fiscal policy is ineffective. Under fixed exchange rates, since the central bank is committed to buying foreign exchange, the capital inflow induces an automatic monetary accommodation of the fiscal expansion, augmenting its effect.

These results, though somewhat specific to the particular structure of the Mundell-Fleming model, showed how the exchange rate regime could fundamentally alter the effectiveness of different policy instruments. In particular, they suggested that fixed exchange rates, open capital accounts, and an activist independent monetary policy form an "impossible trinity."

In practice, the difference between fixed and floating regimes for the autonomy of monetary policy may not be as pronounced as theory would suggest, particularly for developing countries. Few central banks, even when they purport to follow a floating regime, are truly indifferent to exchange rate movements—on the upside because of a loss of export competitiveness, on the downside because of the pass-through to inflation or because of the foreign exchange exposure arising from external debt.[5] Except for very large countries, therefore, the notion of full independence of monetary policy under flexible exchange rates may be largely illusory. Conversely, since capital is never perfectly mobile, there is likely to be at least some scope for an independent monetary policy even under fixed exchange rates.

While the models of Mundell and Fleming were purely deterministic, stochastic implications could be derived by reinterpreting fiscal policy as real shocks, and monetary policy as nominal shocks. Applying the same logic, under high capital mobility floating exchange rates insulate output better against real shocks, while the balance of payments movements under fixed exchange rates offset nominal shocks. Viewed in this light, the relative incidence of nominal and real shocks becomes a key criterion in choosing the exchange rate regime.[6]

The precise configuration of shocks under which fixed exchange rates would be preferable to floating rates stimulated a lively literature that yielded a number of insights. For instance, if capital is relatively immobile, fixed exchange rates provide better insulation of output against shocks to aggregate demand, whereas, under high capital mobility, floating exchange rates are preferable.[7]

This ambiguity arises from the asymmetric effects of trade and capital flows on the balance of payments (or the exchange rate). With low capital mobility, trade flows dominate. Under fixed exchange rates, a positive shock to aggregate demand leads to higher imports and a loss of reserves through the trade deficit. This loss of reserves, unless sterilized, contracts the money supply, partly offsetting the original shock. Under floating rates, by contrast, the trade deficit depreciates the exchange rate. The depreciation increases exports and thus amplifies the shock to aggregate demand.

When capital is highly mobile, the results are reversed. Under fixed exchange rates, the positive demand shock raises interest rates and induces a capital inflow that more than offsets the loss of reserves through the trade deficit. Thus, the money supply increases, exacerbating the demand shock. Under floating rates the capital inflow appreciates the exchange rate. The appreciation reduces exports and thus partly offsets the shock to aggregate demand.

The models yielded a second important insight: In the face of monetary shocks, fixed exchange rates generally provide better insulation of output. In response to a random shock that raises money demand, domestic interest rates increase, depressing aggregate demand and imports. Under a fixed exchange rate, this leads to an increase in reserves—whether because of lower imports (under low capital mobility) or because of larger capital inflows in response to the higher interest rates (under high capital mobility)—and a corresponding expansion in the money supply. In the limiting case, the increase of the money supply perfectly matches the higher money demand, completely insulating output. Under floating exchange rates, by contrast, the higher interest rate leads to an appreciation of the exchange rate, reducing exports and thus exacerbating the negative effect on output.

A few studies took the analysis a step further to ask whether these properties of exchange rate regimes had implications for long-term growth (as opposed to the variation of output around its potential). No strong conclusions emerged from these studies, reflecting the ambiguous effect of greater output volatility on both the level and the growth rate of output.[8]

By exploring the interaction between various types of shocks and country characteristics, studies of the insulating properties of the nominal exchange rate regime developed an entire taxonomy under which fixed exchange rates may be preferable to floating rates—or vice versa. But precisely because there are so many possible configurations, perhaps the most robust conclusion from these studies is that some form of intermediate regime is likely to serve most countries well—a result that stands in stark contrast to the policy credibility literature, reviewed in section 3.3.[9]

3.2 Economic Integration and the Exchange Rate Regime

Adopting an exchange rate peg implies surrendering the nominal exchange rate as an adjustment tool. It follows that the case for pegging between two countries (or for adopting a common currency) is stronger, ceteris paribus, if they are subject to relatively similar and highly correlated output shocks. This is the central insight of the optimum currency area (OCA) literature (Mundell 1961).[10] The ceteris paribus assumption is of some importance: The loss of the exchange rate as an adjustment tool is less serious if alternative adjustment mechanisms—notably wage and price flexibility, factor mobility and fiscal transfer systems—are available; while the gain increases in the extent of trade integration (McKinnon 1963).[11]

The European agenda of greater monetary and economic integration spurred a large literature on whether (parts of) Europe constituted an optimum currency area.[12] The question has typically been answered through a comparison to the states or regions of the United States. The merits of using an existing monetary union as a baseline are debatable since the criteria are endogenous to the exchange rate regime (quite aside from the fact that Mundell's original work was motivated by a concern that the United States itself may not be an optimum currency area). In particular, the stability of the nominal exchange rate may affect the degree of trade integration, which, in turn, may influence the correlation of shocks.

The direction of each of these linkages, however, remains a matter of debate.[13] The first link—the effect of exchange rate variability on international trade—is itself the subject of a large literature. The usual assumption (which underlay, for instance, the push for greater intra-European exchange rate stability) is that lower exchange rate variability reduces uncertainty and risk premia, thereby encouraging greater cross-border trade.[14] At least for the industrialized countries, however, empirical evidence of such effects is weak,[15] although full monetary integration (if not pegged exchange rates as such) appears to be associated with substantially more cross-border trade.[16]

Moreover, even if it could be concluded that fixed exchange rates reduce uncertainty[17] and thereby increase trade integration, the effect on the correlation of shocks—and thus on the case for pegging or monetary union—is ambiguous. While greater trade linkages lead to more specialization, and thus reduce the correlation of supply shocks,[18] they also ease the transmission of demand shocks.[19] The net effect on business cycle correlations is ambiguous.

3.3 Credibility

Although much of the original impetus for monetary union in Europe came from the desire to foster greater integration, the collapse of the Bretton Woods system derailed these plans. By the time the European countries were again reestablishing fixed exchange rates between themselves, the main policy concern had shifted to combating inflation.

In this endeavor, pegged exchange rates were seen as providing a potential nominal anchor, lowering inflationary expectations and helping the central bank to achieve its inflation objective. The theoretical foundation for this argument was laid by the work of Barro and Gordon (1983), who examined a closed-economy game between wage setters and the central bank. In their model, nominal wages are set before the central bank decides on monetary policy (and hence determines the inflation rate). The central bank's objective is to minimize both inflation and unemployment. It has an incentive to create "surprise" inflation in order to reduce realized real wages, thereby raising employment.[20]

However, rational workers, foreseeing this incentive, build it into their demands for nominal wages. Under discretionary monetary policy, the economy thus inherits an inflationary bias but remains at its natural rate of employment. A promise by the central bank not to generate surprise inflation is not credible since, the moment the workers believe this promise and lock into correspondingly low nominal wages, the central bank has the incentive to renege and inflate. Moreover, attempting to disinflate in such an environment may be extremely costly, as an "incredible" disinflation will generate high ex post real wages and correspondingly high unemployment.

There is a way out of this conundrum: If the central bank could credibly commit to low inflation, wage setters would build this expectation into their nominal wage demands, shifting the economy to a low-inflation equilibrium (albeit at the same natural rate of employment). In a nonstochastic setting, such a precommitment equilibrium necessarily raises welfare. In a stochastic setting, a trade-off arises since tying the hands of the central bank, while increasing credibility, also limits its ability to react to shocks.

How can the central bank precommit to low inflation? In a closed-economy setting, it must rely on the repeated game nature of its interaction with wage setters, or on the appointment of hawkish central bankers (in a sufficiently independent central bank) (Rogoff 1985).

In the open economy, pegging the nominal exchange rate to a low-inflation country provides an alternative precommitment device. The peg does not eliminate the underlying incentive to create inflation surprises; it merely imposes a constraint on the central bank's ability to act on that incentive. Since the decision to retain the peg is itself endogenous, pegging the exchange rate provides a precommitment device only to the extent that the perceived (political or other) costs of abandoning the peg outweigh the benefits of generating surprise inflation.[21] Raising the costs of exiting the regime—for example, through the adoption of a hard peg enshrined in law—can thus increase credibility, making it easier for the central bank to achieve and maintain low inflation. Therefore, in contrast to the literature on insulating properties of exchange rate regimes reviewed above, the general conclusion from the policy credibility literature is that the harder the peg, the better.

3.4   A Formal Model

While the literature on macroeconomic performance under alternative regimes is too large to be fully captured within any single framework, we illustrate some key elements in a stylized model. The framework marries two distinct strands of the literature: the analysis of optimal regimes in the face of various types of shocks and the Barro-Gordon policy credibility literature. Indeed, with a little extra work, it can be expanded into a ménage à trois, also incorporating the insights of the optimal currency area literature.

Output is determined by a Lucas-type supply function

$$y = \theta(\pi - \pi^e) + \eta \tag{1}$$

where y is the log of output, π is the inflation rate, π^e is the private sector's expectation of the inflation rate, and θ is a positive constant. η denotes a stochastic shock with mean zero and variance σ_η^2, observed after the private sector sets wages, but before the central bank decides on monetary policy. Workers demand nominal wage increases sufficient to cover expected inflation. Employment is determined by realized real wages. If inflation turns out to be unexpectedly high, real wages are eroded, making it profitable for firms to increase employment and output.

The economy's rate of monetization—the real rate of growth of money demand—depends positively on the long-run real growth of output (which is constant, and normalized to zero), and negatively on expected inflation.[22] In addition, money demand is subject to a shock, ε, observed after the central bank chooses its monetary policy (and hence, after the private sector sets nominal wages). Money market equilibrium is thus given by $\Delta m - \pi = \alpha\Delta\bar{y} - \upsilon\pi^e - \varepsilon$, where α is the income elasticity of money demand and $0 \leq \upsilon < 1$ is the elasticity with respect to expected inflation. Normalizing $\Delta\bar{y} = 0$, and inverting, yields an expression for inflation

$$\pi = \Delta m + \upsilon\pi^e + \varepsilon \tag{2}$$

For simplicity, the banking sector is ignored so that the money supply consists of central bank domestic credit and international reserves: $\Delta m = \Delta dc + \Delta r$. Under fixed exchange rates, the central bank chooses Δdc while the change in reserves is endogenous. Under floating rates, the central bank again chooses Δdc, but does not hold reserves (so $\Delta r = 0$) and the nominal exchange rate is endogenous. The model is closed by assuming purchasing power parity

$$\pi = \pi^* + \Delta e \tag{3}$$

where π^* is the foreign inflation rate, which is assumed to be lower than the domestic inflation rate, and for simplicity is set to zero. The central bank is assumed to have two objectives: stabilizing output around some desired level, $\bar{y}$, and keeping inflation low. The central bank's objective function may thus be written

$$Min\ L = \frac{1}{2}E\{A(y - \bar{y})^2 + \pi^2\} \tag{4}$$

where $E\{\cdot\}$ is the central bank's expectation and A denotes the relative welfare weight placed on output (or, more generally, on the incentive to generate inflation surprises). As the natural level of output is normalized to zero, $\bar{y} > 0$ implies that the central bank is aiming for a level of output above the economy's natural level. Why would it do so? In the original Barro-Gordon setup, it is assumed that unionization of the labor force leads to a socially suboptimal level of employment. Thus, the central bank is tempted to generate surprise inflation, eroding real wages and thereby raising employment and output. Alternatively, as emphasized by Cukierman (1992), this term could equally reflect the incentive to erode the real value of nominal debt, in which case π^e would represent not the expectation of wage setters, but that of bondholders.

3.4.1 Pegged Exchange Rate Regime
The solution under a pegged regime is straightforward. The purchasing power parity condition (3) implies that, as long as the exchange rate remains fixed, inflation must equal the foreign rate of inflation

$$\pi = \pi^* = 0 \tag{5}$$

Since monetary policy can affect neither inflation nor the level of output, the central bank has no incentive to expand the money sup-

ply, hence domestic credit is constant and the expected inflation rate
under rational expectations is zero. Monetary shocks, ε, are passively
absorbed by the change in reserves, $\Delta r = -\varepsilon$, as long as the shock is
not so large as to deplete the central bank's stock of foreign reserves
and force a devaluation. The low inflation, however, comes at the
cost of greater real volatility as the lack of an activist monetary policy implies that the productivity shock cannot be offset:

$$y = \eta \tag{6}$$

To evaluate welfare under alternative regimes, we use the ex ante
expected utility. Substituting (5) and (6) into the loss function (4) and
taking expected values yields

$$L_{Peg} = \frac{1}{2}\{A(\sigma_\eta^2 + \bar{y}^2)\} \tag{7}$$

3.4.2 Floating Exchange Rate Regime
Under a regime of floating exchange rates, reserves are constant and
the central bank is free to pursue an activist monetary policy. Substituting (1) and (2) into (4) and solving for the optimal reaction
function of the central bank yields

$$\Delta dc = \frac{-A\theta\eta + A\theta\bar{y} + A\theta^2(1-v)\pi^e - v\pi^e}{1+A\theta^2} \tag{8}$$

Substituting (8) into (2) then yields the semireduced form for
inflation:

$$\pi = \frac{-A\theta\eta + A\theta\bar{y} + A\theta^2\pi^e}{1+A\theta^2} + \varepsilon \tag{9}$$

Actual inflation is increasing in the central bank's incentive to create
surprise inflation, $\bar{y} > 0$, and in the private sector's expectation of
inflation, π^e. The latter can be obtained by taking the mathematical
expectation of (9). Since the private sector has observed neither η nor
ε at the time expectations are formed, it must use their unconditional
means (zero) in forming its expectations; solving (9) thus yields

$$\pi^e = A\theta\bar{y} \tag{10}$$

The incentive of the central bank to create inflation surprises is
thus incorporated into private sector expectations. The central bank
therefore cannot systematically surprise the private sector. This is

evident from the reduced form for output, which is independent of $\bar{y}$:

$$y = \theta(\pi - \pi^e) = \frac{A\theta^2\eta}{1 + A\theta^2} + \theta\varepsilon \qquad (11)$$

While the central bank is unable to systematically fool the private sector, it cannot credibly commit itself to not trying to do so. This imparts an inflationary bias to the economy:

$$\pi = \frac{-A\theta\eta}{1 + A\theta^2} + A\theta\bar{y} + \varepsilon \qquad (12)$$

Substituting (11) and (12) into the objective function, and taking expectations based on the central bank's information set, yields the ex ante loss under a floating exchange rate:

$$L_{Flt} = \frac{1}{2}\left\{(1 + A\theta^2)\left(\frac{A\sigma_\eta^2}{(1 + A\theta^2)^2} + \sigma_\varepsilon^2 + A\bar{y}^2\right)\right\} \qquad (13)$$

3.4.3 Comparison of Regimes

Comparing (7) with (13) gives the conditions under which a peg is preferable to a float. It is useful to start with some special cases. Suppose that $\bar{y} = 0$, so that the central bank has no incentive to create surprise inflation. Then

$$L_{Peg} > L_{Flt} \quad \textit{iff} \quad A\sigma_\eta^2 > \frac{A\sigma_\eta^2}{(1 + A\theta^2)} + (1 + A\theta^2)\sigma_\varepsilon^2 \qquad (14)$$

Suppose, further, that there are only real productivity shocks and no (unanticipated) monetary shocks, so that $\sigma_\varepsilon^2 = 0$. Under these conditions, it is evident from (14) that the expected loss under the pegged regime is greater, and hence the floating regime is preferable.[23] On the other hand, if there are only monetary shocks and no real productivity shocks, then $L_{Peg} < L_{Flt}$. Hence the pegged regime is preferable.

The results accord with the traditional intuition that a floating exchange rate better insulates output against real shocks (since inflation and the exchange rate adjust, thus absorbing part of the shock); while under fixed exchange rates, reserve movements automatically offset unanticipated monetary shocks. What about inflation? Ignoring the term $A\bar{y}$, average inflation under the two regimes is the same. Assuming that the partner country has a low and steady rate of inflation, $\pi^* \approx 0$, the variance of inflation will be higher under floating exchange rates.

The second special case abstracts from the stochastic shocks to focus on the policy credibility issue. Assuming that $\sigma_\eta^2 = 0$ and $\sigma_\varepsilon^2 = 0$, but $\bar{y} > 0$ (so that the central bank has an incentive to generate inflation surprises), it is apparent from (5) and (12) that inflation is lower under the pegged exchange rate regime. This, of course, relies on the assumption that the foreign inflation rate is zero—a reasonable approximation when the home country, traditionally a high-inflation country, is pegging to a low-inflation partner (so that inflation in the partner country is negligible). If the foreign central bank instead chooses its inflation rate analogous to (12), and if productivity shocks in the two countries are perfectly correlated, then the pegged exchange rate regime fares no worse in the face of productivity shocks—consistent with the central insight of the optimum currency area literature. The home country does, however, inherit the foreign country's monetary shock under pegged exchange rates. Crucially, if the foreign central bank faces the same incentive to create surprise inflation, $\bar{y} = \bar{y}^* > 0$, then pegging the exchange rate does not remove the home country's inflationary bias. This suggests that pegging the exchange rate among countries that already have low and similar inflation rates—such as the major industrialized countries—would bring few additional anti-inflationary benefits.

What imparts the lower inflation under pegged exchange rates? It reflects both a "discipline" effect operating through monetary growth (under the pegged regime $\Delta m_{Peg} = 0$ while under the floating regime $\Delta m_{Flt} = (1 - v)A\theta\bar{y} > 0$) and a "confidence" or "credibility" effect working through inflation expectations (expected inflation under the pegged regime equals zero, but is positive under the floating regime, $\pi_{Flt}^e = A\theta\bar{y} > 0$). This confidence effect is reflected in a higher money demand, implying, from (2), a lower inflation rate for a *given* growth rate of the money supply.

Comparing (6) and (11), output is the same under the two regimes: $y_{Flt} = y_{Peg} = 0$. It follows that welfare under the floating regime is lower. The traditional Barro-Gordon result thus holds: The inability of the central bank to precommit to low inflation in the floating exchange rate regime creates both the expectation, and, ex post, the realization of higher inflation. However, since this inflation is anticipated, it provides no benefit in terms of generating higher employment and output: It is simply a deadweight loss.

In practice, neither of the two special cases is likely to dominate, creating trade-offs between the benefits of adopting a peg (and hence eliminating the Barro-Gordon inflationary bias) and losing the ability to offset real shocks. The outcome of the cost-benefit analysis depends on country characteristics; no single exchange rate regime is appropriate for all countries at all times (Frankel 1999).

In countries with histories of high inflation (or new states lacking a monetary policy track record) a pegged exchange rate may be useful in enhancing the central bank's anti-inflationary credibility. Disinflation without such credibility might entail significant output costs.[24] At the other end of the spectrum, a country with a history of reasonably sound macroeconomic policies, but subject to substantial real shocks, may find the strictures of a peg on monetary policy unjustifiably costly.

3.4.4 Transitions

The preceding discussion did not endogenize the duration of regimes. While a country cannot constantly switch regimes and retain credibility (hence the use of the ex ante expected welfare functions to compare alternative regimes), particular realizations of the shocks may be sufficiently large to force a country to abandon the current regime, most notably when a country with a fixed exchange rate faces a large real shock.[25]

Apart from shocks, a more fundamental time inconsistency problem may arise under pegged rates. The results presented above assumed the pegged regime to be credible, reflected in private sector expectations of zero inflation. From (9), however, it follows that when the private sector expects zero inflation (i.e., when the country has a pegged exchange rate), the central bank's optimal inflation rate is given by

$$\pi_{\pi^e=0} = \frac{A\theta\bar{y}}{1 + A\theta^2} > 0 \qquad (15)$$

(where, for convenience, the stochastic shocks have been set to zero). That is, as soon as the private sector believes that inflation will be zero, the central bank has an incentive to renege on this implicit commitment. Plugging the optimal inflation rate (and resulting output level) into the loss function (and again ignoring stochastic shocks to focus on the policy credibility aspects of the problem) gives

$$L_{Flt\,|\,\pi^e=0} = \frac{1}{2}\left\{\frac{A\bar{y}^2}{(1+A\theta^2)}\right\} \tag{16}$$

which is *lower* than $L_{Peg} = \frac{1}{2}\{A\bar{y}^2\}$. Simply put, if the central bank can fool the public, it will. It follows that for the exchange rate peg (and hence the low inflation equilibrium) to be sustainable, there must be some political or other cost, c, of abandoning the peg. The pegged regime will then be sustained as long as the benefit of deviating is less than the cost

$$L_{Peg} - L_{Flt\,|\,\pi^e=0} < c \Rightarrow \frac{1}{2}\{A\bar{y}^2\} - \frac{1}{2}\left\{\frac{A\bar{y}^2}{(1+A\theta^2)}\right\} < c \tag{17}$$

Rearranging (17) yields $\bar{y} < \sqrt{2c(1+A\theta^2)}/(A\theta)$. The model thus generates the sensible result that for the pegged regime to be sustainable, the temptation to inflate must be sufficiently small compared to the costs of abandoning the peg.

What is less satisfactory about the model is that the cost of abandoning the peg, c, must be pulled out of the air, deus ex machina. In particular, it is not clear why the (political or other) costs of abandoning a peg are greater than those of reneging on a money growth or inflation target.[26]

Is it possible to sustain the pegged exchange rate regime without resorting to extraneous costs of abandoning the peg? De Kock and Grilli (1993) show that, in a repeated game, reputational effects may yield the necessary discipline. However, why would the same reputational mechanism not apply to money or inflation targeting under the floating regime? Herrendorf (1997) provides a possible answer: The exchange rate peg, being under more precise control of the monetary authorities than the inflation rate, enhances the effectiveness of reputation in sustaining the equilibrium because any deviation is immediately revealed to be a deliberate policy action rather than an unfortunate stochastic shock.[27] As such, there may be reputational equilibria that sustain low inflation under pegged exchange rate regimes but not under floating exchange rates.

3.4.5   Other Considerations

The model illustrates the two key roles the nominal exchange rate regime plays: It acts both as a stabilization tool and as a credibility device. These objectives are not always in agreement. A country with a poor inflation record and subject to significant real shocks must decide between the insulating properties of flexible exchange rates and the credibility benefits obtainable by pegging the exchange rate. Beyond credibility and stabilization, other factors enter into the choice of regime. We conclude by briefly touching upon three of these: fiscal constraints, financial fragility, and exits.

With a fixed exchange rate and high capital mobility, fiscal policy has to shoulder the entire burden of macroeconomic stabilization. The ability to do so thus becomes an argument in the choice of regime (Gros 1999). Specifically, very large deficits or debt ratios can undermine confidence if investors expect that the government will seek to monetize the deficit (or erode the value of the public debt), abandoning the peg in the process.[28]

Indeed, the fiscal theory of price determination (Woodford 1994), as applied to the exchange rate regime (Canzoneri, Cumby, and Diba 1998), suggests that a fixed exchange rate regime will not be sustained unless fiscal policy, broadly construed, is sufficiently flexible to respect the government's present value budget constraint at a price level consistent with the exchange rate peg (a "money dominant" regime, in their parlance).

Whether, in fact, pegged regimes elicit the requisite fiscal discipline remains an issue of some contention. Indeed, some models suggest that, far from exerting discipline, fixed exchange rates create an incentive for governments with short time horizons to "cheat," delivering temporary growth through larger deficits (Tornell and Velasco 2000), with the inflationary costs generated by the eventual collapse of the peg borne by their successors.

Another concern is that pegged regimes, most notably hard pegs such as currency boards and dollarization, limit the scope for the central bank's lender-of-last-resort function and may therefore render countries operating under pegged exchange rates especially vulnerable to banking crises.[29] On theoretical grounds the argument is not clear-cut, as the existence of a lender of last resort may generate moral hazard problems, increasing the likelihood of banking crises. We return to this issue in more detail in chapter 8.

A third issue we have sidestepped is forced exits and speculative attacks. In terms of voluntary transitions, the model presented above is applicable: An optimal regime transition occurs if the expected welfare gain exceeds the cost of switching regimes. Exits from fixed exchange rate regimes are however often involuntary, triggered by a speculative attack[30] that can be very costly.[31] Chapter 8 focuses on these issues.

3.5 Conclusions

Perusing the theoretical literature, one is hard pressed not to agree with the old canards about two- and three-handed economists. Almost anything seems possible. Pegged exchange rates may help countries achieve low inflation or allow governments to "cheat," running unsustainable deficits that explode into open inflation when the peg collapses. Conversely, flexible exchange rates may allow smooth adjustment to trade imbalances or exacerbate the effects of speculative capital flows and result in excessive volatility. Although flexible regimes are better at insulating output against real shocks when capital mobility is "high," pegged regimes are preferable when capital mobility is "low."

These ambiguities of the theoretical literature are not cause for despair however; rather, they point to a very rich set of possible relationships that can only be resolved by looking at the empirical evidence. This is our task for the remainder of this book.

Classifying Exchange Rate Regimes

How should a country's exchange rate regime be classified? The textbook answer is simple: Either the exchange rate is "fixed" or it "floats." The richness of real world regimes belies this elegant dichotomy as most governments try to reach some (often uneasy) compromise between the different elements of the impossible trinity —independent monetary policy, rigidly fixed exchange rates, and complete capital mobility (Frankel 1999).

Popular regimes run the gamut from currency boards and traditional pegs to crawling pegs, target zones, and floats, with varying degrees of intervention (table 4.1, see also Edwards and Savastano 1999). Before we can undertake any empirical work, therefore, we must first decide upon the appropriate level of aggregation, and on a methodology for classifying regimes. In this chapter, we take up both of these issues.

4.1 Classification Approaches

Intuitively, a pegged exchange rate is one whose value, in terms of some reference currency or commodity (traditionally gold), does not vary, or varies only within narrow, predefined limits. But an exchange rate peg is much more than that since it implies a formal commitment by the central bank to maintain the parity through foreign exchange intervention and, ultimately, through the subordination of its monetary policy to the exchange rate objective if necessary. In a floating regime, by contrast, the central bank undertakes no such commitment.

This suggests that the exchange rate regime might be best defined by the stated intentions of the central bank (which every IMF member country is required to report and publish each year), yielding a de jure classification.

Table 4.1
Characteristics of different exchange rate regimes

Classification	Subclassification	Regime	Main characteristics
Pegged	*Hard pegs*		*Exchange rate is pegged in a manner that makes a change in parity or an exit from the regime extremely difficult and costly.*
		Dollarization	A foreign currency is used as legal tender, even though in some cases domestic coins are issued. Monetary policy is delegated to the anchor country. Seigniorage accrues to the issuing country.
		Currency boards	The exchange rate is pegged to a foreign (anchor) currency, with the regime and the parity enshrined in law. The law would also specify a minimum amount of international reserves to be held by the central bank to back a certain percentage of a prespecified monetary aggregate. Main difference from dollarization: seigniorage accrues to the home country.
		Monetary union	A group of countries uses a common currency issued by a common regional central bank. Monetary policy is determined at the regional level; seigniorage accrues to the region. No option to adjust par-values internally; externally, the monetary authority issuing the common currency can pursue any exchange rate policy.
	Traditional pegs		*Currency is linked to a single foreign currency or to a basket of currencies. Cost of adjusting the parity or of abandoning the regime lower than in the case of hard pegs.*
		Single currency peg	The exchange rate is pegged to a fixed par-value to a single foreign currency. The central bank is expected to trade at the announced par-value, but the rate is generally adjustable (through discrete devaluations or revaluations) in case of fundamental disequilibria. Credibility is greater the higher the level of central bank reserves, but generally reserves do not fully cover all domestic monetary liabilities, leaving some room for discretionary monetary policy.
		Basket peg	Similar to single currency peg, except that the currency is pegged to a basket consisting of two or more currencies. Basket can be designed according to country-specific criteria or be a composite currency (SDR, or, previously ECU). For country-specific baskets, basket weights may be publicly known or be secret, and may be fixed or variable.

Intermediate regimes	*Floats with rule-based intervention*	*Exchange rate is not pegged at a specific rate, but the central bank intervenes in a predetermined manner to limit exchange rate movements.*
	Cooperative regimes	Cooperating central banks agree to keep the bilateral exchange rates of their currencies within a preset range of each other. Policy instruments include adjustment of domestic monetary policy as well as (joint and coordinated) intervention. Arrangement can impose constraints on monetary policy, the severity of which depends on the relative position of the various currencies.
	Crawling peg	The exchange rate is determined in a rule-based manner, typically adjusting at a predetermined rate or as a function of (actual or expected) inflation differentials. Par value can be set with regard to a single currency or a basket of currencies. In some cases, crawling pegs are combined with bands. Specific design features (such as the degree of adjustment, and the length of time between adjustments) determine whether the system resembles more a fixed or a flexible exchange rate.
	Target zones and bands	Exchange rate is allowed to fluctuate within a preset range; endpoints (which, in the case of bands are fixed, in the case of target zones are a policy goal) defended through intervention. There may be intraband intervention to avoid excess pressure at the margin. In some cases, bands are combined with crawling pegs ("crawling bands"). Degree of exchange rate flexibility is determined by the width of the band or target zone.
	Float with discretionary intervention	*Exchange rate floats but is influenced by significant official intervention.*
	Managed floating	Exchange rates are free to move according to supply and demand. Authorities have a view on the desired level and path of the exchange rate and intervene, but are not bound by any intervention rule. Often accompanied by a separate nominal anchor, such as an inflation target.
Floating regimes	*Free floats*	*Exchange rate is allowed to float freely and the central bank does not intervene in the foreign exchange markets.*
	Float	The exchange rate is determined in the foreign exchange market based on daily supply and demand with minor or no official intervention. Requires little or no official reserves. Exchange rate regime places no restrictions on monetary policy, which often follows an inflation-targeting framework.

The classification emphasizes the importance of public pronounce-
ments as a signal for the private sector's expectations. Pushed to its
extreme, it implies that, in comparing two countries with identical
monetary histories, the announced exchange rate regime still matters
because it conveys information about future policy intentions, thus
influencing expectations and outcomes.

But what is one to make of a putative fixed exchange rate that is
devalued each year (if not more frequently)? Recalcitrant governments have been known to abuse the credibility benefits of fixing
the exchange rate, pursuing expansionary policies inconsistent with
long-term viability of the peg (Tornell and Velasco 1995, 2000).
Clearly, if the central bank does not take its commitment to defend
the parity very seriously, it is not much of a fixed exchange rate regime. Conversely, if the central bank—while abjuring any formal
commitment—nevertheless intervenes heavily in the foreign exchange markets, then the exchange rate can hardly be described as
freely floating.[1]

To the extent that there is a sizable number of such "soft pegs" and
"hard floats," classifying countries solely according to their declared
regime may give misleading results. An alternative de facto classification scheme, therefore, uses the observed behavior of the nominal
exchange rate (and perhaps indicators of monetary policy) to define
the exchange rate regime.[2]

De facto classifications are not without their own drawbacks,
however. Foremost among these is their backward-looking nature.
While the stated de jure regime in principle conveys information
about future policy intentions, observed actions necessarily pertain
to the past. De facto measures thus confront intrinsic difficulties of
capturing the signaling function of announced regime choices that lies
at the core of much of modern thinking about the effect of regimes.

Beyond this fundamental concern, de facto measures must contend with a number of conceptual difficulties and practical problems.
Stability of the nominal exchange rate—typically the most significant
component of de facto measures—may reflect either an absence of
shocks or an active policy offsetting shocks; only the latter warrants
inferences about policy. More generally, since countries have different structures and are subject to different shocks, it is difficult to infer
the underlying exchange rate policy from the observed exchange rate
movement. For example, a small open economy with a narrow export base operating under a pure float will likely experience greater

exchange rate volatility than a larger, more diversified economy also operating under a pure float. Since de facto measures are inherently relative—countries have "more" or "less" fixed exchange rates[3]— the small country might be (correctly) classified as floating, while the larger country might be (incorrectly) assigned to the "fixed" category.

In principle, identification can be achieved by controlling for country characteristics (Calvo and Reinhart 2000a,b; Kaminsky and Schmukler 2001; Levy-Yeyati and Sturzenegger 1999) and by incorporating foreign exchange intervention or interest rate movements into the de facto classification.[4] In practice, neither is straightforward. Interest rates in many developing countries are set administratively, often bearing little relation to what would be the market clearing rates. More important, central banks typically treat intervention data as confidential; information is not available on a consistent basis for large, cross-country data sets.[5]

Some studies use the change in gross reserves as a proxy for intervention, which has serious drawbacks. Just as intentions and actions may differ for the exchange rate regime, so statistics and reality might diverge for data on foreign exchange reserves. As the use of forward markets, swaps, nondeliverable forwards, and a variety of other off-balance sheet instruments by central banks have become more commonplace, gross reserves—even if reported accurately— become ever less informative.[6]

Furthermore, movements in central bank reserves, particularly in low income countries, are also influenced by a plethora of other factors. These might include servicing of foreign debt or payments for bulky purchases such as oil imports or aircraft, which have little to do with intentional foreign exchange intervention but may result in large movements in reported reserves.[7]

A more fundamental identification problem concerns the distinction between intervention undertaken to meet an explicit exchange rate target, and intervention motivated by other policy objectives. Inflation-targeting regimes are a case in point. In a small open economy that is subject to significant exchange rate pass-through to domestic prices, an inflation-targeting framework might place considerable weight on exchange rate stability in the face of nominal shocks,[8] thus yielding a low de facto score of exchange rate flexibility. However, the same framework may dictate considerable exchange rate adjustment in the face of real shocks. Depending on the relative incidence of real and nominal shocks, a de facto scheme may thus classify an inflation-targeting regime as either fixed or flexible. Moreover, as the incidence of shocks varies across time or countries, so will the result of a de facto classification rule, even though the underlying policy regime remains the same.

Ultimately, neither the de jure nor the de facto method is ideal. De jure classifications focus on the stated policy intentions of the monetary authorities; difficulties arise when actual policies diverge from promises. De facto classifications are based on actual movements of the exchange rate (and sometimes, other variables), but are backward looking and may capture exchange rate policy very imperfectly for a variety of reasons.

In our judgment, the drawbacks of the de jure classification are less severe. Most countries claiming to operate under fixed exchange rate regimes indeed maintain stable exchange rates over prolonged periods, while most countries claiming to have floating regimes experience substantial exchange rate variability, albeit occasionally tempered by large foreign exchange interventions. Accordingly, we prefer to use the de jure classification as our main method for categorizing regimes.

Several studies suggest, however, that there are some instances of soft pegs (de jure pegs that act as floats) and hard floats (de jure floats that act as pegs) among our sample countries. To examine the robustness of our findings to classification problems arising from these cases, we complement our de jure classification with a "consensus" classification. This sample consists only of those observations that are classified in the same category (fixed, intermediate, or floating) by both the de jure measure and by a de facto measure that we construct. In essence, the consensus sample drops "hard" floats and "soft" pegs. To preview the results, eliminating these ambiguous cases does not materially affect our findings on inflation performance, but it is of some importance for the growth results.[9]

4.2 The De Jure Classification

Our de jure classification is based on the stated intentions of the monetary authorities, as reported in the International Monetary Fund's *Annual Report on Exchange Arrangements and Exchange Restrictions*.[10] Table 4.2 lists the reported exchange rate regimes, along with their relative frequencies for virtually all IMF member

Table 4.2
De jure classification of exchange rate regimes 1970–1999 (in percent of total observations)

	Full Sample: 1970–1999	1970–1979	1980–1989	1990–1999
Number of observations (in percentage of full sample)		30.4	33.1	36.5
Pegged regimes	**65.4**	**84.8**	**68.4**	**46.6**
(1) Hard pegs	*13.2*	*10.0*	*13.8*	*15.4*
Dollarized	0.6	0.5	0.7	0.6
Currency board	5.2	4.6	4.7	6.1
Monetary union	7.4	4.9	8.4	8.7
(2) Single currency pegs	*32.8*	*61.2*	*27.4*	*13.9*
	32.8	61.2	27.4	13.9
(3) Basket pegs	*19.4*	*13.6*	*27.1*	*17.2*
Published basket pegs	9.8	7.3	13.9	8.1
Secret basket pegs	9.6	6.2	13.3	9.1
Intermediate regimes	**20.4**	**11.0**	**22.5**	**26.4**
(4) Floats with rule-based intervention	*8.4*	*5.9*	*9.5*	*9.6*
Cooperative regimes (EMS)	5.2	3.8	5.7	6.0
Crawling pegs	1.4	1.1	1.3	1.9
Target zones and bands	1.0	0.5	1.8	0.8
Unclassified rule-based systems	0.7	0.5	0.8	0.9
(5) Floats with discretionary intervention	*12.0*	*5.1*	*13.0*	*16.8*
Managed floats with heavy intervention	1.4	0.5	3.2	0.6
Unclassified managed floats	8.1	0.8	6.1	16.1
Other floats	2.4	3.8	3.7	0.1
Floating regimes	**14.2**	**4.3**	**9.1**	**27.0**
(6) Floats	*14.2*	*4.3*	*9.1*	*27.0*
Floats with light intervention	1.5	1.1	2.6	0.8
Floats with no intervention	12.7	3.2	6.5	26.2

countries from 1970 to 1999, some 4,300 observations covering 165 countries.[11]

At its most detailed level, the classification comprises fifteen regimes ranging from hard pegs, such as currency boards and dollarization, to intermediate regimes such as crawling pegs and target zones, to floats with varying degrees of intervention.[12] Single currency pegs are the largest group, accounting for almost one third of the observations, followed by basket pegs and managed floats. Over the entire sample, about one eighth of observations fall into each of the two extreme regimes, hard pegs and pure floats.

Fifteen regimes is too fine a classification for most questions; for the bulk of our empirical analysis, we condense regimes into three groups: pegged, intermediate, and floating. Their respective compositions are indicated in bold type in table 4.2. The right-most columns report the frequency distributions by decade. Over the sample period, the prevalence of pegged regimes has declined sharply, from 85 percent of all observations during the 1970s to less than 50 percent by the 1990s. The sharpest gains were recorded by the floating group, increasing from a mere 4 percent in the 1970s to more than 25 percent during the 1990s (figure 4.1).[13]

On occasion, we also make use of a more detailed, six-way classification. We subdivide the pegged regimes into hard pegs, single currency pegs and basket pegs. Intermediate systems are subdivided into those with publicly known or rule-based intervention (crawling pegs and target zones) versus those with more discretionary intervention. Floating regimes form the final category. Table 4.2 reports the composition of this finer classification, in italic type.

The time pattern for the more detailed classification (figure 4.2) shows that the traditional single currency peg has lost market share, shrinking from 60 percent of observations to less than 15 percent over the sample period. Winners include the pure floats and floats with discretionary intervention, increasing from 9 percent to almost 44 percent, while hard pegs display a more modest increase from 10 to 15 percent.

4.3 Consensus Classification

Since policy actions sometimes differ from stated intentions—most notably in the case of soft pegs and hard floats—it is useful to complement the de jure classification with one based on observed

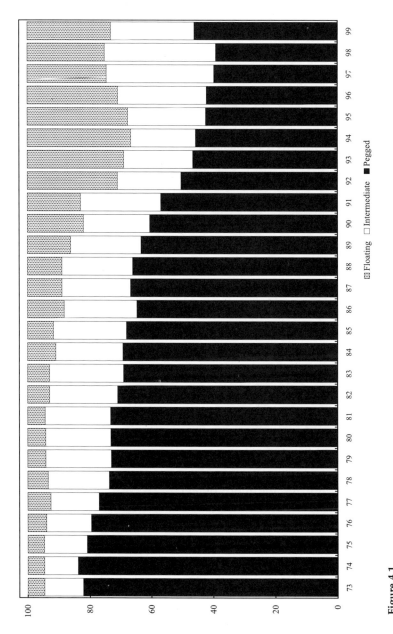

Figure 4.1
Distribution of regimes, 1973–1999 (percent)

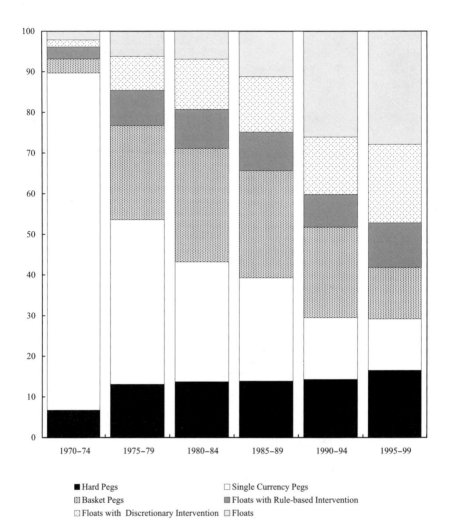

Figure 4.2
Distribution of exchange rate regimes, 1970–1999 (detailed de jure classification)
Source: IMF, *Annual Report on Exchange Arrangements and Exchange Restrictions.*

behavior. To this end, we construct a "consensus classification" that essentially drops soft pegs and hard floats by using the intersection of the de jure classification and a de facto classification that we construct.

We first compute a continuous de facto measure based on observed exchange rate behavior, then convert it into a discrete three-way classification of pegged, intermediate, and floating regimes using the relative frequency distribution of regimes in the de jure classification. The consensus sample then simply consists of all observations for which the two classification methods agree.

The most obvious variable on which to base the de facto measure is the nominal exchange rate itself. As discussed above, stability of the nominal exchange rate may, however, reflect either a deliberate policy of keeping the exchange rate fixed, or an absence of shocks. One option is to augment the measure by incorporating variables such as interest rates and the change in reserves as proxies for intervention. We pursue the simpler approach of using the variability of the nominal exchange rate as the de facto measure, for two reasons. First, our interest lies not in the de facto classification as such, but rather in constructing a robustness check for our empirical results obtained using the de jure classification. Second, the methodological problems identified above are, in our view, too severe to justify the loss of sample size implied by trying to add reserve and interest rate movements to the de facto measure.

Even for our relatively simple de facto measure, several issues arise. First, how should exchange rate volatility be measured? Second, against which reference currency should the volatility be assessed? Figure 4.3 plots examples of two idealized types of nominal exchange rate movement—a crawling peg, and a float without trend—together with their combination (a float with a trend).

While the float with trend is clearly the most volatile, it is less clear how to rank the crawling peg relative to the float without trend. The crawling peg is more predictable, yet the average movement during the year (end point to end point) may well exceed that of a pure float without trend.

For our de facto measure, we attach equal weight to the mean and the volatility of nominal exchange rate changes, creating an annual score based on the mean and the variance of the monthly depreciation rates. We define the continuous de facto measure (referred to in what follows as the z-score) as

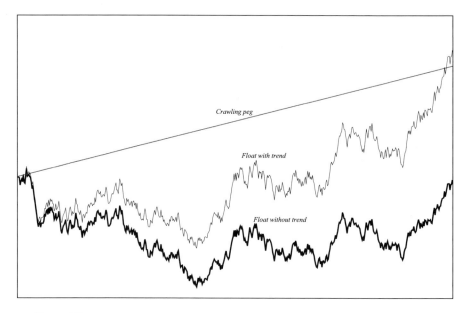

Figure 4.3
De facto measures: An illustration of possible nominal exchange rate movements

$$z = \sqrt{\mu_{\Delta e}^2 + \sigma_{\Delta e}^2}$$

where $\mu_{\Delta e}$ is the average monthly rate of change of the nominal exchange rate during the year and $\sigma_{\Delta e}^2$ is the variance of those monthly changes. For each country in the sample, we compute this measure separately against each of the G7 currencies, the ECU and the SDR, and then select the reference currency yielding the smallest z-score.[14]

To construct a discrete de facto measure comparable to the de jure classification, we drop the (very small) number of observations for which either the de jure or the de facto measure is unavailable. For each sample year, we then map the continuous z-score into a discrete three-way de facto classification (pegged, intermediate, and float) by imposing the relative frequency distribution of the de jure classification for that year.[15]

4.4 A Comparison

The de jure and the de facto classifications are supposed to capture the same concept—the nominal exchange rate regime. If most gov-

Table 4.3
Distribution of de jure and de facto classifications

De jure classification	De facto classification		
	Pegged	Intermediate	Floating
Pegged regimes	2265	378	178
Intermediate regimes	432	270	179
Floating regimes	124	233	254
Total	2821	881	611
Percentage consensus	80.3	30.6	41.6

ernments do what they say and say what they do, one would expect substantial overlap. Table 4.3 compares the de jure and de facto classifications. Along the diagonal of the matrix, both classifications coincide; off-diagonal elements represent divergences between the two classifications. The overlap is greatest for the pegs (where 80 percent are classified in the same way), whereas the distinction between floats and intermediate regimes is hazier. Overall, almost 65 percent of the observations are classified identically under the two schemes. These observations constitute the "consensus" subsample that we will use later for our robustness tests.

The off-diagonal entries provide an indication of the importance of soft pegs and hard floats. Conditional on the de facto classification being correct, soft pegs are those observations that are classified as de jure pegs but de facto floats. There are 178 observations in this category (6 percent of all de jure pegs), while a further 378 (13 percent of all de jure pegs) are classified as intermediate regimes under the de facto classification. At the other end of the spectrum, de jure floats that behave like de facto pegs—hard floats—account for 124 observations (about 20 percent of all de jure floats). About 38 percent of the de jure floats are classified as an intermediate regime under the de facto measure. Again conditional on the correctness of the de facto measure, these observations capture the notion of "fear of floating" proposed by Calvo and Reinhart (2000a).

4.5 Conclusions

Most theoretical analyses rely on an appealingly simple dichotomy between "fixed" and "floating" exchange rates. Empirical work does not enjoy that luxury. The rich diversity of regimes poses two challenges for empirical work: how fine a classification scheme to adopt, and how to classify individual countries.

Trying to squeeze the various regimes into a rigid dichotomization of fixed versus floating ignores important real-world distinctions. On the other hand, too detailed a classification risks losing sight of the forest among the trees. We strike a compromise, using both a broad three-way classification (corresponding to the intuitive notion that countries might have "fixed" or "floating" exchange rate regimes, or an intermediate arrangement) as well as a more detailed, six-way classification.

The second issue concerns the identification of regimes. Are regimes best classified by words—the stated commitment of the central bank—or by actions and behavior, most notably the time path of the nominal exchange rate? There is no clear answer; both approaches have their advantages and drawbacks. We prefer the de jure approach, both because of the central role assigned to signaling and expectations formation in modern macroeconomics, and because of the significant conceptual and practical problems associated with de facto classifications. As a robustness check, we also create a consensus classification that aims to drop the ambiguous cases—soft pegs and hard floats—to examine the sensitivity of our main results to the classification methodology.

5   Facts and Figures

What, then, are the facts? The review of the theoretical literature in chapter 3 suggests an abundance of possible linkages between the nominal exchange rate regime and various macroeconomic variables. At a theoretical level, this multitude of potential linkages—some offsetting, others reinforcing—makes it difficult to establish unambiguous relationships. Determining which linkages dominate, and therefore what is the net influence of the exchange rate regime on the main variables of policy interest, is thus ultimately an empirical issue. Using our regime classifications, we take up this challenge in this chapter and the next.

The discussion is organized around three key sets of macroeconomic variables: nominal and real exchange rates; inflation, money, and interest rates; and output growth and volatility.[1] We begin in this chapter by documenting the unconditional relationships. In chapter 6 we explore the conditional linkages between the exchange rate regime and inflation and growth in a regression framework.

Our empirical analysis is based on a dataset of macroeconomic variables drawn primarily from the International Monetary Fund's *World Economic Outlook* database. The sample covers 147 countries (a subset of the 165 countries for which the exchange rate regime is available) over the period 1970–1999. Taking account of lags and missing values, we have 2,855 observations for most variables.[2]

5.1   Exchange Rates

The most obvious implication of the exchange rate regime concerns the behavior of the nominal exchange rate itself. At first sight, this might appear to be a trivial issue: Presumably, nominal exchange rates are more volatile under floating regimes than under fixed regimes. It turns out, however, that the issue is neither so simple nor so obvious (Bartolini 1996). In particular, the relative volatility of the nominal exchange rate under alternative regimes depends on the time horizon considered.

Under floating exchange rates, there may be significant "noise" (short-term movements that are rapidly reversed). As the horizon lengthens, such temporary movements would cancel out, leading to a decrease in measured volatility. Conversely, nominal exchange rates under pegged regimes may indeed display zero variability (against the reference currency) in the short run. As the horizon lengthens, however, there is a greater likelihood of a change in the parity—a devaluation or a revaluation—which may imply very significant movements of the nominal exchange rate. Of course, "average" volatility may still decrease as the horizon lengthens simply because the nominal exchange rate movement is being spread over a longer period, but the underlying dynamic may be quite different from that of a floating exchange rate.

A second issue concerns the relationship between nominal and real exchange rate variability. There are two starkly different views. One school holds that in a world of integrated financial markets, nominal exchange rates are mainly driven by short-term, highly speculative capital flows, resulting in far greater volatility than justified on the basis of macroeconomic fundamentals.[3] With sticky prices, this nominal volatility implies greater variability of the real exchange rate as well, a point made forcefully by Mussa (1986).

An alternative viewpoint maintains that flexible exchange rates automatically adjust to inflation differentials, implying that movements of the real exchange rate would be less volatile under floating exchange rate regimes. Which view is correct? Again, the answer may depend on the time horizon under consideration. At short horizons, floating exchange rates may be associated with greater volatility of the real exchange rate; at longer horizons, they may help offset inflation differentials, thus reducing real exchange rate volatility.

All this suggests that any discussion of exchange rate volatility must be in reference to the time horizon under consideration. With this in mind, we calculate the volatility of the trade-weighted nominal effective and real effective exchange rates at various horizons, from one to sixty months, for the de jure classification.[4] For each month of a given year, we define the k-horizon volatility as the absolute value of the percentage change of the exchange rate over the previous k months. To calculate the volatility for a given horizon, we average all observations over this horizon. To ensure that the sample is consistent across horizons, observations are dropped if the regime changes during the sixty-month window.[5]

Figure 5.1 graphs the volatility of the nominal effective exchange rate (expressed at annual rates, in percent) for various time horizons and exchange rate regimes. Two features are immediately apparent. First, at all horizons, nominal exchange rate volatility is greater under floating regimes than under pegged or intermediate regimes. Second, there is a general tendency for volatility to decrease with the length of the horizon. Averaging across all regimes, the volatility of the nominal exchange rate halves from 18 percent per year at the one-month horizon, to just under 10 percent per year at the twelve-month horizon and 8 percent per year by the five-year horizon.

There are, however, significant differences across regimes. For floating exchange rates, we observe an initial decline in volatility as the horizon lengthens (consistent with the presence of short-term "noise"). This trend ends, however, at the twelve- to eighteen-month horizon. Not only is the absolute decline in volatility smaller for floating exchange rates compared to other regimes, so is the *relative* decline. Whereas the five-year volatility is about 35 percent of the one-month volatility for pegged exchange rates, for floating exchange rates the corresponding ratio is closer to 60 percent.

The bottom panel of figure 5.1 shows that these results are not robust across country groups. For the higher income countries, the volatility of floating exchange rates decreases monotonically in the length of the horizon. The decline is quite rapid: The five-year volatility is about 35 percent of the one-month volatility—commensurate with the drop-off observed under pegged regimes (and somewhat faster than under intermediate regimes). For these countries, therefore, the bulk of nominal exchange rate movements may indeed represent short-term noise.[6]

For the lower income countries, we observe a starkly different pattern under floating exchange rates. The monotonic decline seen for the higher income countries gives way to a U-shaped relation— in fact, the five-year volatility considerably *exceeds* the one-year volatility. One explanation is that, for these countries, price and exchange rate movements tend to be mutually validating, be it because

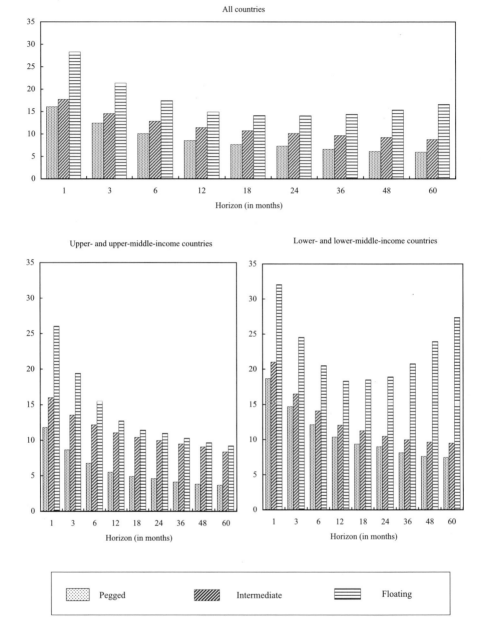

Figure 5.1
Nominal exchange rate volatility at alternative horizons (in percent per year)

the exchange rate depreciates in response to higher inflation or be-cause the central bank allows an exchange rate depreciation to feed into higher prices.

Figure 5.2 turns to real exchange rate volatility, calculated in the same manner at horizons ranging from one to sixty months. The results are rather striking: Averaging across all countries, the vola-tility of the real effective exchange rate at shorter horizons is only slightly greater under floating rates than under fixed rates (some 1 to 2 percent per year), while at the twelve-month horizon, real ex-change rate volatility is actually *lower* under floating regimes. Inter-mediate regimes exhibit the lowest volatility.

The finding seems at odds with conventional wisdom. But again, the distinction between country groups is crucial. For higher income countries, real exchange rate volatility is substantially greater under floating regimes at all horizons, consistent with the view of Mussa (1986) that nominal exchange rate movements in countries with high capital mobility can be an independent source of real exchange rate volatility. In contrast, for the lower income countries there is a much greater tendency of floating exchange rates to offset inflation differ-entials. Accordingly, the volatility of the real exchange rate under floating regimes eventually falls below the volatility observed under pegged regimes.

The sources of real exchange rate variability can be explored more directly by decomposing the movements into nominal exchange rate changes, the inflation differential, and their covariance.[7] If nominal exchange rate movements tend to offset inflation differentials, the negative covariation reduces the volatility of the real exchange rate. As figure 5.3 illustrates, this is the case across all country groups and exchange rate regimes, though the effect is much more pronounced under floating regimes.

Across country groups, the pattern for pegged exchange rates is similar. However, for floating regimes, there are important differences between the high- and low-income countries. First, in high-income countries the movement in nominal exchange rates dominates the movement in relative prices (consistent with Mussa's 1986 stylized fact for industrialized countries); while for the lower income coun-tries, relative price movements are actually a slightly larger source of variation of the real exchange rate.

Second, as documented in figure 5.1, the nominal exchange rate variability under floating rates in lower income countries is U-

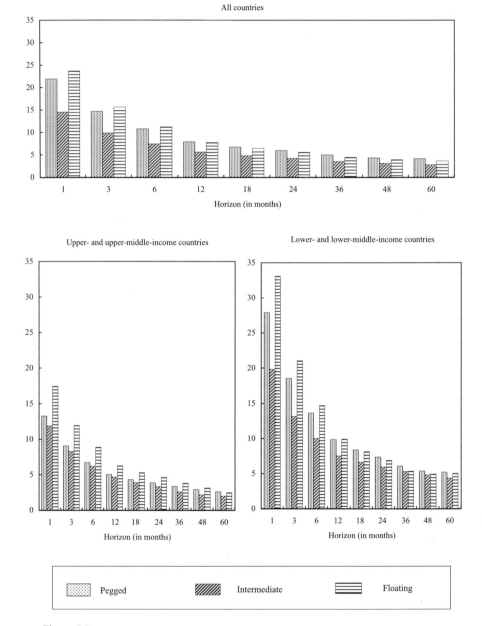

Figure 5.2
Real exchange rate volatility at alternative horizons (in percent per year)

All countries

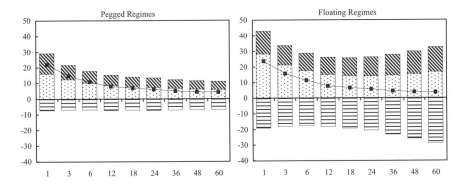

Upper- and upper-middle-income countries

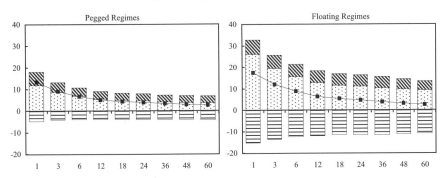

Lower- and lower-middle-income countries

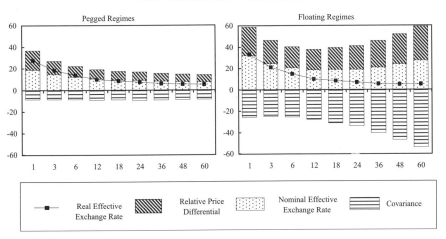

Figure 5.3
Decomposition of real exchange rate volatility at alternative horizons (in percent per year)

shaped in the horizon, as is the volatility of relative prices. These two effects, however, are dominated by the much greater negative covariance between the two series; in consequence, real exchange rate volatility monotonically declines as the horizon lengthens.

To conclude, nominal exchange rate variability is greater under floating regimes than under pegged regimes, not only (trivially) at short horizons but also at longer horizons. For the upper income countries, shorter term movements under floating rates partly represent noise; volatility at longer horizons is thus smaller. For the lower income countries, nominal exchange rate movements tend to be both much larger and more persistent, but since they mostly offset inflation differentials, they serve to reduce real exchange rate variability. By the same token, however, this also means that, instead of providing an anti-inflationary anchor, floating exchange rates may accommodate inflation.

5.2   Inflation, Money, and Interest Rates

Most policy credibility models predict that inflation is lower under pegged exchange rates. The findings of the previous section provide some indirect support for this prediction, at least for lower income countries.

Does inflation in fact differ systematically across exchange rate regimes? Figure 5.4 graphs the relative frequency distribution of inflation rates across various regimes under the de jure classification (for each regime, the bars sum to unity). While observations for pegged regimes cluster at low inflation rates, the distributions for intermediate and floating regimes are more even. But the figure also reveals the existence of a sizable set of low-inflation floats: 13 percent of the floating regime observations occur in the 0–2 percent inflation range, compared to 10 percent of the pegged regime observations. The pattern is even more dramatic for the consensus classification (figure 5.5). Eighty percent of the observations under pegged regimes are below 15 percent per year, compared to less than 40 percent of the floating regime observations (and about 50 percent of the intermediate regime observations). Again, there is a sizable subset of countries with floating regimes yet low inflation; indeed, the distribution is almost bimodal. In chapter 6, we explore the characteristics of this group further.

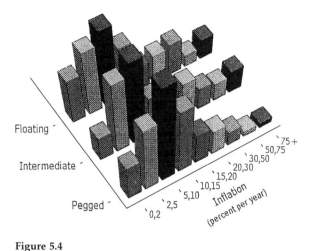

Figure 5.4
Relative frequency distribution of inflation rates by exchange rate regime (de jure classification)

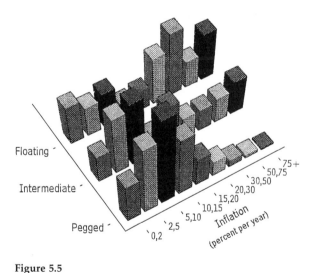

Figure 5.5
Relative frequency distribution of inflation rates by exchange rate regime (consensus classification)

How do these frequency distributions translate into average inflation performance under the various regimes? Inflation averaged 24.3 percent per year under floating regimes, about 10 percentage points higher than under pegged regimes (13.3 percent per year), and slightly above that recorded under intermediate regimes (22 percent per year).

Average inflation rates, however, can be skewed by a few hyperinflationary outliers, which may be particularly important for the statistics on floating regimes. The median avoids this problem but does not readily capture the thickness of the distribution tails. In what follows, therefore, we focus on the scaled inflation rate, given by $\pi/(1+\pi)$, which is robust to hyperinflationary outliers while capturing the mass of the distribution.[8]

The differences across regimes for this scaled inflation rate are more modest, but hardly negligible (table 5.1). On average (scaled) inflation was 3.5 percentage points per year lower under pegged regimes compared to floating regimes (while intermediate regimes do marginally worse than floats). Not surprisingly, the difference between pegs and floats in the consensus classification—which tends to drop soft pegs and hard floats—is considerably greater, at about 15 percentage points per year.

What lies behind this better inflation performance? The most obvious explanation is that money growth is lower under pegged regimes. This is in fact the case: Scaled money growth was 3.5 percentage points per year lower under de jure pegs than under floats (and about 12 percentage points lower in the consensus classification), providing some initial support for the presence of what we termed the "monetary discipline effect" in chapter 3.

The theoretical model also suggests that, in addition to this greater monetary discipline, there may be a confidence effect whereby inflation under pegged regimes is lower, even controlling for money growth. Figure 5.6 takes a first look at this issue, plotting money growth against inflation for pegged and floating regimes.[9] While only impressionistic, the graph suggests that, at annual inflation rates above 10 percent, inflation is indeed lower under pegged regimes for a *given* rate of money growth.

As table 5.1 reveals, this greater monetary discipline does not translate into fiscal discipline: Countries on pegged regimes ran larger fiscal deficits.[10] The difference may reflect the enhanced credibility that the peg affords, allowing such countries to run larger deficits without triggering fears that the debt will be inflated away. Or,

Table 5.1
Inflation, money growth, and interest rates (in percent per year, unless otherwise specified)

	De jure classification			Consensus classification		
	Pegged	Intermediate	Floating	Pegged	Intermediate	Floating
Scaled inflation (average)[1]	9.6	13.9	13.1	7.9	17.2	23.0
Scaled money growth (average)[2]	13.4	18.6	16.9	12.4	21.5	24.7
Nominal interest rate (median)	7.3	12.4	12.3	7.0	14.6	18.3
Real interest rate, ex post (median)	0.7	2.9	3.2	1.7	2.4	1.9
Memorandum items						
Inflation (average)	13.3	22.0	24.3	9.4	30.2	58.8
Inflation (median)	8.0	9.6	9.0	6.9	11.4	21.7
Money growth (average)	17.7	29.3	28.1	15.5	39.2	51.4
Money growth (median)	14.4	18.3	15.5	13.7	18.8	26.7
Government balance, percent of GDP (median)	−3.9	−3.3	−2.8	−3.9	−2.6	−3.8
Observations	1807	606	442	1483	1280	103

[1] Scaled inflation: $\pi/(1+\pi)$.
[2] Scaled money growth: $\mu/(1+\mu)$.

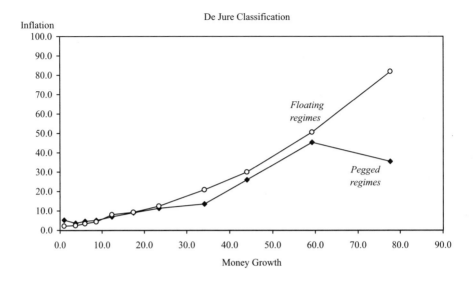

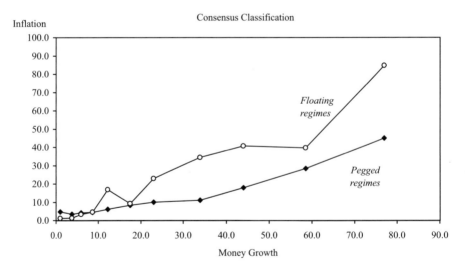

Figure 5.6
Inflation and money growh under alternative exchange rate regimes (in percent per year)

as Tornell and Velasco (1995) argue, it may reflect the willingness of governments with short time horizons to exploit the peg by running large fiscal deficits that eventually burst into open inflation and a collapse of the fixed exchange rate regime. We examine the evidence for cross-regime contamination in the next chapter, and focus on crises in chapter 7.

Perhaps the most direct way to examine credibility effects is through interest rates. If expected inflation is lower under pegged rates, and if real interest rates under pegged rates are either lower or at least not much greater than under floating regimes, then nominal interest rates on comparable assets should be lower under pegged regimes. Unfortunately, interest rates in many of our sample countries were administratively set over much of the sample period, so it is difficult to obtain comparable market-determined interest rates. With this caveat, table 5.1 shows that the median nominal interest rate is indeed lowest under pegged regimes—by some 5 percentage points per year in the de jure classification and 10 percentage points per year in the consensus classification.

A credibility bonus of pegged exchange rates should also be reflected in a smaller risk premium, and thus lower "real" interest rates. Here data problems are even more formidable: apart from the standard problem of using ex post rather than expected inflation rates, recorded real rates in high-inflation countries are quite often significantly negative.[11] With these qualifications in mind, ex post real interest rates are indeed lower under pegged exchange rate regimes.

Of course, the adoption of a pegged exchange rate provides only one of several mechanisms to enhance credibility, alongside the introduction of independent central banks or the appointment of conservative central bankers. For countries that have already adopted such measures, or that enjoy long track records of moderate policy, the adoption of pegs is likely to have only a marginal additional effect. A full assessment of the relative inflation performance across regimes requires controlling for these factors. In chapter 6, we examine the conditional effect of regimes using more formal statistical methods. As a first indication, table 5.2 reports average inflation performance, differentiated by both exchange rate regime and various country characteristics.

For high-income countries,[12] whose inflation rates average about 5 percent per year, pegged exchange rate regimes perform no better—

Table 5.2
Inflation performance under alternative exchange rate regimes and country characteristics (in percent per year)

	De jure classification			Consensus classification		
	Pegged	Intermediate	Floating	Pegged	Intermediate	Floating
Upper-income countries	6.5	7.1	5.7	5.9	5.8	1.6
Upper-middle-income countries	8.4	28.2	13.8	6.6	32.8	23.1
Lower- and lower-middle-income countries	10.6	15.8	18.6	6.6	12.1	28.7
Countries with no current account restrictions	6.9	9.6	10.1	6.3	12.2	18.0
Countries with no capital account restrictions	6.0	8.5	7.1	5.6	11.1	18.4
Very open economies[1]	7.3	8.9	16.0	6.7	6.1	24.2
Countries with low central bank turnover rates[2]	6.9	9.9	10.1	6.4	9.8	20.6

[1] Countries whose ratio to GDP of exports plus imports exceeds 75 percent.
[2] Countries in the bottom quartile of the country distribution of central bank turnover rates.

in fact, rather worse—than floats. Otherwise, it is uniformly the case that pegs show better inflation performance than either floats or intermediate regimes under both the de jure and the consensus classifications.

While the ordering of the three regimes is robust, the size of the inflation differences varies substantially across country groups. Among the lower income countries, where limited policy credibility may be more of an issue, inflation under pegged exchange rates is about 8 percentage points lower than under floats. For the upper middle income countries, the differential is about 5 percentage points per year, which is smaller both in absolute terms and in relation to the inflation rate under a float. Among countries without capital controls, the inflation bonus of pegging the exchange rate, at 1 percentage point, is even smaller, consistent with the notion that capital mobility provides an alternative disciplinary device.

In summary, inflation is generally lower under pegged regimes than under floating regimes, as is money growth. Moreover, inflation is lower under pegged exchange rates for a given rate of money growth. When other disciplinary devices are present, however, the benefit of pegging the exchange rate is smaller. The stylized facts are thus very much consistent with the theoretical model presented in chapter 3.

5.3   Output Growth

Does the lower inflation come at the expense of reduced growth? Analogous to the inflation charts, figures 5.7 and 5.8 graph the frequency distributions of the level of per capita real GDP growth under the de jure and consensus classifications.

Comparing de jure pegs to de jure floats yields no clear pattern, except perhaps the more dispersed distribution of growth rates under pegged regimes, with a larger proportion of observations both at the very low range (negative per capita growth) and at the upper end (5 percent per year and above).

Dropping hard floats and soft pegs makes a significant difference. As figure 5.8 reveals, pegged regimes do markedly better than floating regimes under the consensus classification, with a greater proportion of observations at the upper end of the distribution and a smaller proportion at the very low end. In both classifications, intermediate regimes do best.

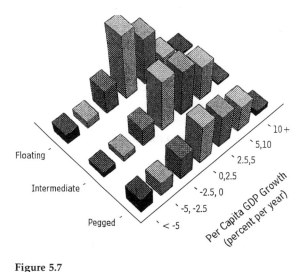

Figure 5.7
Relative frequency distribution of per capita GDP growth rates by exchange rate regime (de jure classification)

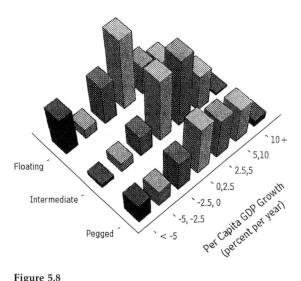

Figure 5.8
Relative frequency distribution of per capita GDP growth rates by exchange rate regime (consensus classification)

These patterns are reflected in the average and median growth rates (table 5.3). In the de jure classification, pegged and floating regimes are precisely matched at an average growth rate of 1.2 percent per year, while intermediate regimes do twice as well. Looking across subgroups, growth rates under pegs and floats are similar for lower income countries and countries with current account convertibility. Pegged exchange rates do somewhat better in very open economies and higher income countries, and somewhat worse in countries with full capital mobility.

As noted earlier, dropping the soft pegs and hard floats changes the picture considerably. In the consensus sample, average growth under floating rates is negative and some 2.25 percentage points lower than under pegged regimes. Again, intermediate regimes do best.

Of course, the nominal exchange rate regime is not the only determinant of growth. Indeed, growth theory does not suggest that it is even a particularly important factor. In the next chapter, therefore, we turn to the conditional effect of the exchange rate regime on growth controlling for various other factors.

For the moment, it suffices to note that two of the most obvious candidates for a link between the exchange rate regime and growth—the investment and trade openness ratios—do vary systematically across regimes. Investment rates are about 2 percent of GDP higher under pegged regimes than under floats, while trade openness (the ratio of imports plus exports to GDP) is about 20 percentage points greater; moreover, these differences hold across various country groupings.

It is tempting to conclude that pegged exchange rates foster greater trade integration or investment, and thereby promote faster growth. While this may be true, it cannot be the whole story. Intermediate regimes, which have lower investment and openness ratios than pegged regimes, have the highest GDP growth rates. The explanation of the growth patterns must thus await the full conditional analysis undertaken in chapter 6.[13]

To conclude, GDP growth is highest for countries with intermediate exchange rate regimes. Pegs perform about as well as floating regimes in the de jure classification, and significantly better in the consensus classification. However, the reasons for these differences are not readily apparent: Investment and trade openness, the most

Table 5.3
Growth, investment, and openness (in percent per year, unless otherwise specified)

	De jure classification			Consensus classification		
	Pegged	Intermediate	Floating	Pegged	Intermediate	Floating
Real GDP growth per capita (average)	1.2	2.4	1.2	1.3	2.6	−0.9
Real GDP growth per capita (median)	1.5	2.4	1.8	1.6	2.7	0.5
Investment ratio (in percent of GDP)	22.0	22.5	20.0	22.1	21.7	18.3
Trade openness (in percent of GDP)[1]	76.0	70.3	56.4	78.2	68.9	57.2
Export growth[2]	4.9	8.4	7.0	4.8	7.2	8.8
Memorandum items						
Number of observations	1807	606	442	1280	103	100
Real GDP growth per capita (average)						
Upper- and upper-middle-income countries	2.1	2.5	1.7	2.1	2.9	0.7
Lower- and lower-middle-income countries	0.8	2.4	0.7	0.9	2.1	−1.5
Countries without current account restrictions	1.3	2.6	1.4	1.2	3.3	−1.2
Countries without capital account restrictions	1.1	2.6	1.6	1.1	3.4	−0.4
Very open economies	1.8	2.9	0.5	1.7	4.8	−2.5

[1] Ratio to GDP of imports of goods and services and of exports of goods and services.
[2] Volume of exports of goods and services.

likely channels, vary across regimes in ways that do not easily correlate with observed differences in GDP growth.[14]

5.4   Output Volatility

While theoretical models are largely silent on the implications of the exchange rate regime for long-run growth, there is a significant body of literature on the stabilizing properties of exchange rate regimes.[15] As discussed in chapter 3, fixed exchange rates should be better at stabilizing output in the face of nominal shocks. Conversely, assuming nominal wages and prices are sticky, fixed exchange rates impede adjustment to real shocks, exacerbating their effect on the volatility of output.

The latter effect seems to dominate (table 5.4). The standard deviation of real GDP around its HP-filtered trend, or of real GDP growth, is some 0.5 to 1.5 percent per year higher under pegged regimes than under floating regimes (the only exception being the lower income countries under the consensus classification).[16]

Furthermore, at least for the de jure classification, the difference between pegged and floating regimes is larger for the higher income countries (where nominal rigidities are likely to be more prevalent). Intermediate regimes have the lowest volatility under the de jure classification, but not in the consensus classification.

5.5   Conclusions

In this chapter, we took an initial look at the stylized facts about macroeconomic performance under alternative exchange rate regimes. At all horizons, nominal exchange rates are more volatile under floating regimes than under pegged regimes. For the higher income countries, much of this movement appears to be short-term noise; for the lower income countries, floating exchange rates mostly offset inflation differentials.

This pattern has implications for the real exchange rate as well. For the higher income countries, real exchange rate variability is greater under floating regimes than under pegged regimes at all horizons. For the lower income countries, the offsetting nature of nominal exchange rate movements means that, at horizons of one year or above, real exchange rate variability is lower under floating regimes than under pegged regimes.

Table 5.4
Volatility[1] (in percent per year, unless otherwise specified)

	De jure classification			Consensus classification		
	Pegged	Intermediate	Floating	Pegged	Intermediate	Floating
Real GDP growth volatility	3.4	2.1	2.3	3.5	2.3	3.6
Real GDP volatility[2]	2.8	1.9	2.0	2.9	2.3	2.7
Consumption growth volatility	5.9	3.0	3.8	6.1	3.1	5.8
Consumption share volatility	2.8	1.6	2.0	2.9	1.9	2.8
Memorandum items						
Number of observations	1777	594	426	1258	102	89
Upper- and upper-middle-income						
Real GDP growth volatility	3.2	2.0	1.7	3.4	2.5	2.5
Real GDP volatility[2]	2.6	1.8	1.6	2.8	2.2	1.7
Lower- and lower-middle-income						
Real GDP growth volatility	3.5	2.1	2.9	3.5	1.8	4.1
Real GDP volatility[2]	2.9	2.0	2.5	3.0	2.4	3.1

[1] Calculated as the three-year moving standard deviation.
[2] Percentage deviation of output from HP-fitted trend.

Viewed from another angle, floating exchange rates are more accommodative of inflation: With the exception of the major industrialized nations, countries with floating regimes have experienced higher inflation. The inflation differential reflects both higher money growth rates, and a larger inflationary impact of a given rate of money growth.

While the inflation results are quite robust, the evidence on output growth is more equivocal. Pegged regimes perform about as well as floats in the de jure classification, and considerably better in the consensus classification. In both classifications, intermediate regimes perform best. The results on real volatility are somewhat stronger, suggesting greater volatility under pegged exchange rates, particularly for the higher income countries.

These stylized facts are merely suggestive, since inflation and growth are likely to depend on much more than just the exchange rate regime. In the next chapter, therefore, we turn to regression analysis to examine the effects of the exchange rate regime, controlling for at least some of these other factors.

6

Inflation, Growth, and the Exchange Rate Regime

Chapter 5 documented stylized facts about macroeconomic performance under alternative exchange rate regimes. For inflation, the findings are largely consistent with the predictions of the policy credibility models. For growth, the unconditional results are more equivocal, although the large differences in investment and openness ratios across regimes might translate into growth differentials once other factors are taken into account. This suggests that the link between the exchange rate regime and macroeconomic performance warrants further examination—for inflation, to see whether the results are robust; for growth, to see whether any firm conclusions can be drawn at all.

In this chapter, we go beyond the stylized facts by estimating regressions that relate inflation and growth to the exchange rate regime and various other determinants suggested by the literature. We then subject these base specifications to a series of tests to establish whether the estimated relationships are robust.

6.1 Inflation: Baseline Specification

To examine the conditional link between inflation and the exchange rate regime, we regress the scaled inflation rate (which we refer to simply as "inflation," π, in what follows) on two exchange rate regime dummies for pegged (*Peg*) and intermediate (*Int*) regimes respectively. Floating regimes are the excluded category (so that the coefficients on *Peg* and *Int* should be interpreted as the inflation differential relative to a floating exchange rate regime).

Of course, inflation is likely to depend on much more than just the exchange rate regime. The theoretical model in chapter 3 suggests that higher real GDP growth, Δy, by raising money demand, should reduce inflation. Conversely, faster growth of the money supply, Δm, should be associated with higher inflation.

Beyond the variables explicitly included in the theoretical model, the literature suggests a number of other potential determinants of inflation. Romer (1993) argues that greater trade openness (the ratio of exports plus imports to GDP, *Open*) raises the costs of a monetary expansion, which, by the logic of the policy credibility models, should imply lower inflation in more open economies.[1]

The policy credibility literature suggests that an independent, "conservative" central banker can help solve the time consistency problem (Rogoff 1985). Although it is difficult to measure the conservatism of the central bank governor, Cukierman (1992) uses the turnover rate (*CBTurn*) of the central bank governor as an (inverse) proxy for central bank independence, on the grounds that less independent central bank governors can be fired more easily. A higher turnover rate of the central bank governor should therefore be associated with higher inflation. Other factors include inflationary terms-of-trade shocks (*TofT*) (Fischer 1993) and the fiscal balance (*GovGDP*), either because of direct money financing, or simply by contributing to aggregate demand pressures.

In addition, we include annual dummies in the regression to capture shocks that are common across countries, but vary over time, such as oil price shocks. The baseline equation therefore becomes[2]

$$\pi = \beta_0 + \beta_{Peg}Peg + \beta_{Int}Int + \beta_{Mon}\Delta m + \beta_4\Delta y + \beta_5 Open$$
$$+ \beta_6 CBTurn + \beta_7\Delta TofT + \beta_8 GovGDP + \varepsilon \qquad (1)$$

To interpret the results, we need to take account of the possibility that money growth itself is endogenous to the nominal exchange rate regime. Since money growth is included as one of the conditioning variables in the regression, any indirect effects of the exchange rate regime operating through money growth would not be picked up by the coefficients on the regime dummies. To illustrate, suppose that the growth rate of the money supply depends upon the exchange rate regime

$$\Delta m = \alpha_0 + \alpha_{Peg}Peg + \alpha_{Int}Int + \eta \qquad (2)$$

where *Peg* and *Int* are dummy variables for pegged and intermediate regimes, and η is a random shock. Suppose further that the inflation rate depends upon money growth, the exchange rate regime, and a vector of other conditioning variables, z:

$$\pi = \beta_0 + \beta_{Peg}Peg + \beta_{Int}Int + \beta_{Mon}\Delta m + \beta_j z_j + \varepsilon \qquad (3)$$

The direct effect of the exchange rate regime on inflation, conditional on money growth—what we termed the "confidence effect" above—is given by the coefficient β_{Peg} (β_{Int} for intermediate regimes). From (2), however, there is also an indirect effect on inflation through the money growth channel, given by $\beta_{Mon}\alpha_{Peg}$.[3] Since Peg is a dummy variable, an estimate of α_{Peg} is given by the difference in the average growth rates of the money supply under pegged and floating regimes, $\alpha_{Peg} = \overline{\Delta m}_{Peg} - \overline{\Delta m}_{Flt}$ (and likewise for α_{Int}). The full effects of the exchange rate regime on inflation, combining the confidence and discipline effects, can therefore be obtained from (3) as $\gamma_{Peg} = \beta_{Peg} + \beta_{Mon}(\overline{\Delta m}_{Peg} - \overline{\Delta m}_{Flt})$. Below we report both the confidence effect alone, β_{Peg}, and this combined effect, γ_{Peg}.[4]

Table 6.1 reports the coefficients for alternative samples. Panel 1 refers to the de jure classification of exchange rate regimes, and panel 2 to the consensus classification. Within each panel, the coefficients on the regime dummies in the first column capture the sum of the confidence and the discipline effects, $\gamma_{Peg} = \beta_{Peg} + \beta_{Mon}(\overline{\Delta m}_{Peg} - \overline{\Delta m}_{Flt})$. The coefficient in the second column reports the confidence effect alone, β_{Peg}. The difference between the two columns thus captures the discipline effect.

The various independent variables enter the regression with the expected signs and are statistically significant (with the exception of the terms of trade). Faster money growth and lower GDP growth are associated with higher inflation, while more open economies, countries with larger fiscal balances, and those with more independent central banks exhibit lower inflation.

Turning to the exchange rate regime, we observe that inflation under pegged regimes is 10.5 percentage points per year lower than under floating rates. At 13.5 percentage points, the inflation differential vis-à-vis intermediate regimes is larger. Of the difference between pegged and floating exchange rates, 4.8 percentage points are associated with lower money growth, and the remaining 5.7 percentage points represent the "confidence" effect.[5]

From panel 2 of table 6.1, under the consensus classification, the difference in inflation rates between pegged and floating regimes is

Table 6.1
Inflation base regression
$\pi = \beta_0 + \beta_{Peg}Peg + \beta_{Int}Int + \beta_{Mon}\Delta m + \beta_4\Delta y + \beta_5 Open + \beta_6 CBTurn + \beta_7 \Delta TofT + \beta_8 GovGDP + \varepsilon$

	De jure exchange rate classification				Consensus classification			
	Unconditional on money growth[1]		Conditional on money growth		Unconditional on money growth[1]		Conditional on money growth	
	coef.	t-stat.	coef.	t-stat.	coef.	t-stat.	coef.	t-stat.
All countries								
Constant	0.084	6.29***	0.084	6.29***	0.146	4.77***	0.146	4.77***
Pegged regimes	−0.105	−9.53***	−0.057	−6.72***	−0.214	−8.09***	−0.142	−6.76***
Intermediate regimes	0.030	3.46***	0.012	1.40	−0.034	−1.40	−0.018	−0.73
Money growth	0.507	9.93***	0.507	9.93***	0.209	4.25***	0.209	4.25***
Real GDP growth	−0.956	−3.36***	−0.956	−3.36***	−0.324	−1.07	−0.324	−1.07
Trade openness	−0.031	−5.99***	−0.031	−5.99***	−0.025	−3.93***	−0.025	−3.93***
Central bank turnover rate	0.100	6.64***	0.100	6.64***	0.059	3.56***	0.059	3.56***
Terms of trade growth	−0.010	−0.37	−0.010	−0.37	0.014	0.40	0.014	0.40
Government balance	−0.287	−3.87***	−0.287	−3.87***	−0.202	−2.65***	−0.202	−2.65***
Number of observations, R^2	1946	0.26	1946	0.26	862	0.42	862	0.42
Upper-income countries								
Constant	0.027	2.77***	0.027	2.77***	0.013	1.01	0.013	1.01
Pegged regimes	0.006	0.76	0.010	1.54	0.036	3.49***	0.007	0.62
Intermediate regimes	0.009	1.07	0.010	1.25	0.043	4.92***	0.012	1.78*
Number of observations, R^2	577	0.50	577	0.50	164	0.65	164	0.65

Upper-middle-income countries

Constant	0.099	3.37***	0.099	3.37***	0.195	4.13***	0.195	4.13***
Pegged regimes	-0.113	-4.28***	-0.092	-3.08***	-0.255	-5.39***	-0.193	-3.97***
Intermediate regimes	0.127	2.25**	0.051	1.72*	0.025	0.53	-0.044	-0.94
Number of observations, R^2	402	0.65	402	0.65	248	0.83	248	0.83

Lower- and lower-middle-income countries

Constant	0.118	8.45***	0.118	8.45***	0.151	5.06***	0.151	5.06***
Pegged regimes	-0.087	-9.17***	-0.015	-1.42	-0.197	-8.93***	-0.075	-3.37***
Intermediate regimes	-0.034	-3.44***	-0.010	-0.99	-0.174	-6.72***	-0.071	-3.08***
Number of observations, R^2	967	0.51	967	0.51	450	0.59	450	0.59

Asterisks denote statistical significance at the 10 percent (*), 5 percent (**), and 1 percent (***) levels, respectively.

[1] Direct effect of exchange rate regime on inflation, plus indirect effect through money growth given by $\beta_{Peg} + \beta_{Mon}(\overline{\Delta m_{Peg}} - \overline{\Delta m_{Flt}})$ and $\beta_{Int} + \beta_{Mon}(\overline{\Delta m_{Int}} - \overline{\Delta m_{Flt}})$ for pegged and intermediate regimes, respectively.

twice as large—about 21 percentage points per year (of which 7 percentage points are associated with lower money growth, and 14 percentage points with greater confidence).[6]

Taken together, the results suggest that pegging the exchange rate can substantially improve inflation performance, with the full anti-inflationary benefits—particularly through the confidence channel—accruing to those countries that maintain a hard peg and avoid frequent devaluations.

Differentiating across the three income groups, the results are weakest for the upper income (industrialized) countries, for which the differences in inflation rates across regimes are negligible and statistically insignificant. As discussed in chapter 3, if the industrialized countries are pegging their exchange rates to each other, and if they all face Barro-Gordon type time inconsistency problems, pegged exchange rates do not remove the inflationary bias of these countries as a group. Another possible explanation is that these countries have strong institutional frameworks and enjoy low inflation rates anyway, so that the exchange rate regime makes little difference.

This is demonstrated by splitting the full sample into low inflation observations (those below 10 percent per year) and high inflation observations (those above 10 percent per year), and reestimating the regression for the two subsamples. As table 6.2 indicates, the difference in inflation between pegged and floating regimes holds at inflation rates above 10 percent per year, but not below. (The cutoff of 10 percent per year is just about right: If the low inflation sample is defined to include inflation rates of 12 percent per year or below, the coefficient on the Peg dummy becomes negative and statistically significant).

Table 6.2 also reports regressions for a variety of other subsamples, each capturing alternative ways (other than the exchange rate regime) through which countries can gain policy credibility. These samples include countries with no current account restrictions (IMF Article VIII countries), countries with no capital controls (as defined by the IMF's *Annual Report on Exchange Arrangements and Restrictions*), countries with especially low rates of turnover of the central bank governor, and countries that are particularly open to international trade.

For countries without current account restrictions, high trade openness ratios, or low central bank turnover rates, the difference in inflation performance between pegged and floating regimes remains. Abjuring capital controls, on the other hand, does seem to provide an alternative means of gaining policy credibility. Inflation in these countries averages less than 10 percent per year, and the de jure exchange rate regime makes only a marginal difference to their inflation performance (in the consensus classification, however, the difference remains pronounced, at about 17 percentage points per year).

6.2 Inflation: Extensions and Robustness Tests

The results suggest a rather strong link between the exchange rate regime and inflation performance. In this section, we check whether the results are robust.

6.2.1 A Finer Classification
We begin by disaggregating the three de jure exchange rate regimes into their more detailed six-way classification: hard pegs, single currency pegs, basket pegs, rule-based flexible systems, floats with discretionary intervention, and pure floats. We include dummies for the first five regimes, leaving pure floats as the omitted category. The coefficients on the regime dummies, reported in table 6.3, should thus be interpreted as inflation differentials relative to a pure float.

Hard pegs (currency boards and dollarization) perform best, with a 15 percentage point inflation differential vis-à-vis pure floats, split roughly equally into the discipline and confidence effects. Basket pegs do somewhat better than single currency pegs. The confidence effect, however, is slightly greater for the latter, consistent with the view that, compared to basket pegs, the transparency and simplicity of a single currency peg should foster greater credibility (Frankel, Schmukler, and Servén 2000b).

Despite the general tendency for inflation to be higher under more flexible regimes, average inflation under pure floats is some 8 percent per year lower than under floating regimes with discretionary intervention. This gives some support to the contention that "extreme regimes"—strict pegs or pure floats—perform particularly well. Alternatively, the finding may be an indication that countries with generally good macroeconomic fundamentals can better afford to allow their exchange rate to float freely (whether endogeneity of regime choice can account for the good inflation performance of

Table 6.2
Inflation base regression alternative samples

$$\pi = \beta_0 + \beta_{Peg}Peg + \beta_{Int}Int + \beta_{Mon}\Delta m + \beta_4\Delta y + \beta_5 Open + \beta_6 CBTurn + \beta_7\Delta TofT + \beta_8 GovGDP + \varepsilon$$

| | De jure exchange rate classification | | | | Consensus classification | | | |
| | Unconditional on money growth[1] | | Conditional on money growth[2] | | Unconditional on money growth[1] | | Conditional on money growth[2] | |
	coef.	t-stat.	coef.	t-stat.	coef.	t-stat.	coef.	t-stat.
Low inflation observations[3]								
Constant	0.024	6.36***	0.024	6.36***	0.018	2.52**	0.018	2.52**
Pegged regimes	0.001	0.28	−0.003	−1.21	0.003	0.48	−0.001	−0.11
Intermediate regimes	0.010	4.34***	0.005	2.31**	0.017	2.51**	0.013	2.02**
Number of observations, R^2	1130	0.23	1130	0.23	540	0.30	540	0.30
High inflation observations[4]								
Constant	0.235	5.88***	0.235	5.88***	0.271	3.12***	0.271	3.12***
Pegged regimes	−0.098	−4.47***	−0.046	−3.17***	−0.199	−5.39***	−0.108	−3.23***
Intermediate regimes	0.004	0.29	0.005	0.33	0.005	0.13	0.010	0.28
Number of observations, R^2	816	0.30	816	0.30	322	0.49	322	0.49
Countries without current account restrictions								
Constant	0.062	5.97***	0.062	5.97***	0.084	4.19***	0.084	4.19***
Pegged regimes	−0.089	−9.59***	−0.056	−6.98***	−0.138	−6.90***	−0.071	−3.73***
Intermediate regimes	0.012	1.34	0.006	0.71	−0.036	−1.74*	−0.025	−1.21
Number of observations, R^2	1083	0.28	1083	0.28	465	0.66	465	0.66
Countries without capital account restrictions								
Constant	0.049	3.92***	0.049	3.92***	0.083	1.93*	0.083	1.93*
Pegged regimes	−0.015	−1.45	−0.017	−1.60	−0.173	−4.75***	−0.065	−1.89*
Intermediate regimes	0.039	4.74***	0.016	1.75*	−0.101	−2.78***	−0.024	−0.70
Number of observations, R^2	578	0.59	578	0.59	229	0.69	229	0.69

Low central bank turnover rate[5]								
Constant	0.073	3.70***	0.073	3.70***	0.182	3.56***	0.182	3.56***
Pegged regimes	−0.061	−2.72***	−0.034	−3.43***	−0.236	−4.50***	−0.141	−4.21***
Intermediate regimes	0.002	0.12	0.016	1.32	−0.157	−3.06***	−0.071	−1.89*
Number of observations, R²	663	0.33	663	0.33	297	0.48	297	0.48
Open economies[6]								
Constant	0.088	4.90***	0.088	4.90***	0.148	4.15***	0.148	4.15***
Pegged regimes	−0.132	−5.00***	−0.088	−4.21***	−0.201	−6.47***	−0.139	−4.14***
Intermediate regimes	−0.070	−3.00***	−0.041	−2.06**	−0.157	−4.92***	−0.106	−3.13***
Number of observations, R²	652	0.34	652	0.34	370	0.61	370	0.61

Asterisks denote statistical significance at the 10 percent (*), 5 percent (**), and 1 percent (***) levels, respectively.

[1] Direct effect of exchange rate regime on inflation, plus indirect effect through money growth given by $\beta_{Peg} + \beta_{Mon}(\overline{\Delta m_{Peg}} - \overline{\Delta m_{Flt}})$ and $\beta_{Int} + \beta_{Mon}(\overline{\Delta m_{Int}} - \overline{\Delta m_{Flt}})$ for pegged and intermediate regimes, respectively.

[2] Direct effect of exchange rate regime on inflation, controlling for money growth given by β_{Peg} and β_{Int} for pegged and intermediate regimes, respectively.

[3] Inflation below 10 percent per year.

[4] Inflation 10 percent per year or above.

[5] Central bank turnover rate below 5 percent per year.

[6] Sum of exports plus imports greater than 75 percent of GDP.

Table 6.3
Inflation regressions detailed de jure classification

| | De jure exchange rate classification | | | |
| | Unconditional on money growth[1] | | Conditional on money growth[2] | |
	coef.	t-stat.	coef.	t-stat.
All countries				
Constant	0.085	6.31***	0.085	6.31***
Hard pegged regimes	−0.148	−9.68***	−0.076	−7.06***
Single currency pegged regimes	−0.084	−7.39***	−0.058	−5.64***
Basket pegged regimes	−0.110	−9.27***	−0.051	−6.11***
Rule-based flexible regimes	−0.036	−3.91***	−0.004	−0.46
Float with discretionary intervention	0.078	7.00***	0.024	2.32**
Money growth	0.488	9.37***	0.488	9.37***
Real GDP growth	−0.975	−3.44***	−0.975	−3.44***
Trade openness	−0.029	−5.66***	−0.029	−5.66***
Central bank turnover rate	0.099	6.62***	0.099	6.62***
Terms of trade growth	−0.010	−0.37	−0.010	−0.37
Government balance	−0.292	−3.96***	−0.292	−3.96***
Number of observations, R^2	1946	0.26	1946	0.26

Asterisks denote statistical significance at the 10 percent (*), 5 percent (**), and 1 percent (***) levels, respectively.
[1] Direct effect of exchange rate regime on inflation, plus indirect effect through money growth.
[2] Direct effect of exchange rate regime on inflation, controlling for money growth.

pegged regimes is taken up below). Otherwise, the results for this more detailed classification are very much consistent with those for the three-way categorization into pegged, intermediate, and floating regimes.

6.2.2 Contamination

Are the results driven by "contamination" across regimes? For example, fixing the exchange rate may allow the government to "cheat," delivering apparently good inflation performance during its tenure while leaving a legacy of a collapsing peg and high inflation to its successors. (At least in the de jure classification, fiscal deficits have on average been larger under pegged regimes.) If so, using the contemporaneous exchange rate classification would inappropriately attribute inflation that had developed under the pegged regime to the subsequent floating period.

The problem can be addressed either by dropping the first few years following any regime change from the dataset or, more stringently, by reclassifying the first few years of any floating regime under the previous peg. An alternative is to drop the fiscal balance from the regression, on grounds that pegged regimes might be associated with larger deficits, and that by conditioning on the deficit, this channel for pegged exchange rates to adversely affect inflation is being purged from the regression. As specifications (1)–(4) in table 6.4 indicate, none of the modifications changes the qualitative results—pegged regimes continue to exhibit both confidence and discipline benefits.

6.2.3   Fixed Effects

Does the association between pegged regimes and low inflation stem from the sample's cross-sectional dimension, from its time dimension, or from both? The panel results suggest that countries operating under pegged exchange rates have lower inflation on average. This does not imply, however, that a country switching from a floating to a pegged regime will enjoy a lower inflation rate (even ignoring transitional dynamics) as the results could be driven entirely by country-specific factors. To address this possibility, we reestimate the panel regression, including country-specific fixed effects.

As the fifth panel in table 6.4 shows, the imputed effect of the exchange rate regime does indeed become somewhat smaller. The total inflation differential between pegged and floating regimes declines from 10.5 to 7 percentage points per year in the de jure classification, and from 21.5 to 15 percentage points per year in the consensus classification. In both cases, however, the coefficients remain highly significant.

6.2.4   Endogeneity of Regime Choice

The results reported so far strongly suggest that countries operating under pegged exchange rate regimes enjoy lower inflation. As discussed in chapter 3, the decision to adopt a specific exchange rate regime itself depends on a variety of factors, potentially raising econometric problems. Specifically, if countries enjoying low inflation—for whatever reason—are more likely to adopt pegged rates, then the coefficient on the pegged regime dummy may suffer from simultaneity bias.

Table 6.4

Inflation regression robustness checks

$$\pi = \beta_0 + \beta_{Peg}Peg + \beta_{Int}Int + \beta_{Mon}\Delta m + \beta_4\Delta y + \beta_5 Open + \beta_6 CBTurn + \beta_7\Delta TofT + \beta_8 GovGDP + \varepsilon$$

	De jure exchange rate classification				Consensus classification			
	Unconditional on money growth[1]		Conditional on money growth[2]		Unconditional on money growth[1]		Conditional on money growth[2]	
	coef.	t-stat.	coef.	t-stat.	coef.	t-stat.	coef.	t-stat.
(1) Dropping two years following regime change								
Constant	0.085	5.89***	0.085	5.89***	0.152	3.88***	0.152	3.88***
Pegged regimes	−0.099	−8.84***	−0.054	−6.23***	−0.230	−3.84***	−0.154	−5.76***
Intermediate regimes	0.026	2.94***	0.012	1.38	−0.012	−0.33	0.000	0.01
Number of observations, R^2	1765	0.25	1765	0.25	714	0.44	714	0.44
(2) Dropping five years following regime change								
Constant	0.075	4.68***	0.075	4.68***	0.227	2.99***	0.227	2.99***
Pegged regimes	−0.049	−1.65*	−0.028	−2.55**	−0.382	−4.34***	−0.236	−3.51***
Intermediate regimes	0.023	2.22**	0.021	2.05**	0.219	1.22	0.150	0.85
Number of observations, R^2	1267	0.31	1267	0.31	439	0.53	439	0.53
(3) Classifying first five years of floating regime under previous peg								
Constant	0.077	4.73***	0.077	4.73***	0.155	2.93***	0.155	2.93***
Pegged regimes	−0.078	−5.40***	−0.038	−3.24***	−0.222	−3.33***	−0.146	−3.82***
Intermediate regimes	0.037	3.40***	0.023	2.06**	−0.009	−0.21	0.004	0.10
Number of observations, R^2	1765	0.24	1765	0.24	699	0.43	699	0.43
(4) Dropping fiscal balance								
Constant	0.082	6.10***	0.082	6.10***	0.146	4.72***	0.146	4.72***
Pegged regimes	−0.105	−9.28***	−0.056	−6.47***	−0.215	−8.03***	−0.143	−6.71***
Intermediate regimes	0.031	3.57***	0.012	1.42	−0.039	−1.56	−0.022	−0.89
Number of observations, R^2	1946	0.25	1946	0.25	862	0.42	862	0.42

(5) Fixed effects estimation

Constant	0.127	2.82***	0.127	2.82***	0.112	1.75*	0.112	1.75*
Pegged regimes	−0.071	−4.10***	−0.062	−5.11***	−0.150	−7.21***	−0.093	−4.64***
Intermediate regimes	0.003	0.24	0.000	−0.05	−0.035	−1.69*	−0.021	−1.04
Number of observations, R^2	1946	0.58	1946	0.58	862	0.75	862	0.75

Asterisks denote statistical significance at the 10 percent (*), 5 percent (**), and 1 percent (***) levels, respectively.

[1] Direct effect of exchange rate regime on inflation, plus indirect effect through money growth, given by $\beta_{Peg} + \beta_{Mon}(\overline{\Delta m_{Peg}} - \overline{\Delta m_{Flt}})$ and $\beta_{Int} + \beta_{Mon}(\overline{\Delta m_{Int}} - \overline{\Delta m_{Flt}})$ for pegged and intermediate regimes, respectively.

[2] Direct effect of exchange rate regime on inflation, controlling for money growth given by β_{Peg} and β_{Int} for pegged and intermediate regimes, respectively.

To address this issue, we develop a simultaneous equation frame-work that allows explicitly for the endogeneity of regime choice. In this framework, inflation depends upon whether the country has an exchange rate peg, *Peg*, and upon a vector of other characteristics, z_1, comprising the independent variables included in the regressions reported earlier:

$$\pi = z_1\beta_1 + \gamma_1 Peg + \eta_1 \tag{4}$$

The decision to peg is assumed to depend upon the inflation rate, as well as other country characteristics, z_2:[7]

$$Peg^* = z_2\beta_2 + \gamma_2\pi + \eta_2 \tag{5}$$

Peg^* is an unobserved "desire" to peg the exchange rate and η cap-tures nonsystematic factors. $Peg = 1$ if, and only if, $Peg^* > 0$. If $\gamma_2 < 0$ (countries with high inflation are less likely to maintain an exchange rate peg), then the anti-inflationary benefit of pegging, obtained by OLS regressions, is overstated.

Using the simultaneous equation framework, we can estimate the residual effect of a pegged exchange rate regime on inflation, con-trolling for the endogeneity of the choice of regime. We first estimate the *fully* reduced form of the regime choice, obtained by substituting (4) into (5)

$$Peg = z\beta + \eta \tag{6}$$

where $z = [z_1, z_2]$ includes all of the independent variables, and η is a composite error term. The predicted values for $\widehat{Peg}$ from this probit are then substituted into the semireduced form of the inflation re-gression (4) with the appropriate correction for the standard error (Maddala 1989).

In principle, the nonlinearity of the probit function is sufficient for identifying the inflation regression; in practice, an explicit exclusion restriction makes a more compelling case for identification. We use two restrictions, on country size and on export concentration. The literature on exchange rate regime choice suggests that smaller countries and countries with geographically concentrated exports are more likely to have a pegged exchange rate. There is, however, little reason to believe that either country size or export concentra-tion influences inflation.

Since it is difficult to find plausible instruments that distinguish between pegged and intermediate regimes, we use a dichotomous classification (for this section only), grouping intermediate and floating regimes together. The inflation regression is thus not comparable to the results reported above, where intermediate and floating regimes were separated. To provide a benchmark, we first reestimate the simple OLS regression for this dichotomous classification. The results, given in the bottom panel of table 6.5, indicate a differential of 11.7 percentage points per year in favor of pegged regimes (and 13.5 percentage points per year under the consensus classification).

Turning to the simultaneous equation framework, it is reassuring to note that, as hypothesized, smaller countries and countries with greater geographic concentration of exports are in fact more likely to have an exchange rate peg (table 6.5, top panel).[8] In all, the probit correctly predicts some 70 to 80 percent of the observations.

The second-stage inflation regression suggests that the OLS estimates may indeed be subject to some simultaneity bias. In the two-stage simultaneous equation framework, the inflation differential in favor of pegged regimes falls from 11.7 to 7.2 percentage points per year for the de jure classification and from 13.5 to 9.8 percentage points per year for the consensus classification. Nonetheless, the benefit of pegged regimes for lowering inflation remains both economically and statistically significant.[9]

6.3 Growth: Baseline Specification

Growth, even more than inflation, is likely to depend upon much more than just the exchange rate regime; indeed, the large empirical literature on economic growth suggests a plethora of possible determinants. Accordingly, we turn to regression analysis to examine the effect of the exchange rate regime on growth, controlling for these other factors.

To capture factor accumulation, we include the ratio of investment to GDP and the average number of years of schooling of the population. To control for convergence or "catch-up" effects, we use the log of the ratio of the country's per capita GDP to that of the United States (both in 1970, and measured in international prices). In addition, we include openness to trade, the tax-to-GDP and budget balance-to-GDP ratios (averaged over the previous three years to reduce problems of endogeneity and cyclical dependency), terms of trade shocks, population growth, and population size, as well as

Table 6.5
Inflation: Simultaneous equation model[1]

	De jure exchange rate classification		Consensus classification	
	coef.	t-stat.	coef.	t-stat.
First-stage probit estimation[2]				
Constant	0.590	4.50***	0.777	3.47***
Population	-0.372	-16.14***	-0.289	-6.86***
Export concentration	0.006	2.98***	0.014	3.88***
Money growth	4.348	8.89***	-1.954	-6.70***
Real GDP growth	5.823	2.42**	16.543	3.62***
Trade openness	-0.223	-2.67***	-0.230	-1.79*
Central bank turnover rate	0.046	0.34	0.232	1.01
Terms of trade growth	0.156	0.52	0.746	1.38
Government balance	-1.459	-1.90*	-5.031	-3.38***
Number of observations, percent correctly predicted	1946	71.8	862	82.4

	De jure exchange rate classification				Consensus classification			
	Unconditional on money growth		Conditional on money growth		Unconditional on money growth		Conditional on money growth	
	coef.	t-stat.	coef.	t-stat.	coef.	t-stat.	coef.	t-stat.
Second-stage regression								
Constant	0.032	3.87***	0.032	3.87***	0.093	4.16***	0.093	4.16***
Pegged regimes	−0.072	−7.61***	−0.015	−4.29***	−0.098	−14.04***	−0.025	−4.30***
Money growth	0.497	8.41***	0.497	8.41***	0.242	8.62***	0.242	8.62***
Real GDP growth	−0.831	−3.07***	−0.831	−3.07***	−0.393	−1.31	−0.393	−1.31
Trade openness	−0.033	−5.74***	−0.033	−5.74***	−0.015	−3.30***	−0.015	−3.30***
Central bank turnover rate	0.100	6.37***	0.100	6.37***	0.045	3.42***	0.045	3.42***
Terms of trade growth	−0.007	−0.24	−0.007	−0.24	0.016	0.57	0.016	0.57
Government balance	−0.275	−3.66***	−0.275	−3.66***	−0.286	−4.18***	−0.286	−4.18***
Number of observations, R^2	1946	0.18	1946	0.18	862	0.57	862	0.57
Memorandum item: OLS estimates								
Constant	0.032	7.11***	0.032	7.11***	0.042	5.24***	0.042	5.24***
Pegged regimes	−0.117	−12.46***	−0.060	−10.44***	−0.135	−13.03***	−0.053	−5.96***
Money growth	0.498	10.18***	0.498	10.18***	0.273	10.11***	0.273	10.11***
Real GDP growth	−0.832	−3.16***	−0.832	−3.16***	−0.570	−1.84*	−0.570	−1.84*
Trade openness	−0.034	−6.71***	−0.034	−6.71***	−0.021	−4.79***	−0.021	−4.79***
Central bank turnover rate	0.100	6.63***	0.100	6.63***	0.040	3.05***	0.040	3.05***
Terms of trade growth	−0.007	−0.26	−0.007	−0.26	0.001	0.03	0.001	0.03
Government balance	−0.274	−3.80***	−0.274	−3.80***	−0.217	−3.46***	−0.217	−3.46***
Number of observations, R^2	1946	0.22	1946	0.22	862	0.58	862	0.58

Asterisks denote statistical significance at the 10 percent (*), 5 percent (**), and 1 percent (***) levels, respectively.
[1] Pegged regimes versus intermediate and floating regimes.
[2] Probit estimation of fully reduced form of regime choice.

annual and regime dummies. The estimated regression is thus given by

$$\Delta y^{pc} = \beta_0 + \beta_{Peg} Peg + \beta_{Int} Int + \beta_{Inv} InvGDP + \beta_{Open} Open$$

$$+ \beta_5 \Delta TofT + \beta_6 Sch + \beta_7 TaxGDP + \beta_8 GovGDP$$

$$+ \beta_9 \log(y_0 / y_0^{US}) + \beta_{10} \Delta Pop + \beta_{11} \log(Pop) + \varepsilon \tag{7}$$

We examine both whether the exchange rate regime influences growth directly (measured by the coefficients on the *Peg* and *Int* dummies) and whether it exerts any indirect effects—for instance, by promoting greater openness to international trade or higher investment.[10]

A number of studies have argued that greater trade openness contributes to economic growth, both by increasing allocative efficiency and by accelerating the transfer of technical knowledge. A recent study by Frankel and Rose (2001) shows that trade openness is higher among countries sharing a common currency; such countries, therefore, should enjoy faster output growth. Since the stylized facts presented in chapter 5 suggest that countries with pegged exchange rate regimes are considerably more open, the results of Frankel and Rose are of obvious interest.

Just as we did for the inflation regressions, we estimate the indirect effect of the exchange rate regime operating through trade openness as $\beta_{Open}(\overline{Open}_{Peg} - \overline{Open}_{Flt})$. We calculate the indirect effect operating through the investment ratio analogously.

The estimated coefficients are reported in table 6.6. With the exception of the tax burden and the budget balance, the independent variables enter with the expected sign and are statistically significant. Higher investment in physical or human capital is associated with faster per capita GDP growth, as are greater openness and positive terms of trade developments. Larger countries (as measured by population size) tend to grow faster, but faster population growth itself is associated with lower (per capita) GDP growth. A higher initial income level is associated with lower GDP growth, consistent with conditional convergence.

Under the de jure classification, both pegged and intermediate regimes are associated with better growth performance compared to floating regimes, though only the latter difference is statistically significant. Across income groups, the results are not robust. Pegged regimes are associated with faster growth among the lower income countries, but with slower growth among the higher income countries (only the latter difference is significant). The conditional and unconditional coefficients are very close, suggesting that any link between the exchange rate regime and growth does *not* operate through either trade openness or investment.[11]

Overall, the differences in growth performance are neither paltry nor spectacular. They imply that, over a twenty-five-year period, and controlling for other determinants, per capita output in a country with a pegged or intermediate regime would be some 10 to 20 percent higher than in a country that had maintained a floating regime.

Dropping soft pegs and hard floats makes a dramatic difference. The growth differential for pegs jumps from 0.4 percentage points under the de jure classification to 2.5 percentage points under the consensus classification; for intermediate regimes, the difference increases from 0.6 to 3.3 percentage points.[12] The increase in the estimated growth effects between the de jure and the consensus classification is not surprising in itself. The consensus sample drops the floats with stable exchange rates. If exchange rate stability is correlated with greater macroeconomic stability more generally, the excluded observations are likely to be fast growers within the floating group. Similarly, the consensus sample excludes the least stable pegs, which are likely to be the underperformers of their group. The differences, however, are sufficiently large to warrant closer scrutiny of the results.

6.4 Growth: Extensions and Robustness Tests

To assess robustness, we begin with the more disaggregated regime classification, and then check whether the results are driven by contamination across regimes, country-specific effects, and the possible endogeneity of the regime choice.

6.4.1 A Finer Classification

Disaggregating the de jure exchange rate regimes into their more detailed classification (table 6.7) suggests that the relationship between growth and exchange rate flexibility is far from monotonic. Hard pegs and traditional single currency pegs fare no worse than

Table 6.6
Per capita real GDP growth regressions

$$\Delta y^{pc} = \beta_0 + \beta_{Peg}Peg + \beta_{Int}Int + \beta_{Inv}InvGDP + \beta_{Open}Open + \beta_5\Delta TofT + \beta_6Sch + \beta_7TaxGDP + \beta_8GovGDP + \beta_9\log(y_0/y_0^{US}) + \beta_{10}\Delta Pop + \beta_{11}\log(Pop) + \varepsilon$$

| | De jure exchange rate classification | | | | | | Consensus exchange rate classification | | | | | |
| | Unconditional on investment[1] | | Unconditional on trade openness[2] | | Conditional on openness and investment[3] | | Unconditional on investment[1] | | Unconditional on trade openness[2] | | Conditional on openness and investment[3] | |
	coef.	t-stat.	coef.	t-stat.	coef.	t-stat.	coef.	t-stat.	coef.	t-stat.	coef.	t-stat.
All countries												
Constant	0.001	0.19	0.001	0.19	0.001	0.19	−0.025	−3.01***	−0.025	−3.01***	−0.025	−3.01***
Pegged regimes	0.004	1.51	0.006	2.02**	0.004	1.34	0.027	4.07***	0.028	4.31***	0.025	3.91***
Intermediate regimes	0.007	2.69***	0.007	2.52**	0.006	2.33**	0.034	5.21***	0.034	5.12***	0.033	4.96***
Investment ratio	0.040	1.81*	0.040	1.81*	0.040	1.81*	0.035	0.94	0.035	0.94	0.035	0.94
Trade openness	0.012	4.07***	0.012	4.07***	0.012	4.07***	0.013	2.98***	0.013	2.98***	0.013	2.98***
Terms of trade growth	0.030	2.27**	0.030	2.27**	0.030	2.27**	0.065	3.67***	0.065	3.67***	0.065	3.67***
Average years of schooling	0.002	3.27***	0.002	3.27***	0.002	3.27***	0.004	3.24***	0.004	3.24***	0.004	3.24***
Tax ratio	−0.014	−1.29	−0.014	−1.29	−0.014	−1.29	−0.003	−0.16	−0.003	−0.16	−0.003	−0.16
Government balance	0.016	0.71	0.016	0.71	0.016	0.71	−0.051	−1.61	−0.051	−1.61	−0.051	−1.61
Initial income/U.S. income	−0.025	−4.42***	−0.025	−4.42***	−0.025	−4.42***	−0.033	−3.78***	−0.033	−3.78***	−0.033	−3.78***
Population growth	−0.612	−5.54***	−0.612	−5.54***	−0.612	−5.54***	−0.655	−4.14***	−0.655	−4.14***	−0.655	−4.14***
Population size	0.004	5.26***	0.004	5.26***	0.004	5.26***	0.004	3.28***	0.004	3.28***	0.004	3.28***
Number of observations, R^2	1762	0.17	1762	0.17	1762	0.17	759	0.24	759	0.24	759	0.24
Upper- and Upper-middle-income countries												
Constant	0.010	1.91*	0.010	1.91	0.010	1.91	−0.008	−0.78	−0.008	−0.78	−0.008	−0.78
Pegged regimes	−0.010	−2.65***	0.000	0.05	−0.008	−2.26**	0.004	0.39	0.016	1.74*	0.006	0.64
Intermediate regimes	−0.001	−0.37	0.002	0.76	−0.001	−0.21	0.015	1.94*	0.019	2.39**	0.015	1.94*
Number of observations, R^2	806	0.25	806	0.25	806	0.25	307	0.33	307	0.33	307	0.33

Lower- and lower-middle-income

	Coef.	t	Coef.	t	Coef.	t	Coef.	t	Coef.	t	Coef.	t
Constant	-0.002	-0.34	-0.002	-0.34	-0.002	-0.34	-0.031	-2.84***	-0.031	-2.84***	-0.031	-2.84***
Pegged regimes	0.005	1.24	0.004	0.96	0.004	0.98	0.033	3.83***	0.031	3.47***	0.031	3.46***
Intermediate regimes	0.009	2.19**	0.005	1.04	0.005	1.17	0.040	3.88***	0.036	3.26***	0.037	3.34***
Number of observations, R^2	956	0.19	956	0.19	956	0.19	452	0.24	452	0.24	452	0.24

Countries without current account restrictions

	Coef.	t	Coef.	t	Coef.	t	Coef.	t	Coef.	t	Coef.	t
Constant	0.004	0.82	0.004	0.82	0.004	0.82	-0.028	-2.53**	-0.028	-2.53**	-0.028	-2.53**
Pegged regimes	0.003	0.96	0.005	1.64*	0.003	0.83	0.031	3.52***	0.034	3.93***	0.031	3.63***
Intermediate regimes	0.005	1.66*	0.006	1.96**	0.004	1.47	0.040	4.73***	0.043	5.05***	0.040	4.76***
Number of observations, R^2	985	0.20	985	0.20	985	0.20	428	0.25	428	0.25	428	0.25

Countries without capital account restrictions

	Coef.	t	Coef.	t	Coef.	t	Coef.	t	Coef.	t	Coef.	t
Constant	-0.001	-0.09	-0.001	-0.09	-0.001	-0.09	-0.046	-2.87***	-0.046	-2.87***	-0.046	-2.87***
Pegged regimes	-0.004	-0.85	0.006	1.12	-0.003	-0.59	0.023	1.54	0.032	2.28**	0.025	1.73*
Intermediate regimes	0.005	0.97	0.010	2.17**	0.006	1.13	0.034	2.25**	0.042	2.81***	0.036	2.37**
Number of observations, R^2	494	0.25	494	0.25	494	0.25	185	0.36	185	0.36	185	0.36

Asterisks denote statistical significance at the 10 percent (*), 5 percent (**), and 1 percent (***) levels, respectively.

[1] Allows for direct effect of exchange rate regime on growth plus indirect effects through investment, given by $\beta_{Peg} + \beta_{IGDP}(\overline{InvGDP}_{Peg} - \overline{InvGDP}_{Flt})$ and $\beta_{Int} + \beta_{IGDP}(\overline{InvGDP}_{Int} - \overline{InvGDP}_{Flt})$ for pegged and intermediate regimes, respectively.

[2] Allows for direct effect of exchange rate regime on growth plus indirect effects through trade, given by $\beta_{Peg} + \beta_{Open}(\overline{Open}_{Peg} - \overline{Open}_{Flt})$ and $\beta_{Int} + \beta_{Open}(\overline{Open}_{Int} - \overline{Open}_{Flt})$ for pegged and intermediate regimes, respectively.

[3] Allows for only direct effects of exchange rate regime on growth.

Table 6.7
Per capita GDP growth regressions: Detailed de jure classification

	De jure exchange rate classification					
	Unconditional on investment[1]		Unconditional on trade openness[2]		Conditional on investment and trade openness	
	coef.	t-stat.	coef.	t-stat.	coef.	t-stat.
All countries						
Constant	−0.006	−1.22	−0.006	−1.22	−0.006	−1.22
Hard peg	0.001	0.31	0.005	1.13	0.001	0.23
Single currency peg	−0.002	−0.45	0.000	−0.12	−0.001	−0.44
Basket peg	0.010	3.01***	0.011	3.30***	0.009	2.74***
Rule-based flexible	0.008	2.59***	0.008	2.58***	0.007	2.39**
Float with discretionary intervention	0.007	2.12**	0.006	2.00**	0.006	1.83*
Investment ratio	0.035	1.56	0.035	1.56	0.035	1.56
Trade openness	0.013	4.27***	0.013	4.27***	0.013	4.27***
Terms of trade growth	0.033	2.51**	0.033	2.51**	0.033	2.51**
Average years of schooling	−0.020	−1.86*	−0.020	−1.86*	−0.020	−1.86*
Tax ratio	0.008	0.33	0.008	0.33	0.008	0.33
Government balance ratio	−0.024	−4.01***	−0.024	−4.01***	−0.024	−4.01***
Initial income/U.S. income	−0.591	−5.36***	−0.591	−5.36***	−0.591	−5.36***
Population growth	0.002	3.08***	0.002	3.08***	0.002	3.08***
Population size	0.004	5.36***	0.004	5.36***	0.004	5.36***
Number of observations, R^2	1762	0.18	1762	0.18	1762	0.18

Asterisks denote statistical significance at the 10 percent (*), 5 percent (**), and 1 percent (***) levels, respectively.
[1] Allows for direct effect of exchange rate regime on growth plus indirect effects through investment.
[2] Allows for direct effect of exchange rate regime on growth plus indirect effects through trade.

free floats; on the other hand, basket pegs and various intermediate regimes are associated with about 1 percentage point per year faster growth compared to free floats.

6.5 Contamination

Returning to the three-way regime classification, the results are moderately robust to controlling for contamination effects across regimes (table 6.8): Excluding the years after regime changes preserves the sign pattern, although some of the coefficients become insignificant.

Table 6.8
Per capita real GDP growth regressions: Robustness checks

$$\Delta y^{pc} = \beta_0 + \beta_{Peg} Peg + \beta_{Int} Int + \beta_{Inv} InvGDP + \beta_{Open} Open + \beta_5 \Delta ToT + \beta_6 Sch + \beta_7 TaxGDP + \beta_8 GovGDP + \beta_9 \log(y_0/y_0^{US}) + \beta_{10} \Delta Pop + \beta_{11} \log(Pop) + \varepsilon$$

	De jure exchange rate classification						Consensus exchange rate classification					
	Unconditional on investment[1]		Unconditional on trade openness[2]		Conditional on investment and trade openness[3]		Unconditional on investment[1]		Unconditional on trade openness[2]		Conditional on investment and trade openness[3]	
	coef.	t-stat.	coef.	t-stat.	coef.	t-stat.	coef.	t-stat.	coef.	t-stat.	coef.	t-stat.
(1) Dropping two years following regime change												
Constant	0.004	0.92	0.004	0.92	0.004	0.92	−0.019	−1.88*	−0.019	−1.88*	−0.019	−1.88*
Pegged regimes	0.002	0.57	0.003	1.17	0.001	0.42	0.019	2.44**	0.021	2.84***	0.018	2.36**
Intermediate regimes	0.008	2.98***	0.007	2.89***	0.007	2.67***	0.027	3.54***	0.027	3.70***	0.026	3.42***
Number of observations, R^2	1606	0.20	1606	0.20	1606	0.20	620	0.26	620	0.26	620	0.26
(2) Dropping five years following regime change												
Constant	0.006	1.27	0.006	1.27	0.006	1.27	−0.019	−1.49	−0.019	−1.49	−0.019	−1.49
Pegged regimes	0.003	0.89	0.005	1.52	0.003	0.89	0.008	0.70	0.011	0.98	0.008	0.69
Intermediate regimes	0.012	4.03***	0.013	4.18***	0.012	4.00***	0.043	2.75***	0.041	2.72***	0.042	2.78***
Number of observations, R^2	1218	0.20	1218	0.20	1218	0.20	378	0.24	378	0.24	378	0.24
(3) Fixed effects estimation												
Constant	0.098	2.01**	0.098	2.01**	0.098	2.01**	−0.038	−0.59	−0.038	−0.59	−0.038	−0.59
Pegged regimes	−0.004	−0.80	0.002	0.33	−0.003	−0.56	0.017	1.63	0.032	2.67***	0.021	1.96*
Intermediate regimes	−0.005	−1.01	−0.002	−0.37	−0.003	−0.58	0.019	1.94*	0.027	2.74***	0.023	2.37**
Number of observations, R^2	1762	0.29	1762	0.29	1762	0.29	759	0.39	759	0.39	759	0.39

Asterisks denote statistical significance at the 10 percent (*), 5 percent (**), and 1 percent (***) levels, respectively.

[1] Allows for direct effect of exchange rate regime on growth plus indirect effects through investment, given by $\beta_{Peg} + \beta_{InvGDP}(\overline{InvGDP}_{Peg} - \overline{InvGDP}_{Flt})$ and $\beta_{Int} + \beta_{InvGDP}(\overline{InvGDP}_{Int} - \overline{InvGDP}_{Flt})$ for pegged and intermediate regimes respectively.

[2] Allows for direct effect of exchange rate regime on growth plus indirect effects through trade, given by $\beta_{Peg} + \beta_{Open}(\overline{Open}_{Peg} - \overline{Open}_{Flt})$ and $\beta_{Int} + \beta_{Open}(\overline{Open}_{Int} - \overline{Open}_{Flt})$ for pegged and intermediate regimes respectively.

[3] Allows for only direct effects of exchange rate regime on growth.

6.5.1 Fixed Effects

In contrast to the inflation results, country-specific factors do seem to play a large role in explaining output growth. The estimated effects of the exchange rate regime become correspondingly weaker. In the de jure classification, the growth differential in favor of pegged and intermediate regimes disappears entirely, though both remain positive and statistically significant in the consensus classification (table 6.8, panel 3).

6.5.2 Endogeneity of Regime Choice

If countries enjoying faster growth are better able to maintain an exchange rate peg, then the positive association between pegged regimes and growth performance may partly reflect simultaneity bias.

We correct for the potential bias by estimating a simultaneous equation in which the decision to have a pegged exchange rate depends on GDP growth, among other factors. As before, we collapse the number of regimes to two, though this time we compare pegs and intermediate regimes to floating regimes (the question of interest being whether floats fare worse than other regimes). We use an exclusion restriction on export concentration to help identify the second stage (growth) regression.[13]

The bottom panel of table 6.9 reports the simple OLS regression results to provide a benchmark using the dichotomous classification of regimes. Pegged and intermediate regimes exhibit a growth advantage of close to 1 percentage point per year in the de jure classification and almost 3 percentage points in the consensus classification.

Controlling for simultaneity bias (table 6.9, middle panel), the growth differential disappears for the de jure classification, and falls to about one-half of 1 percentage point per year (with barely statistically significant coefficients) in the consensus classification.[14]

Overall, and in line with the theoretical literature, the results do not suggest a strong link between the exchange rate regime and real GDP growth. There is some evidence that countries with pegged (and particularly intermediate) regimes grow faster than countries with floating regimes. Much of this growth bonus disappears, however, once country-specific effects and the possibility of simultaneity bias are taken into account.

6.6 Output Volatility

The theoretical literature suggests that pegged exchange rates will be associated with greater output volatility when there are real shocks (assuming nominal rigidities exist elsewhere in the economy). Some support for this was found in the stylized facts presented in chapter 5.

Of course, output volatility depends on factors other than just the exchange rate regime. To examine the conditional effect of the exchange rate regime on output volatility, we control for the variability of the terms of trade and of the investment ratio. In line with the regressions above, additional controls include population growth, average years of schooling, the tax ratio, the fiscal balance, and the conditional convergence variable. We use two alternative measures of output volatility: the standard deviations of real GDP growth and the percentage deviation of real GDP from its HP-filtered trend.

The results for the two measures, presented in tables 6.10 and 6.11, are very similar, and suggest that pegged exchange rates are associated with greater output volatility of about one-third to one-half of 1 percentage point per year. The effect is particularly pronounced for higher income countries, which are more likely to have sticky nominal wages and prices. In the consensus sample, however, the signs are reversed, with pegged (and intermediate) regimes being associated with significantly lower volatility. The findings may be reconciled by noting that the consensus float category includes all countries that experience significant exchange rate movements, among which are countries going through severe economic turmoil but excludes pegs with similarly pronounced movements. As such, the results for the consensus sample may be less a reflection of the properties of the regime than of the circumstances of the particular countries in the sample.[15]

6.7 Conclusions

In this chapter, we set out to examine whether the stylized facts reported in chapter 5 stand up to closer scrutiny. On inflation, the results are compelling. Across a range of subsamples and alternative specifications, inflation is lower under pegged exchange rates, reflecting both lower money growth (the discipline effect) and greater confidence in the currency (the credibility effect).

Table 6.9
Per capita GDP growth: Simultaneous equation model[1]

First-stage probit estimation[2]

	De jure exchange rate classification		Consensus exchange rate classification	
	coef.	t-stat.	coef.	t-stat.
Constant	2.078	12.33***	2.516	8.00***
Export concentration	−0.011	−4.42***	−0.012	−2.35**
Investment ratio	5.509	6.66***	9.758	5.34***
Trade openness	−0.251	−2.27**	0.014	0.06
Terms of trade growth	0.783	1.49	−0.034	−0.03
Average years of schooling	−0.166	−7.37***	−0.386	−6.48***
Tax ratio	1.798	4.42***	−0.292	−0.33
Government balance ratio	−1.358	−1.48	1.097	0.55
Initial income/U.S. income	−0.546	−2.77***	2.596	4.26***
Population growth	−0.838	−0.25	9.575	1.12
Population	−0.207	−7.08***	−0.424	−6.61***
Number of observations, percent correctly predicted	1762	82.7	759	91.7

Second-stage regression

	De jure exchange rate classification						Consensus exchange rate classification					
	Unconditional on investment		Unconditional on trade openness		Conditional on investment		Unconditional on investment		Unconditional on trade openness		Conditional on investment	
	coef.	t-stat.	coef.	t-stat.	coef.	t-stat.	coef.	t-stat.	coef.	t-stat.	coef.	t-stat.
Constant	−0.003	−0.25	−0.003	−0.25	−0.003	−0.25	−0.010	−0.70	−0.010	−0.70	−0.010	−0.70
Pegged and intermediate	0.002	0.78	0.002	0.84	0.001	0.25	0.003	1.29	0.004	1.61	0.002	0.72

Investment ratio	0.064	2.42**	0.064	2.42**	0.044	1.20	0.044	1.20
Trade openness	0.011	3.35***	0.011	3.35***	0.013	2.99***	0.013	2.99***
Terms of trade growth	0.033	2.50**	0.033	2.50**	0.058	3.55***	0.058	3.55***
Average years of schooling	0.002	1.91*	0.002	1.91*	0.003	2.49**	0.003	2.49**
Tax ratio	-0.018	-1.42	-0.018	-1.42	-0.002	-0.11	-0.002	-0.11
Government balance ratio	0.009	0.40	0.009	0.40	-0.047	-1.52	-0.047	-1.52
Initial income/U.S. income	-0.021	-3.56***	-0.021	-3.56***	-0.029	-3.44***	-0.029	-3.44***
Population growth	-0.650	-6.05***	-0.650	-6.05***	-0.697	-4.68***	-0.697	-4.68***
Population size	0.004	3.65***	0.004	3.65***	0.003	2.33**	0.003	2.33**
Number of observations, R^2	1762	0.11	1762	0.11	759	0.14	759	0.14
Memorandum item; OLS estimates								
Constant	-0.005	-2.24**	-0.005	-2.24**	-0.025	-4.44***	-0.025	-4.44***
Pegged and intermediate	0.007	2.92***	0.008	3.08***	0.028	4.95***	0.030	5.15***
Investment ratio	0.061	2.94***	0.061	2.94***	0.030	0.93	0.030	0.93
Trade openness	0.011	3.62***	0.011	3.62***	0.014	3.14***	0.014	3.14***
Terms of trade growth	0.032	2.55**	0.032	2.55**	0.059	3.56***	0.059	3.56***
Average years of schooling	0.002	2.84***	0.002	2.84***	0.003	3.24***	0.003	3.24***
Tax ratio	-0.020	-1.93*	-0.020	-1.93*	-0.002	-0.11	-0.002	-0.11
Government balance ratio	0.010	0.43	0.010	0.43	-0.049	-1.60	-0.049	-1.60
Initial income/U.S. income	-0.020	-3.79***	-0.020	-3.79***	-0.031	-3.81***	-0.031	-3.81***
Population growth	-0.647	-6.08***	-0.647	-6.08***	-0.701	-4.76***	-0.701	-4.76***
Population size	0.004	5.43***	0.004	5.43***	0.004	3.69***	0.004	3.69***
Number of observations, R^2	1762	0.12	1762	0.12	759	0.17	759	0.17

Asterisks denote statistical significance at the 10 percent (*), 5 percent (**), and 1 percent (***) levels, respectively.

1 Pegged and intermediate regimes compared to floating regimes.

2 Probit estimation of regime choice.

Table 6.10
Volatility of output[1]

| | De jure exchange rate classification | | | | Consensus exchange rate classification | | | |
| | Unconditional on investment | | Conditional on investment | | Unconditional on investment | | Conditional on investment | |
	coef.	t-stat.	coef.	t-stat.	coef.	t-stat.	coef.	t-stat.
All countries								
Constant	0.035	12.47***	0.035	12.47***	0.046	8.61***	0.046	8.61***
Pegged regimes	0.003	2.31*	0.002	1.81*	-0.007	-2.17**	-0.007	-2.14**
Intermediate regimes	-0.003	-2.16**	-0.002	-1.88*	-0.007	-2.23**	-0.007	-2.13**
Number of observations, R²	1874	0.10	1874	0.10	808	0.12	808	0.12
Upper- and upper-middle-income countries								
Constant	0.029	6.87***	0.029	6.87***	0.028	4.11***	0.028	4.11***
Pegged regimes	0.005	3.53***	0.004	2.72***	0.001	0.36	0.002	0.49
Intermediate regimes	0.002	1.70*	0.003	1.99**	-0.001	-0.45	0.000	0.06
Number of observations, R²	865	0.16	865	0.16	315	0.17	315	0.17
Lower- and lower-middle-income countries								
Constant	0.040	10.05***	0.040	10.05***	0.055	7.13***	0.055	7.13***
Pegged regimes	0.001	0.44	0.001	0.33	-0.012	-2.37**	-0.012	-2.37**
Intermediate regimes	-0.008	-3.82***	-0.008	-3.70***	-0.014	-2.38**	-0.014	-2.36**
Number of observations, R²	1009	0.09	1009	0.09	493	0.15	493	0.15
Countries without current account restrictions								
Constant	0.034	10.38***	0.034	10.38***	0.046	7.54***	0.046	7.54***
Pegged regimes	0.003	1.72*	0.002	1.26	-0.009	-2.33**	-0.009	-2.30**
Intermediate regimes	-0.002	-1.21	-0.001	-0.89	-0.009	-2.46**	-0.009	-2.34**
Number of observations, R²	1038	0.15	1038	0.15	459	0.18	459	0.18

Countries without capital account restrictions

Constant	0.035	6.03***	0.035	6.03***	0.060	4.37***	0.060	4.37***
Pegged regimes	0.007	2.41**	0.006	1.88*	−0.011	−1.56	−0.010	−1.52
Intermediate regimes	−0.000	−0.07	0.000	0.18	−0.016	−2.19**	−0.015	−2.12**
Number of observations, R²	514	0.20	514	0.20	186	0.26	186	0.26

Asterisks denote statistical significance at the 10 percent (*), 5 percent (**), and 1 percent (***) levels, respectively.
[1]Three-year centered moving standard deviation of the deviation of real GDP from its HP-filtered trend.

Table 6.11
Volatility of real GDP growth[1]

	De jure exchange rate classification				Consensus exchange rate classification			
	Unconditional on investment		Conditional on investment		Unconditional on investment		Conditional on investment	
	coef.	t-stat.	coef.	t-stat.	coef.	t-stat.	coef.	t-stat.
All countries								
Constant	0.020	7.06***	0.020	7.06***	0.035	5.21***	0.035	5.21***
Pegged regimes	0.002	1.45	0.002	1.16	-0.013	-3.06***	-0.013	-3.07***
Intermediate regimes	-0.004	-2.32**	-0.004	-2.12**	-0.012	-2.47**	-0.012	-2.61***
Number of observations, R^2	1878	0.10	1878	0.10	811	0.10	811	0.10
Upper- and upper-middle-income countries								
Constant	0.011	3.81***	0.011	3.81***	0.019	2.52**	0.019	2.52**
Pegged regimes	0.006	3.30***	0.004	2.54**	0.000	0.09	0.001	0.14
Intermediate regimes	0.003	1.57	0.003	1.78*	-0.001	-0.17	0.000	0.03
Number of observations, R^2	869	0.18	869	0.18	318	0.21	318	0.21
Lower- and lower-middle-income countries								
Constant	0.026	5.87***	0.026	5.87***	0.043	4.65***	0.043	4.65***
Pegged regimes	0.001	0.40	0.001	0.35	-0.018	-2.87***	-0.018	-2.91***
Intermediate regimes	-0.011	-3.99***	-0.011	-3.90***	-0.024	-2.93***	-0.024	-3.05***
Number of observations, R^2	1009	0.09	1009	0.09	493	0.11	493	0.11
Countries without current account restrictions								
Constant	0.018	5.43***	0.018	5.43***	0.036	4.07***	0.036	4.07***
Pegged regimes	0.002	1.32	0.001	0.78	-0.014	-2.81***	-0.014	-2.74***
Intermediate regimes	-0.004	-1.93*	-0.003	-1.49	-0.016	-3.15***	-0.014	-2.82***
Number of observations, R^2	1042	0.15	1042	0.15	462	0.16	462	0.16

Countries without capital account restrictions

Constant	0.021	3.61***	0.021	3.61***	0.043	2.74***	0.043	2.74***
Pegged regimes	0.009	2.80***	0.008	2.14**	-0.008	-1.05	-0.007	-0.93
Intermediate regimes	-0.001	-0.35	-0.000	-0.03	-0.023	-2.87***	-0.020	-2.74***
Number of observations, R^2	518	0.19	518	0.19	189	0.26	189	0.26

Asterisks denote statistical significance at the 10 percent (*), 5 percent (**), and 1 percent (***) levels, respectively.

[1] Three-year centered moving standard deviation of real GDP growth.

The link between the exchange rate regime and growth is much less robust. While we find some evidence that countries with pegged and intermediate regimes perform better, much of this can be explained by country-specific effects or simultaneity bias. Perhaps the best one can say is that the growth performance of pegged regimes is no worse than that of floating regimes. There is at least some evidence, however, that countries with pegged exchange rate regimes experience greater output volatility.

7   Macroeconomic Stabilization and the Exchange Rate Regime

The results reported in the last two chapters take a bird's-eye view of the relationship between a country's exchange rate regime and its inflation performance. By comingling periods of rising, steady and declining inflation, the results pertain to the "long-run" or average behavior of inflation under alternative regimes. Quite aside from any such long-run considerations, pegged exchange rates have also been advocated as a means of achieving rapid disinflation. In this chapter, we narrow our focus to the role of the exchange rate regime in stabilization programs.

As noted in chapter 3, a substantial literature explores exchange rate–based stabilizations (ERBS). Most empirical studies on ERBS have focused on the higher inflation members of the European Monetary System[1], and on the hyperinflation stabilizations in Israel (Bruno et al. 1988) and the Southern Cone countries of Latin America. The experience of these countries has sometimes been characterized as the "ERBS Syndrome." A rapid drop in domestic real interest rates triggers a consumption boom that, together with a real appreciation due to inertial inflation, widens the current account deficit and depletes reserves, often leading to the collapse of the peg and a resurgence of inflation.[2]

Recent work by Hamann (1999) suggests, however, that this pattern may be specific to this small group of countries. In a larger set of disinflation episodes, he finds few differences between money-based and exchange rate–based stabilizations. Here we examine the evidence within our own sample, with a view to answering two questions. First, are exchange rate–based stabilizations more prone to failure than money-based programs? Second, are exchange rate–based stabilizations—whether successful or not—more costly than money-based programs?

In the second part of the chapter, we illustrate the complexity of disinflation attempts with case studies of three recent exchange rate–based stabilizations. The first, Bulgaria, is generally considered to have been a success; the second, Turkey, ended in spectacular failure. The third, Argentina, lies in between, experiencing a sustained disinflation, but also, ultimately, a collapse of the exchange rate regime.

7.1 Disinflation Programs: Success and Failure

Our first task is to define what we mean by a stabilization program or episode. For countries suffering hyperinflation, the challenge is to bring inflation down from hundreds or even thousands of percent per year to low double digits. Yet, disinflation programs have also been undertaken by many industrialized countries with the aim of reducing inflation from the low double digits to the low single digits. In between these two extremes are countries trying to reduce inflation from perhaps 30 or 40 percent per year to the low or mid-teens.

Since it is unlikely that these very different types of stabilization programs share the same dynamics, we use three alternative definitions of disinflation programs, based on the starting level of inflation. A low disinflation episode is one in which the starting inflation rate is below 20 percent per year and declines by at least 5 percentage points over two years. Similarly, moderate (high) disinflations are those in which the initial inflation rate is between 20 and 50 percent per year (above 50 percent per year) and falls by at least 10 percentage points (at least 20 percentage points) over the following two years.

Definitions of Disinflation Episodes

Low	$\pi_{t_0-2} < 20\%$, and $\pi_{t_0-2} - \pi_{t_0} \geq 5\%$
Moderate	$20\% < \pi_{t_0-2} \leq 50\%$, and $\pi_{t_0-2} - \pi_{t_0} \geq 10\%$
High	$\pi_{t_0-2} > 50\%$, and $\pi_{t_0-2} - \pi_{t_0} \geq 20\%$

Applying these criteria to our panel of countries yields a data-determined set of disinflation episodes. Since we are interested in the link between disinflation and the exchange rate regime, we drop all episodes in which the regime changes over the two-year disinflation period. (This is more common in the consensus classification so the total number of episodes is correspondingly smaller.)

7.1.1 The Likelihood of Success

Next, we divide episodes into successes and failures. Success is defined as a lasting disinflation, which we assess in two ways. The weaker definition classifies an episode as a *successful stabilization* if the inflation rate does not rebound above its *original* level in years $t_0 + 3$ to $t_0 + 5$: $\pi_{t_0+j} \leq \pi_{t_0-2}$ $j = 1, 2, 3$. A stronger criterion requires that the inflation rate not exceed its new lower level $\pi_{t_0+j} \leq \pi_{t_0}$ $j = 1, 2, 3$ in the poststabilization period, years $t_0 + 1$ to $t_0 + 3$. We refer to such cases as *durable* disinflations (figure 7.1).

Table 7.1 summarizes the various stabilization attempts, comprising 277 "low," 266 "moderate," and 106 "high" disinflation episodes. For low and moderate disinflations, the proportion of stabilizations undertaken under pegged regimes is strikingly high, ranging from about two-thirds to more than three-quarters (with an even higher proportion under the consensus classification of exchange rate regimes). For the high disinflation episodes, the distribution across regimes is rather more even.

How lasting are these stabilization attempts? For the full sample, about three-quarters of all attempts are "successful" (that is, inflation does not exceed its original level for at least five years from the starting date of the disinflation program). Using the stricter definition of a "durable" disinflation (over the subsequent three years, inflation does not rise above its new lower level), only one-quarter to one-fifth of low and moderate disinflation programs survive. The survival rate for high inflation countries is slightly greater, at about one-third.

Are exchange rate–based stabilizations more likely to fail? For disinflations starting from a low initial inflation rate, the answer is *yes*, though the difference is small. Seventy percent of stabilizations undertaken under pegged regimes are classified as successful, while for intermediate and floating regimes, the ratio of successful stabilizations is closer to 80 percent. In terms of the stricter criterion of a durable disinflation, pegs and floats are comparable (about a 20 percent survival rate), while the survival rate for intermediate regimes is closer to 30 percent.

For disinflations under pegged regimes starting from moderate and high inflation rates, the picture reverses: about 45 percent of

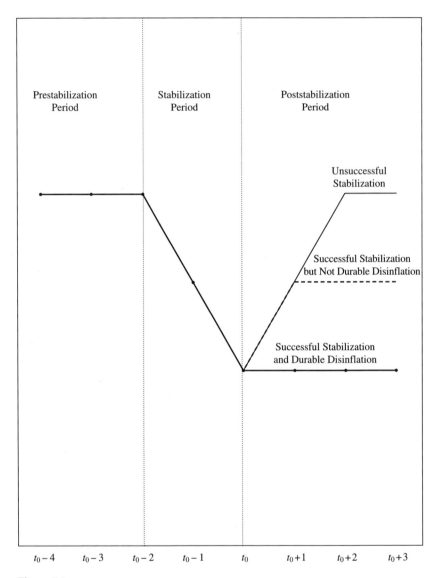

Figure 7.1
Alternative definitions of successful disinflation episodes

disinflation attempts achieve durable disinflation under pegs, compared to 25 to 30 percent under intermediate or floating regimes.

Taken as a whole, the evidence thus does not support the contention that stabilization attempts based on pegged exchange rates are any more prone to failure than others. If anything, pegged regimes are slightly *more* successful in achieving durable disinflation when the initial inflation rate is at least moderately high, although the difference is not statistically significant.[3]

In chapter 6 we documented the confidence and discipline benefits of pegging the exchange rate. Do these still persist when we limit our attention to countries that, regardless of their exchange rate regime, have embarked on disinflation programs, presumably accompanied by the appropriate supporting monetary and fiscal policies? Table 7.2 reports the results.

Consistent with our earlier findings, pegging the exchange rate during disinflation brings the least benefit when the initial level of inflation is already low. When disinflation starts from moderate or high initial inflation rates, pegged exchange rate regimes again exhibit both confidence and discipline effects.

For moderate disinflations, pegged exchange rates are associated with about 3 percentage points lower inflation, split equally between the discipline and confidence effects. Restricting the sample to durable disinflations raises the effect to 4 percentage points, largely reflecting the confidence effect. For countries starting from high inflation rates, this differential doubles, but now the confidence effect vanishes, and the benefit derives almost entirely from the greater discipline on money growth that pegged regimes impose.[4]

Stabilization attempts under pegged exchange rates are thus no more prone to failure than those undertaken under floating regimes. Furthermore, pegged exchange rates are if anything associated with a disinflation bonus, reflecting the greater discipline and confidence they engender. Why, then, are exchange rate–based stabilizations viewed as particularly risky?

There are a number of possible answers. Successful stabilization under pegged exchange rates might come at the cost of greater output losses, and thus a higher sacrifice ratio. The economic cost of failure might be higher under pegged regimes. Alternatively, it may simply be the case that such failures are more visible, entailing significant political costs (which, of course, is part of the reason pegged exchange rates provide greater policy credibility). To evaluate these

Table 7.1
Disinflation attempts under alternative exchange rate regimes

	De jure classification				Consensus classification			
	Total	Pegged	Intermediate	Floating	Total	Pegged	Intermediate	Floating
Low: Inflation below 20 percent per year in year $t_0 - 2$, at least 5 percentage point decline between year $t_0 - 2$ and year t_0								
Number	277	218	31	28	168	164	3	1
Proportion of total	100.0	78.7	11.2	10.1	100.0	97.6	1.8	0.6
Proportion of disinflation attempts with:								
Inflation in $t_0 + 1$ below inflation in $t_0 - 2$	94.2	92.7	100.0	100.0	92.9	92.7	100.0	100.0
Inflation in $t_0 + 2$ below inflation in $t_0 - 2$	83.0	82.1	87.1	85.7	82.1	82.3	66.7	100.0
Inflation in $t_0 + 3$ below inflation in $t_0 - 2^1$	72.2	70.6	77.4	78.6	67.9	68.9	33.3	0.0
Inflation in $t_0 + 1$ below inflation in t_0	44.4	41.7	58.1	50.0	44.0	43.3	100.0	0.0
Inflation in $t_0 + 2$ below inflation in t_0	26.0	22.9	38.7	35.7	25.6	25.6	33.3	0.0
Inflation in $t_0 + 3$ below inflation in t_0^2	19.5	17.9	29.0	21.4	19.6	20.1	0.0	0.0
Moderate: Inflation above 20 percent and below 50 percent per year in year $t_0 - 2$, at least 10 percentage point decline between year $t_0 - 2$ and year t_0								
Number	226	142	40	44	116	96	9	11
Proportion of total	100.0	62.8	17.7	19.5	100.0	82.8	7.8	9.5
Proportion of disinflation attempts with:								
Inflation in $t_0 + 1$ below inflation in $t_0 - 2$	97.8	96.5	100.0	100.0	97.4	96.9	100.0	100.0
Inflation in $t_0 + 2$ below inflation in $t_0 - 2$	85.8	87.3	82.5	84.1	87.1	87.5	77.8	90.9
Inflation in $t_0 + 3$ below inflation in $t_0 - 2^1$	71.2	77.5	57.5	63.6	69.0	74.0	22.2	63.6
Inflation in $t_0 + 1$ below inflation in t_0	53.1	51.4	65.0	47.7	50.9	47.9	77.8	54.5
Inflation in $t_0 + 2$ below inflation in t_0	37.2	35.2	45.0	36.4	36.2	32.3	55.6	54.5
Inflation in $t_0 + 3$ below inflation in t_0^2	23.9	23.2	27.5	22.7	24.1	22.9	22.2	36.4

High: Inflation above 50 percent per year in year $t_0 - 2$, at least 20 percentage point decline between year $t_0 - 2$ and year t_0

Number	106	32	39	35	43	11	14	18
Proportion of total	100.0	30.2	36.8	33.0	100.0	25.6	32.6	41.9
Proportion of disinflation attempts with:								
Inflation in $t_0 + 1$ below inflation in $t_0 - 2$	89.6	84.4	87.2	97.1	83.7	72.7	78.6	94.4
Inflation in $t_0 + 2$ below inflation in $t_0 - 2$	83.0	81.3	76.9	91.4	79.1	90.9	50.0	94.4
Inflation in $t_0 + 3$ below inflation in $t_0 - 2$[1]	75.5	81.3	64.1	82.9	69.8	81.8	42.9	83.3
Inflation in $t_0 + 1$ below inflation in t_0	48.1	53.1	41.0	51.4	48.8	45.5	35.7	61.1
Inflation in $t_0 + 2$ below inflation in t_0	39.6	43.8	35.9	40.0	39.5	45.5	21.4	50.0
Inflation in $t_0 + 3$ below inflation in t_0[2]	32.1	43.8	25.6	28.6	30.2	45.5	14.3	33.3

[1] Constitutes successful stabilization.
[2] Constitutes durable disinflation.

Table 7.2
Inflation regressions: De jure classification

$$\pi = \beta_0 + \beta_{Peg} Peg + \beta_{Int} Int + \beta_{Mon} \Delta m + \beta_4 \Delta y + \beta_5 Open + \beta_6 CBTurn + \beta_7 \Delta TofT + \beta_8 GovGDP + \varepsilon$$

	All disinflation observations				Durable disinflations			
	Unconditional on money growth[1]		Conditional on money growth[2]		Unconditional on money growth[1]		Conditional on money growth[2]	
	coef.	t-stat.	coef.	t-stat.	coef.	t-stat.	coef.	t-stat.
Low: Inflation below 20 percent per year in year $t_0 - 2$, at least 5 percentage point decline between year $t_0 - 2$ and year t_0								
Constant	0.043	6.79***	0.043	6.79***	0.054	5.30***	0.054	5.30***
Pegged regimes	0.002	0.20	0.007	1.01	0.007	0.53	0.008	0.61
Intermediate regimes	0.010	1.11	0.009	1.06	0.032	2.55**	0.023	2.28**
Number of observations, R^2	277	0.07	277	0.07	54	0.27	54	0.27
Moderate: Inflation above 20 percent and below 50 percent per year in year $t_0 - 2$, at least 10 percentage point decline between year $t_0 - 2$ and year t_0								
Constant	0.095	11.55***	0.095	11.55***	0.133	10.29***	0.133	10.29***
Pegged regimes	-0.031	-2.72***	-0.012	-1.35	-0.042	-2.57**	-0.032	-1.92*
Intermediate regimes	0.021	1.63	0.007	0.56	-0.025	-1.29	-0.036	-1.74*
Number of observations, R^2	226	0.14	226	0.14	54	0.20	54	0.20
High: Inflation above 50 percent per year in year $t_0 - 2$, at least 20 percentage point decline between year $t_0 - 2$ and year t_0								
Constant	0.266	9.24***	0.266	9.24***	0.364	7.42***	0.364	7.42***
Pegged regimes	-0.071	-1.93*	0.004	0.10	-0.138	-1.66*	-0.013	-0.21
Intermediate regimes	0.011	0.30	0.042	1.16	-0.185	-2.22**	-0.046	-0.85
Number of observations, R^2	106	0.32	106	0.32	34	0.51	34	0.51

Asterisks denote statistical significance at the 10 percent (*), 5 percent (**), and 1 percent (***) levels, respectively.

[1] Direct effect of exchange rate regime on inflation, plus indirect effect through money growth, given by $\beta_{Peg} + \beta_{Mon}(\overline{\Delta m}_{Peg} - \overline{\Delta m}_{Flt})$ and $\beta_{Int} + \beta_{Mon}(\overline{\Delta m}_{Int} - \overline{\Delta m}_{Flt})$ for pegged and intermediate regimes, respectively.

[2] Direct effect of exchange rate regime on inflation, controlling for money growth given by β_{Peg} and β_{Int} for pegged and intermediate regimes, respectively.

possibilities, we next explore whether successful disinflation programs under pegged regimes are very different from those undertaken under floating or intermediate regimes; and whether the costs of failure under pegged exchange rates differ from those under other regimes.

7.1.2 Characteristics of Successful and Unsuccessful Stabilization Programs

We begin by looking at the characteristics of successful and unsuccessful stabilization programs, aggregated across all regimes (table 7.3). For the moment, we focus exclusively on our weaker criterion of success—namely, that inflation not exceed its prestabilization level.

Our interest lies in identifying the factors leading to the success or failure of disinflation programs. To this end, we compare the behavior of both policy variables (money growth, fiscal deficit) and the more endogenous macroeconomic variables (real exchange rate, current account balance, output growth) prior to the onset of the disinflation program (years $t_0 - 2$ to t_0) to their behavior during, and immediately following, the initial stabilization (years $t_0 + 1$ to $t_0 + 3$).

For moderate disinflations, successful stabilization is associated with a decline in the annual inflation rate from 19.3 percent to 10.6 percent; in unsuccessful cases, inflation falls from 19.9 to 13.3 percent. Failed stabilizations are associated with a more pronounced consumption boom (measured in real terms), although the current account deficit is only slightly larger, and the real exchange rate is actually more depreciated. The essential differences seem to lie in the performance of the policy variables. The fiscal deficit is some 2 percent of GDP larger, and money growth is more than 8 percentage points per year higher in programs that failed.

However, the immediate output consequences of failure are small: If anything, the level of output is higher in failed stabilizations than in successful ones. In the latter, however, the swing between pre-stabilization and poststabilization growth is appreciably greater.

The differences are more dramatic when stabilization commences from a high inflation rate. Here, the inflation rate roughly halves from 98 percent to 48 percent per year in successful programs, while rising by 10 percentage points in unsuccessful cases. The swing in growth is also greater: Growth rises from −3 percent per year to about 1.3 percent per year in successful stabilizations, while falling

Table 7.3
Characteristics of successful and unsuccessful stabilizations and disinflations (medians, in percent per year, unless otherwise specified)

	Stabilization				Durable disinflation			
	Successful		Unsuccessful		Successful		Unsuccessful	
	Years t_0-2 to t_0	Years t_0+1 to t_0+3	Years t_0-2 to t_0	Years t_0+1 to t_0+3	Years t_0-2 to t_0	Years t_0+1 to t_0+3	Years t_0-2 to t_0	Years t_0+1 to t_0+3
Low: Inflation below 20 percent per year in year t_0-2, at least 5 percentage point decline between year t_0-2 and year t_0								
Inflation	11.6	7.2	12.8	8.2	12.2	7.0	11.9	7.5
Money growth	16.9	13.1	18.2	15.4	16.5	10.8	17.5	14.5
Government balance[1]	-3.9	-3.9	-5.6	-4.9	-3.8	-4.0	-4.1	-4.3
Current account[1]	-3.2	-3.3	-3.9	-4.0	-1.8	-2.1	-3.7	-3.8
Per capita real GDP growth	1.4	1.7	1.8	1.8	1.5	1.1	1.4	1.9
Output[2]	100.0	104.3	100.0	104.6	100.0	103.1	100.0	105.2
Consumption[1]	64.7	64.0	67.9	66.5	66.7	63.3	65.5	65.1
Real consumption[2]	100.0	107.7	100.0	110.0	100.0	106.3	100.0	99.7
Real exchange rate[3]	100.0	100.1	100.0	87.6	100.0	105.3	100.0	108.9
Real exchange rate[4]	100.0	101.9	100.0	90.1	100.0	106.4	100.0	98.3
Moderate: Inflation above 20 percent and below 50 percent per year in year t_0-2, at least 10 percentage point decline between year t_0-2 and year t_0								
Inflation	19.3	10.6	19.9	13.3	21.5	10.5	18.5	11.3
Money growth	22.5	18.0	24.0	26.5	26.1	17.8	22.6	19.2
Government balance[1]	-3.7	-2.9	-5.4	-5.1	-4.3	-2.4	-3.7	-3.3
Current account[1]	-4.0	-4.4	-5.3	-4.9	-2.9	-3.9	-4.6	-4.9
Per capita real GDP growth	0.7	1.7	1.5	2.0	0.8	2.2	0.9	1.6
Output[2]	100.0	103.4	100.0	106.2	100.0	104.5	100.0	103.6
Consumption[1]	69.0	70.4	69.3	67.1	65.4	66.2	69.3	71.4

Real consumption[2]	100.0	110.8	100.0	114.4	100.0	104.4	100.0	98.9
Real exchange rate[3]	100.0	100.0	100.0	93.5	100.0	110.8	100.0	111.5
Real exchange rate[4]	100.0	100.1	100.0	93.9	100.0	105.1	100.0	97.6
High: Inflation above 50 percent per year in year $t_0 - 2$, at least 20 percentage point decline between year $t_0 - 2$ and year t_0								
Inflation	97.9	47.8	78.4	87.9	332.3	56.3	80.2	51.1
Money growth	88.6	50.2	60.9	79.8	186.9	52.8	61.3	50.5
Government balance[1]	-5.2	-3.6	-4.4	-5.1	-2.7	-2.4	-5.8	-4.9
Current account[1]	-3.0	-3.8	-3.5	-2.5	-1.7	-3.2	-3.9	-3.9
Per capita real GDP growth	-3.1	1.3	-0.1	-1.1	-3.7	2.3	-1.7	0.8
Output[2]	100.0	100.5	100.0	98.8	100.0	99.1	100.0	100.7
Consumption[1]	69.1	71.6	68.7	69.9	67.8	68.8	69.1	72.4
Real consumption[2]	100.0	108.6	100.0	114.1	100.0	110.1	100.0	91.2
Real exchange rate[3]	100.0	99.6	100.0	76.4	100.0	112.7	100.0	109.9
Real exchange rate[4]	100.0	98.5	100.0	79.3	100.0	115.2	100.0	91.4

[1] In percent of GDP.
[2] Index, prestabilization period = 100.
[3] Through year $t_0 + 2$; index, prestabilization period = 100.
[4] Through year $t_0 + 3$; index, prestabilization period = 100.

by 1 percentage point in unsuccessful programs. Again, the main distinguishing characteristic is neither the real exchange rate nor the current account deficit (which is smaller in unsuccessful programs) but the policy variables. The fiscal deficit falls from 5 percent of GDP to 3.6 percent of GDP in successful stabilizations but widens from 4.5 percent of GDP to 5 percent of GDP in unsuccessful cases. The rate of money growth is almost 30 percentage points per year higher in failed programs.

7.1.3   Differences across Regimes

Are there significant differences in these patterns across exchange rate regimes? For successful stabilizations, inflation roughly halves under either pegged or floating regimes, with a rather more dramatic decline for pegged regimes starting from high inflation (table 7.4). The change in the level of output is comparable under pegged and floating regimes (with rather better performance of the intermediate regimes), as is the difference in real GDP growth rates before and after stabilization. For successful stabilizations, there is thus little evidence of a sizable difference in the sacrifice ratio between pegged and floating regimes. Interestingly, the fiscal adjustment tends to be smaller, and the current account deficit larger under pegged regimes, suggesting that the confidence effects of pegging the exchange rate may grant countries some fiscal leeway.

What about the costs of *failed* stabilization attempts? For moderate disinflations, failure under pegged exchange rates entails a marginal decline in the growth rate but not in the level of output, while failed attempts under floating and intermediate regimes are associated with a pickup in growth. For disinflations starting from high inflation rates, growth increases significantly under both pegged and floating regimes. Again, therefore, the evidence does not support the contention that exchange rate–based stabilizations are especially costly, even when they fail.

7.1.4   Durable Disinflations and Failed Stabilizations

Does the picture change when we focus on the tougher criterion of durable disinflation? The right-hand panels of figures 7.2 to 7.5 compare these episodes under pegged and floating regimes. Pegged exchange rates are associated with lower money growth and lower inflation (figure 7.2), and a faster rebound in real GDP growth (figure 7.3). On the other hand, the improvement in fiscal balances is smaller, as is the appreciation of the real exchange rate.

The left-hand panels of figures 7.2 to 7.5 depict failed stabilizations (corresponding to table 7.4). In these figures, some elements of the "ERBS syndrome" are more easily discerned. Among countries that fail to stabilize, those with pegged exchange rates experience a sharper real exchange rate appreciation (which begins before the disinflation is achieved), a more pronounced boom in consumption, and a significantly wider current account deficit.

Contrasting failed stabilizations to durable disinflations (the left-hand versus the right-hand panels of figures 7.2 to 7.5) reveals that the main difference is *not*, as is commonly asserted, the real exchange rate appreciation (figure 7.4). Rather, the essential distinction is the extent of fiscal adjustment. The reduction in the fiscal deficit is much larger in countries that achieved a durable decline in inflation rates than in those that failed to stabilize. In the latter, the lack of sufficient fiscal adjustment is reflected in an upsurge of inflation, in particular under floating regimes, where any semblance of monetary discipline seems to be lost as the program collapses (figure 7.2).

We conclude that the results of earlier studies, based primarily on the experience of a select group of countries, do not readily extend to a broader set of countries, a finding consistent with the results reported by Hamann (1999). Some stabilization programs succeed, and many fail. But success or failure seems to have relatively little to do with the exchange rate regime. In particular, stabilization attempts based on pegged exchange rate regimes are no more prone to failure than others—if anything, they are somewhat more likely to succeed. Nor are the output costs of such programs—whether they succeed or fail—any greater. Moreover, the discipline and confidence effects of pegged exchange rate regimes, identified in chapter 6, seem to carry over to disinflation episodes as well.

That said, some elements of the exchange rate–based stabilization syndrome seem to survive scrutiny. Compared to failures under other regimes, pegged exchange rate–based programs are characterized by a greater appreciation of the real exchange rate, a larger boom in private consumption, and a wider current account deficit.

It bears emphasizing, however, that the key distinction between failed stabilizations and durable disinflations is not the behavior of these variables, but rather the extent of fiscal adjustment and monetary discipline achieved.[5]

Table 7.4
Characteristics of successful and unsuccessful stabilizations under alternative exchange rate regimes (in percent per year, unless otherwise specified)

	Pegged regimes				Intermediate regimes				Floating regimes			
	Successful		Unsuccessful		Successful		Unsuccessful		Successful		Unsuccessful	
	Years t_0-2 to t_0	Years t_0+1 to t_0+3	Years t_0-2 to t_0	Years t_0+1 to t_0+3	Years t_0-2 to t_0	Years t_0+1 to t_0+3	Years t_0-2 to t_0	Years t_0+1 to t_0+3	Years t_0-2 to t_0	Years t_0+1 to t_0+3	Years t_0-2 to t_0	Years t_0+1 to t_0+3
Low: Inflation below 20 percent per year in year t_0-2, at least 5 percentage point decline between year t_0-2 and year t_0												
Inflation	11.2	7.2	12.9	8.3	14.1	7.9	9.6	2.7	12.1	6.3	10.3	8.1
Money growth	17.0	13.1	18.9	16.0	18.1	12.3	14.2	13.6	14.4	15.3	12.1	15.3
Government balance[1]	-3.9	-3.9	-5.6	-5.1	-10.0	-8.1	-8.0	-5.3	-2.1	-2.1	-0.9	-3.4
Current account[1]	-3.5	-3.8	-3.8	-4.0	-3.0	-2.1	-8.0	-4.0	-1.0	-1.1	-3.6	-2.3
Per capita real GDP growth	1.4	1.5	1.8	1.8	1.2	2.5	3.9	1.0	1.0	1.2	2.5	1.4
Output[2]	100.0	103.9	100.0	105.2	100.0	106.9	100.0	105.3	100.0	101.1	100.0	103.7
Consumption[1]	66.9	65.3	68.0	67.7	65.8	65.4	67.3	65.4	61.2	61.2	62.9	63.9
Real exchange rate[3]	100.0	99.6	100.0	87.5	100.0	105.1	100.0	90.7	100.0	99.2	—	—
Real exchange rate[4]	100.0	101.1	100.0	89.3	100.0	103.8	100.0	90.9	100.0	101.8	—	—
Real consumption[2]	100.0	108.9	100.0	110.4	100.0	106.6	100.0	109.8	100.0	105.8	100.0	109.5
Moderate: Inflation above 20 percent and below 50 percent per year in year t_0-2, at least 10 percentage point decline between year t_0-2 and year t_0												
Inflation	16.7	9.3	17.9	11.4	25.7	11.8	25.2	16.8	25.8	12.4	24.0	20.6
Money growth	20.6	15.4	23.3	24.5	34.2	24.8	26.5	28.5	32.6	23.5	28.9	31.7
Government balance[1]	-4.1	-3.7	-6.0	-6.2	-4.0	-3.2	-4.7	-3.0	-3.3	-1.9	-2.2	-3.1
Current account[1]	-4.0	-5.0	-5.8	-6.6	-4.2	-3.1	-4.4	-4.9	-3.8	-4.5	-6.3	-1.6
Per capita real GDP growth	0.3	1.6	2.2	1.9	1.4	3.3	1.5	2.3	0.6	1.3	-0.1	3.0

Output²	102.7	100.0	105.1	100.0	109.5	100.0	108.5	100.0	103.1	100.0	107.9
Consumption¹	70.9	71.3	69.3	68.9	64.8	69.1	67.1	72.6	72.4	75.6	68.2
Real exchange rate³	96.3	100.0	90.5	100.0	106.5	100.0	120.2	100.0	104.6	100.0	67.9
Real exchange rate⁴	97.6	100.0	92.9	100.0	108.0	100.0	118.8	100.0	102.3	100.0	72.2
Real consumption²	108.0	100.0	114.4	100.0	112.3	100.0	114.7	100.0	114.0	100.0	106.7
High: Inflation above 50 percent per year in year $t_0 - 2$, at least 20 percentage point decline between year $t_0 - 2$ and year t_0											
Inflation	193.6	81.7	91.3	85.1	53.6	99.7	88.9	124.4	44.2	40.6	31.3
Money growth	108.7	62.6	65.0	82.4	52.0	60.1	102.7	105.0	48.5	42.1	39.9
Government balance¹	-4.8	-5.1	-7.4	-4.9	-2.9	-4.8	-5.0	-5.9	-3.9	-4.0	-1.5
Current account¹	-1.5	-4.2	-6.0	-2.9	-2.9	-2.4	-1.3	-5.3	-6.1	-3.5	-0.9
Per capita real GDP growth	-3.7	-3.2	0.6	0.3	1.7	0.3	-2.8	-5.7	1.0	-0.5	1.2
Output²	100.0	100.0	102.0	100.0	102.4	100.0	96.0	100.0	98.0	100.0	105.1
Consumption¹	63.6	65.3	70.8	66.7	69.9	69.1	69.1	78.3	78.5	70.2	67.4
Real exchange rate³	100.0	100.0	118.3	100.0	99.9	100.0	60.9	100.0	99.6	100.0	54.8
Real exchange rate⁴	100.0	100.0	109.5	100.0	100.5	100.0	59.5	100.0	98.4	100.0	58.3
Real consumption²	114.3	114.4	118.8	100.0	109.6	100.0	115.8	100.0	99.7	100.0	110.3

¹ In percent of GDP.
² Index, prestabilization period = 100.
³ Through year $t_0 + 2$; index, prestabilization period = 100.
⁴ Through year $t_0 + 3$; index, prestabilization period = 100.

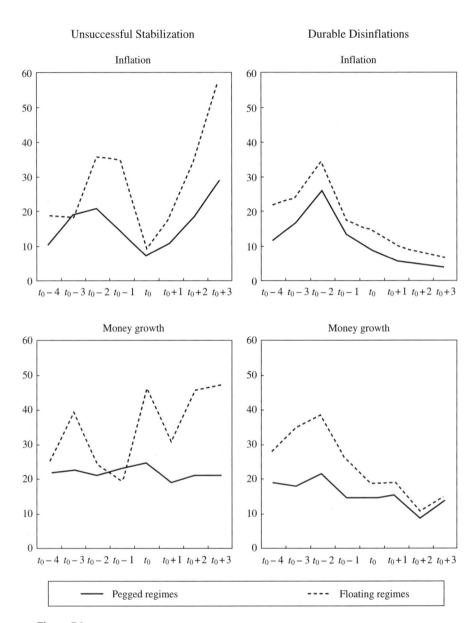

Figure 7.2
Inflation and money growth (medians, in percent per year)

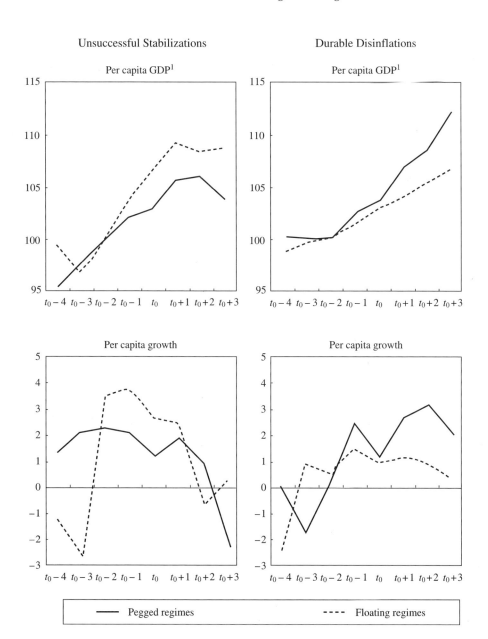

Figure 7.3
Per capita GDP and per capita growth (medians)
[1] Index, year $t_0 - 2 = 100$.

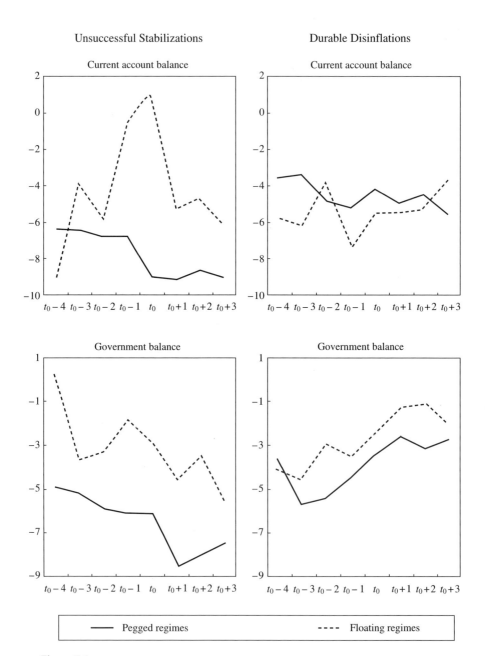

Figure 7.4
Current account balance and government balance (medians, in percent of GDP)

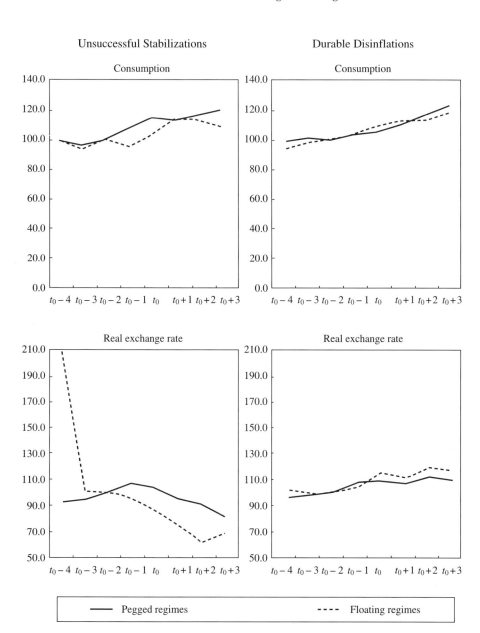

Figure 7.5
Consumption and real exchange rate (medians, index year $t_0 - 2 = 100$)

7.2   Case Studies

The results presented above, based on our panel dataset, do not suggest that exchange rate–based stabilizations are particularly prone to failure. Such summary statistics, however, necessarily abstract from much of the complexity of actual disinflation programs. In this section, we flesh out the cross-sectional evidence by exploring three recent exchange rate–based disinflation programs. Two of these—Bulgaria and Turkey—are chosen deliberately outside the Southern Cone (Argentina, Chile, Uruguay) Latin American experience.

7.2.1   Bulgaria

Bulgaria embarked on the transition to a market economy in 1989. As in many other transition economies, the road proved to be rocky. Bulgaria battled with an unsettled political framework and macroeconomic instability; progress on structural reforms was initially slow.

Macroeconomic policy remained stuck in a stop-and-go cycle. In the early 1990s Bulgaria undertook no fewer than four money-based stabilization attempts, supported by standby arrangements with the International Monetary Fund (1991, 1992, 1994, and 1996). Only the first of these was completed, with attempts at monetary discipline repeatedly succumbing to the need to provide liquidity to the government, parts of the banking system, and state-owned enterprises.

Early reforms of the financial sector exacerbated existing weaknesses. The mono-banking system had been divided into a central bank and a group of state-owned commercial banks in the late 1980s, soon followed by the entry of private banks. But regulation and supervision of the banking sector did not keep pace. Both public and private banks lent excessively to essentially unproductive enterprises, funded by borrowing from the central bank. Attempts to tighten monetary policy resulted in a liquidity crisis. Rumors about the state of the banking sector subsequently led to repeated bank runs, prompting renewed central bank support.[6]

The combination of financial sector fragility and unstable macroeconomic policies planted the seeds for a systemic crisis, which erupted in late 1996. In January 1997, the annualized inflation rate soared to almost 500 percent, by March, it had reached 2000 percent.

The accelerating inflation activated the familiar feedback loops. The Olivera-Tanzi effect and collapsing output undermined the fiscal accounts, with tax revenues plummeting from about 40 percent of GDP in 1996 to 15 percent of GDP by February 1997. The printing press ran overtime to cover the shortfall and to prop up the faltering banking sector. As inflation accelerated, so did currency substitution, further reducing the base for the inflation tax. The flight to hard currencies depreciated the exchange rate from 487 Lev/U.S.$ in January to 1588 Lev/U.S.$ by March, while foreign exchange reserves plummeted to a scant two months of imports. By March, Bulgaria found itself on the brink of hyperinflation.

7.2.1.1 The Currency Board After four failed money-based stabilizations, it was widely agreed that a clear and credible break from past policies was essential to restore confidence. One option attracting increasing support since the fall of 1996 was the introduction of a currency board.

Proponents argued that to break inflationary expectations and impose monetary discipline, the central bank had to be stripped of its ability to provide further liquidity support to the government and the banking sector. Most critics did not dispute the potential benefits of a currency board in lowering inflation and real interest rates (an issue of particular concern in light of the rapidly worsening public sector debt dynamics), but argued that Bulgaria could not meet the necessary preconditions for its adoption.

Among the reservations expressed perhaps the most important concerned the fragility of the banking system. Given the limited lender of last resort facilities that would be available under a hard peg, a crisis appeared all but unavoidable. Moreover, the low level of foreign exchange reserves meant that either the backing of base money would have to be far below customary levels for a currency board, or there would be a need for a large up-front devaluation.

While the debate unfolded, the continuing inflation resolved most of these objections. Fiscal sustainability was helped by the erosion of the real value of public debt, while banks, which held a large share of their assets in foreign currency denominated instruments, saw their capitalization improve as the real value of their liabilities contracted. Over the same period, the depreciation, coupled with a halt to extensive central bank intervention, solved the problem of insufficient reserve coverage.

These developments however did little to arrest inflation, which continued to ratchet up, finally tilting the political consensus decisively in favor of a drastic break from the past. The new government taking office in April 1997 was thus able to agree on the adoption of a currency board with substantial public support.

The currency board, introduced on July 1, 1997, was enshrined in a new central bank law. The Lev was tied to the Deutsche mark (DM) at an exchange rate of 1,000 Lev to one DM, with the central bank required to hold sufficient foreign exchange and gold assets at all times to cover all its liabilities, including government deposits, and to buy and sell Lev against DM on demand and without limit.

The currency board was augmented by several auxiliary measures. Most importantly, a fiscal reserve account held as a government deposit in the central bank was created to consolidate central government deposits and the accounts of the major extrabudgetary funds. The balance of the account represents the funds available to the government at any given time. Maintaining a minimum balance in the account, as required under Bulgaria's IMF-supported program, provides assurance of the government's ability to honor its budgetary commitments without recourse to monetary financing and thus forms an important source of stability and credibility.

Responding to the perceived need for a lender of last resort, the currency board operates with excess reserve coverage (initially amounting to one-fifth of total foreign reserves), effectively granting the central bank a limited lender of last resort capacity.

7.2.1.2 Stabilization Results Following the introduction of the currency board, annual inflation fell to 13 percent by mid-1998 and to less than 2 percent by the end of 1998. The official interest rate declined from a peak of more than 200 percent to 5.3 percent in October 1998, while retail interest rates moved closer to German levels as soon as the currency board was introduced (figures 7.6 and 7.7).

The stabilization gains have broadly persisted, despite significant shocks such as the Russian crisis of mid-1998 and the fallout from the Balkan conflict. Inflation, after having increased to around 12 percent in 2000 has declined again to less than 5 percent at the end of 2001. Interest rates remain in line with euro rates. The currency board continues to enjoy widespread support, and Bulgaria has declared its intention to maintain the arrangement until Euro-

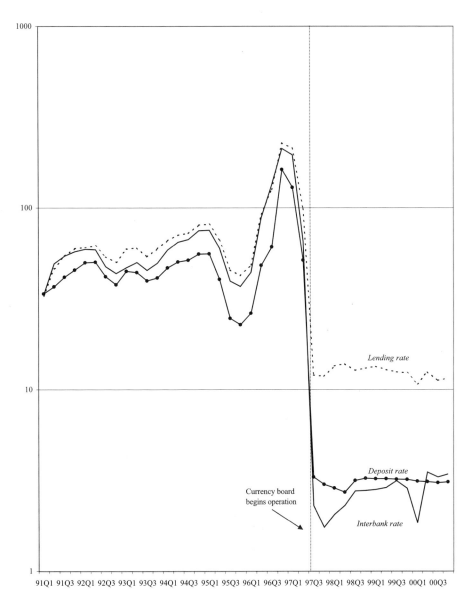

Figure 7.6
Bulgaria interest rates (in percent per year, logarithmic scale)

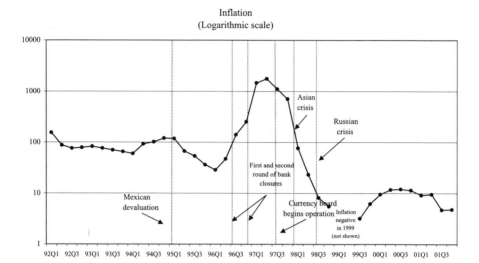

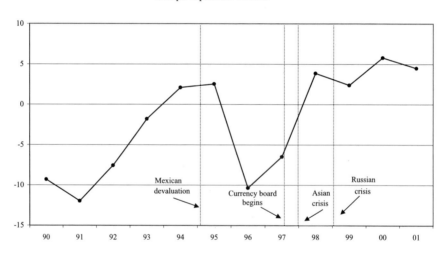

Figure 7.7
Bulgaria: inflation and growth (in percent per year)

pean Union accession and eventual European Monetary Union membership.

7.2.2 Turkey 1999–2000

Starting in the mid-1960s, Turkey started to suffer from chronically high inflation rates. With some respites, inflation ratcheted up steady over the following three decades: averaging 20 percent during the 1970s, 40 percent in the early 1980s, and 85 percent by the mid-1990s. Volatile inflation was matched by erratic output growth, with repeated boom and bust cycles around a low long-term trend of 2.5 percent per year (figure 7.8).

Underlying this poor inflation performance were monetized fiscal deficits, emerging during the 1970s and persisting through the 1980s and 1990s. As money velocity increased—in response to high actual and expected inflation—extracting the same amount of seignorage revenue from the shrinking monetary base required ever increasing inflation rates (Dornbusch, Sturzenegger, and Wolf 1990).[7]

Inflationary expectations also had a direct impact on public finances (Moalla-Fetini 1999). High and volatile inflation translated into high nominal interest rates, which in turn sharply raised the cost of attempting disinflation, thus validating the inflationary expectations. Even when the authorities tried to improve the primary balance, as in 1994–1995, nominal interest rates remained stubbornly high, undermining the adjustment of the overall deficit and ultimately the success of the disinflation program.

In early 1998, confronted by the prospect of a slide into hyperinflation, the Turkish authorities embarked upon a money-based stabilization program.[8] Broad money growth was reduced from 118 percent in 1997 to 76 percent in 1998, while the nominal exchange rate was depreciated in line with inflation.

While the program initially succeeded in reducing inflation— from 100 percent in 1997 to 70 percent in 1998—the lack of a well-publicized expectations anchor, together with adverse shocks and a failure to tackle the structural roots of the fiscal weaknesses, undermined policy credibility. Ex post real interest rates soared, reaching more than 40 percent per year by 1999. Growth plummeted from 8 percent in 1997 to 4 percent in 1998 and −6 percent by 1999. The high real interest rates in turn put the public debt dynamics on a clearly unsustainable path. The public sector debt ratio doubled in the space of two years, to almost 40 percent of GDP by 1999.

Inflation and Nominal Exchange Rate Depreciation[1]

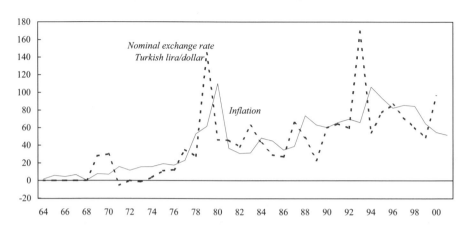

Per Capita Real GDP Growth

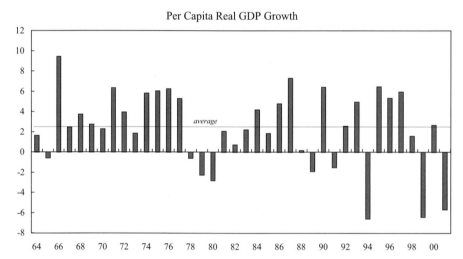

Figure 7.8
Turkey: inflation, nominal exchange rate depreciation and per capita real GDP growth
(in percent per year)
Source: International Financial Statistics.
[1] Average of period; Turkish lira per U.S. dollar.

In short, Turkey presented a textbook case for an exchange rate–based stabilization program, with one important wrinkle: Too rapid a fall in inflation threatened a ballooning of real interest payments on the existing government debt.[9]

7.2.2.1   The December 1999 Disinflation Program   The solution was sought in a combination of a crawling peg (with the central bank committing to the rate of crawl, preannounced for one year at a time), buttressed by currency-board-like rules (full backing for base money and, essentially, zero growth of central bank credit).

An important innovation of the new exchange rate regime was an explicit, preannounced exit strategy (taking the form of a band around the central rate of crawl, beginning eighteen months into the program and widening progressively at the rate of 15 percentage points per year).[10] This was intended to address a common concern about hard pegs—that, once entered, they may be difficult to exit without triggering a crisis (see chapter 8). Since the hard crawling peg was intended only as an interim device to achieve disinflation, it was hoped that announcing the exit strategy at the outset of the program would lessen the risk that markets might interpret the eventual exit adversely.

Underpinning the disinflation effort was a substantial fiscal adjustment—the primary balance improved by more than 5 percent of GDP—as well as structural reforms intended to put the public finances in better order and to strengthen the previously lax supervision of the banking sector.

7.2.2.2   The Aftermath   At first, the program was remarkably successful. Annualized inflation fell from around 70 percent in December 1999 to about 45 percent in November 2000. Treasury bill rates, which had exceeded 140 percent in January 1999 and were still above 90 percent in October, plunged in anticipation of the program,[11] falling below 40 percent in December 1999. The fall in interest rates (figure 7.9) implied substantial fiscal savings and, together with substantial capital inflows, helped fuel a dramatic recovery of output, with growth rebounding from −6 percent in 1999 to 6 percent in 2000.

But the program soon began to exhibit some of the symptoms of the ERBS syndrome. Inertial inflation above the crawling rate led to a real appreciation of some 10 to 15 percent. Coupled with a boom in

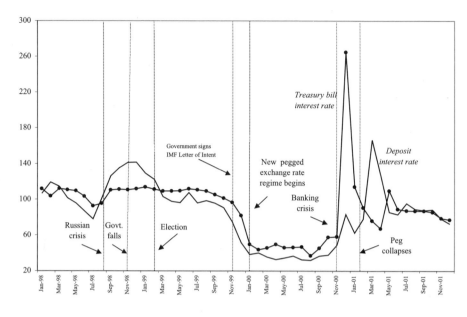

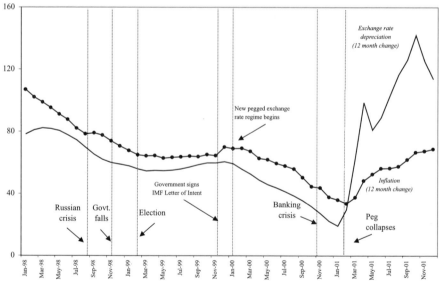

Figure 7.9
Turkey: interest rates, inflation and depreciation of nominal exchange rate (in percent per year)

domestic demand, which rose by more than 10 percent, and a sharp increase in world oil prices, the current account deficit widened to 5 percent of GNP in 2000. Meanwhile, the government failed to tighten fiscal policy further—indeed, on some measures, the stance was loosened—despite clear signs that the economy was overheating. By the summer of 2000, all the warning signs of a failing ERBS program were in place.

The proximate trigger of the eventual crisis came from the banking system. In November 2000 two of the largest banks began cutting their credit lines to some smaller banks. These responded by a distress sale of treasury bills, spiking yields on government securities and triggering margin calls, which prompted a flight to quality that pushed yields yet higher.

The central bank was thus presented with a classic dilemma between maintaining its external commitments or safeguarding the stability of the financial system. The internal objective proved decisive: as interbank interest rates soared above 100 and later above 1000 percent per year, the central bank injected massive amounts of liquidity, increasing net domestic assets by the equivalent of 70 percent of base money, promptly losing some $6 billion of foreign exchange reserves. On the brink of failure, the program was, temporarily, salvaged when the central bank applied the monetary brakes in the context of a strengthened policy package and the promise of additional support from the international community. Yet, the rescue effort proved short-lived. With its credibility fatally damaged, the program lingered on for another three months before a political crisis brought about the final collapse, a devaluation of some 30 percent, and a resurgence of inflation.

7.2.3 Argentina (1991–2001)

7.2.3.1 Background Argentina has a long history of monetary instability, high inflation, and low growth. During the 1980s, a series of orthodox and heterodox stabilization programs failed as chronically large money-financed deficits led to demonetization, capital flight, and pervasive dollarization.[12] By mid-1989, the economy was in hyperinflation, with monthly inflation rates reaching 300 percent. Output fell by more than 6 percent, investment declined by 25 percent, and, due to disintermediation, M3 declined to just 5 percent of GDP.

Following Carlos Menem's electoral victory, a more drastic stabilization package was announced, including asset freezes, a conversion of domestic debt, and the abolition of remuneration on required reserves (which had previously been an important source of money creation).[13] The fall in inflation and the stabilization of the exchange rate proved short-lived, however, undermined by central bank credits in late 1990 to the social security system and to several banks experiencing deposit runs.

In the face of yet another failed stabilization program, Argentina was ready for a novel approach. Domingo Cavallo, appointed to the position of minister of economy in January 1991, pushed the idea of a currency board as a means of depoliticizing monetary policy (or, more precisely, the money-financing of fiscal deficits).[14] Congress passed the Convertibility Law in March 1991. The law established a fixed parity of 10,000 australes to the dollar (which later became one Argentine peso per dollar following the monetary reform in 1992), as part of a comprehensive stabilization package that also included enacting fiscal policy measures, eliminating wage indexation, and granting legal tender status to the U.S. dollar.[15] While the new exchange rate regime was broadly based on a currency board arrangement (CBA), it differed from a classic currency board in a number of respects, intended to provide some scope for an activist monetary policy.[16]

7.2.3.2 Performance The new regime initially proved remarkably successful (figure 7.10). Inflation fell from several thousand percent in 1989–1990 to less than 25 percent in 1992—the lowest rate in more than twenty years. Per capita output growth, which had had been negative through most of the 1980s, reached more than 8 percent in 1991–1992 and more than 4 percent in the two subsequent years. Capital inflows allowed money and credit to triple between 1991 and 1993, raising the ratio of broad money to GDP from 10.5 to 18.5 percent. Currency substitution remained high, however, at around 50 percent of deposits.

In 1995, the Argentinean CBA weathered its first major financial crisis. In the aftermath of the collapse of the Mexican peg in December 1994—the so-called Tequila crisis—Argentina experienced significant capital outflows, reaching some 5 percent of GDP in the first quarter of 1995. Withdrawals from the banking sector contracted demand deposits by 18 percent in the space of only three months,

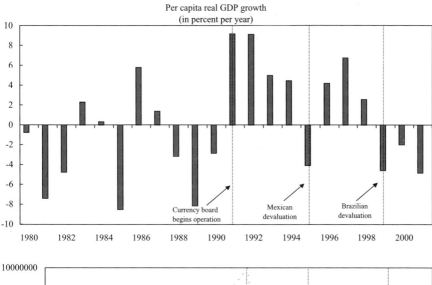

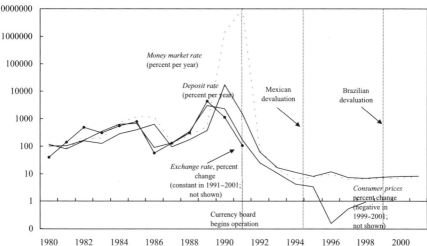

Figure 7.10
Argentina: Macroeconomic indicators, 1980–2001
Source: International Monetary Fund, *WEO*, and *IFS*.

and the attendant capital outflows put the arrangement to a severe test. Domestic interest rates, which had averaged about 10 percent on peso deposits, rose to 15 percent. Although interest rates on dollar deposits also rose, the spread between peso and dollar rates widened—reaching some 5 to 6 percentage points—suggesting both a lack of liquidity and doubts about the sustainability of the currency board (figure 7.11).

The Argentine authorities reiterated their commitment to the currency board regime and responded with a number of measures, including a reduction of reserve requirements, tighter fiscal policy, and an IMF-supported program. These measures proved sufficient to restore confidence. By mid-1995, capital inflows had resumed, reaching 10 percent of GDP by the end of 1995. The economy rebounded robustly, with growth reaching 4 percent in 1996 and almost 7 percent in 1997.

The second major crisis, following the collapse of the Brazilian peg in early 1999, altered priorities. The economy entered the doldrums. Growth slowed to 2.5 percent in 1998 and turned negative in 1999. The appreciation of the trade-weighted real exchange rate implied by the Brazilian devaluation, together with the growth slowdown, again raised questions about the political sustainability of Argentina's currency board regime, which were soon reflected in widening spreads of peso over U.S. dollar interest rates. Within the context of the forthcoming presidential elections, a debate ensued on whether outright dollarization might be preferable to maintaining the currency board with its strictures on monetary policy, or whether the pegged exchange rate regime should be abandoned in favor of a floating exchange rate regime.

Proponents of dollarization argued that it would eliminate the persistent spread between U.S. dollar and peso interest rates which, by now, had reached some 1.5 to 3 percentage points, in part because of the talk of abandoning the currency board regime. Opponents of dollarization noted that it would not solve the problem of high U.S. dollar interest rates, which were mostly being driven by the public-sector deficits (a primary deficit of about 1 percent of GDP and an overall deficit of 4 percent of GDP).[17] In any event, the issue was resolved when the United States, while not opposing dollarization as such, made it clear that Argentina would not be granted a voice in U.S. monetary policy decisions, nor would the Federal Reserve act as lender of last resort for Argentine banks; even the prospect of shar-

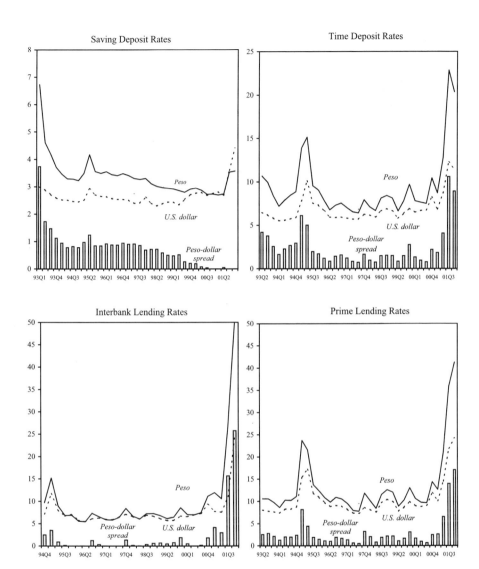

Figure 7.11
Argentina: Interest rates
Source: Central Bank of Argentina.

ing some of the seigniorage seemed remote. Eventually, a consensus
emerged that the costs of dollarization would be too high.

At the same time, fiscal policy was loosened considerably in the
run up to the elections. The overall public sector deficit doubled
from 2 percent of GDP in 1998 to more than 4 percent of GDP in
1999, nearly all reflecting an increase in noninterest expenditure. The
newly elected government of President Fenando de la Rua affirmed
its commitment to the currency board regime and, in late 1999,
attempted to tighten fiscal policy, albeit with limited success.

Through 2000 and 2001, the government took a series of increasingly desperate steps to jumpstart the economy and to continue
funding itself. In March 2001, Domingo Cavallo was brought back as
minister of economy. He immediately unveiled his Competitiveness
Law—harkening back to the Convertibility Law that had introduced
the currency board in 1991—which imposed a financial transactions
tax and raised tariffs. In April, Cavallo introduced a bill to repeg the
peso to a basket consisting of the U.S. dollar and the euro—on
grounds that the strength of the dollar, to which the peso had been
pegged, had hurt Argentina's export competitiveness.[18] A further
measure, introduced two months later, provided a preferential exchange rate for exporters.

The government undertook various fiscal adjustment measures
and swapped government bonds into longer-term instruments. But it
proved impossible to break the cycle of rising interest rates and falling growth. Public sector debt ballooned rapidly from 50 percent of
GDP in 2000 to more than 60 percent by 2001. The government
needed to raise some $15 billion simply to roll over its maturing
debts, and an additional $20 billion to meet its cash deficit and short-
term debt—the equivalent of almost 40 percent of all emerging
market bond issuance. By the end of 2001, spreads on Argentine
debt had reached 3,000 basis points, and it was clear that the debt
dynamics were no longer sustainable.

On December 1, facing a massive run on deposits, the authorities
introduced wide-ranging controls on banking and foreign exchange
transactions. Amid the ensuing social and political unrest, Cavallo
was forced to resign as minister of economy on December 19, and de
la Rua as President on December 20. Three interim presidents
(Puerta, Saá, and Camaño) followed; on January 1, 2002, Eduardo
Duhalde, chosen by Congress, was sworn in to complete de la

Rua's term. Meanwhile, on December 23, President Adolfo Saá had declared default on foreign debt.

The end of the currency board came on January 6, 2002. The Law of Public Emergency and Reform granted the president special powers to devalue the peso and reform the economy. The peso was devalued to 1.40 per dollar for certain transactions, but most transactions were to take place at a floating rate. Dollar deposits in banks were "pesofied" at 1.40 peso per dollar, but mortgages below $100,000 were valued at 1 peso per dollar. These measures, together with the default on government bonds, pushed much of the banking system into technical bankruptcy. On April 23, Congress passed a law reinforcing the legal basis of the freeze on withdrawal of bank deposits—"el corralito." These events placed strong pressure on the peso, which was soon trading at rates of up to four pesos per U.S. dollar.

7.2.3.3 Role of the Currency Board Argentina's experience inevitably raises the question of whether the currency board was responsible for the collapse of the stabilization program—indeed, of the entire economy—not least because proponents of the CBA had been quick to claim credit for early successes. In analyzing the role of the currency board, it is useful to consider two separate questions. First, did the exchange rate peg become overvalued, undermining export competitiveness and, ultimately, growth? Second, did the strictures on monetary policy implied by the currency board result in a liquidity squeeze upon the economy? And relatedly, did persistent expectations of a devaluation—unfulfilled until 2002—mean that nominal and real interest rates were exceptionally high, thus dampening economic activity?

7.2.3.4 Real Exchange Rate The real effective exchange rate certainly appreciated markedly under the currency board regime, rising by some 50 percent between 1991 and 2001 (figure 7.12).[19] This reflected both the strength of the U.S. dollar (to which the peso was pegged) vis-à-vis the currencies of the European countries (which make up a significant share of Argentina's exports), devaluations of some of Argentina's major trading partners (most notably Brazil, in early 1999), as well as some persistence of inflation in the early years of the currency board regime. But much of the real appreciation took place immediately following the stabilization in 1991, and to the

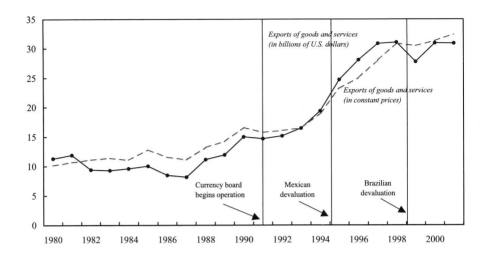

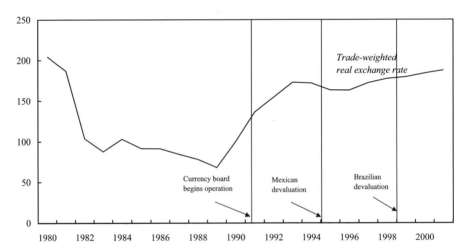

Figure 7.12
Argentina: Exports and real exchange rate
Source: International Monetary Fund, World Economic Outlook database.

extent that the nominal exchange rate overshot during the hyper-inflation, the real appreciation may have been nothing more than a return to equilibrium.[20]

Some evidence comes from the performance of exports. In volume terms, exports of goods and services rose by an *average* of 34 percent per year between 1991 and 1998 (27 percent in value terms)—at a time when the cumulative increase in the real exchange rate was 30 percent. Thereafter, export growth did slow down (from about 25 percent in 1997 to about 3 percent in 1998), and following the Brazilian devaluation in early 1999, Argentina's export growth turned negative. It may be tempting to conclude that Brazil's devaluation—and the consequent appreciation of Argentina's real exchange rate—was responsible for the slowdown in Argentina's export performance. Yet the slowdown started in 1998, and even with Brazil's devaluation, Argentina's real exchange rate rose by only 1 percent in 1999 relative to 1998 (4 percent in 2000). Rather than the real exchange rate appreciation, therefore, it is more plausible that slowing economic activity in Argentina's trading partners was responsible for the deterioration in export performance.[21]

Would exports have fared much better under a floating exchange rate regime? Even if such a regime had implied a real depreciation (which is unlikely, at least in the immediate aftermath of the stabilization in 1991), empirical evidence suggests only a limited impact on exports and the trade balance. Thomas (2002) estimates import and export functions, separating commodities (for which the world price is given) from manufactures. His results indicate that a 20 percent real depreciation would raise export volumes by only 2.5 percent and the peso value of export revenues by 8 percent, while inelastic demand for imports means that import expenditures in peso terms would rise by about 5 percent. Overall, the trade balance would improve by about 1 percent of GDP. Moreover, at around 10 percent of the economy, the share of exports is too small for the real exchange rate to have a significant impact on overall GDP growth. For instance, using Thomas's estimates and assuming a 20 percent real depreciation, the 2.5 percent growth of exports would raise real GDP growth by less than one-third of 1 percentage point.

Taken as whole, therefore, it is hard to make a convincing case that the real appreciation under the currency board regime was responsible for the growth slowdown or the spiraling debt dynamics. During much of the period of the real appreciation, export growth was robust, although the share of exports in the economy has always been low.

7.2.3.5 Monetary Policy and Interest Rates
An alternative hypothesis is that the currency board regime circumscribed the central bank's ability to provide domestic credit, which in turn may have limited banking system credit to the economy and dampened economic activity. Tight monetary conditions may be manifested in high real interest rates or, under certain circumstances, in quantity rationing.

Between 1994 and the end of 2000, peso real lending rates in Argentina averaged 11 percent per year (rising to 20 percent in the first half of 1995 during the Tequila crisis). Real overnight interbank rates averaged some 7 percent per year. To put this in perspective, during the same period, real lending interest rates averaged 67 percent per year in Brazil, 9 percent in Mexico, and 12 percent in Chile. It seems unlikely, therefore, that interest rates in Argentina would have been much lower with a floating exchange rate regime. Argentine real interest rates did rise sharply in the latter half of 2001, reaching 40 to 50 percent by year-end as it became increasingly apparent that the exchange rate regime and the debt dynamics were unsustainable, but this can hardly explain the recession that had started in 1998.

To assess whether there was quantity rationing of loanable funds, it is useful to consider the banking system's lending capacity, defined as total assets (which equals liabilities) minus cash-in-vault, required liquidity reserves held at the central bank, and equity. By increasing its liabilities—either by accepting deposits or borrowing abroad or (when possible) borrowing from the central bank—the banking system is able to increase its capacity to provide loans to either the private or the public sector. The evolution of banking system lending capacity, thus defined, is shown in figure 7.13. Although central bank loans to the banking system became negligible under the currency board regime, the steady growth of deposits and capital inflows (except in 1995) allowed an expansion of banks' lending capacity until 1998. In 1998, there was a temporary decline in lending capacity, but this had recovered by mid-1999, albeit at a much lower growth rate. It was only in mid-2001, with falling deposits, that banks' lending capacity declined appreciably.[22]

Again, therefore, while it is difficult to arrive at a definitive judgment, neither the evidence on interest rates nor the behavior of credit

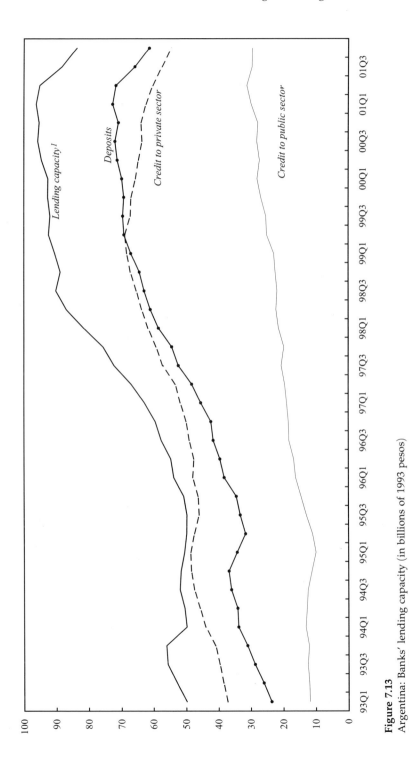

Figure 7.13
Argentina: Banks' lending capacity (in billions of 1993 pesos)
Source: Central Bank of Argentina.
[1] Lending capacity is defined as assets minus cash-in-vault minus equity; assets exclude "other asset accounts."

supply and demand suggests that tight monetary conditions can explain the slowdown of growth that started in 1998.

7.2.3.6 Beyond the Exchange Rate Regime Ultimately, Argentina's problem was one of unsustainable public debt dynamics, partly reflecting the slowdown of output growth after 1998. Beyond the effects of the currency board regime that, as argued previously, are not compellingly large, what explains the growth slowdown? A full account is beyond the scope of this book, but one explanation is that structural reforms petered out, especially during President Menem's second term, in part because of political compromises as he sought a third term in office. Among the reforms, those of the labor market were most pressing. Even during the boom years, 1991–1998, the unemployment rate averaged 14 percent. Historically, Argentina's labor regulations had been highly protective of individual workers' interests, with "lifetime" hiring practices, high barriers to dismissal, and numerous fringe benefits. A series of reforms in the early 1990s strove to make the labor market less rigid, but as the decade progressed, these (and other planned) reforms were either diluted or, in some cases, entirely reversed.[23] In this view, therefore, the growth spurt between 1991 and 1998 mostly reflected a rebound from the hyperinflationary years and the benefits of initial reforms that could not be sustained over the longer term because of structural rigidities of the economy.

The root of the unsustainable debt dynamics was fiscal profligacy. This had a number of dimensions, including the uneasy fiscal relations between the provinces and the central government that were never resolved. In every year from 1992 to 2001, both the federal government and the public sector ran overall deficits, even when the economy was booming. Public sector debt rose steadily throughout this period, almost doubling from 33 percent of GDP in 1992 to 63 percent of GDP by 2001. When the economy entered a downturn in 1999, therefore, constraints on obtaining additional funding meant that there was almost no scope for an expansionary fiscal policy. More speculatively, had there not been such a buildup of public debt, the economy might well have weathered the downturn without a crisis.

In sum, the currency board regime probably played only a minor role in the failure of Argentina's decade-long stabilization episode. While Argentina's real exchange rate did appreciate under its exchange rate peg, its experience does not really match the classic ERBS syndrome. For one thing, the regime lasted much longer than most failed exchange rate–based stabilization programs; for another, the collapse came in the midst of a deep and enduring recession, not a boom. In one sense, however, the experience does follow the ERBS syndrome—the pegged exchange rate regime instilled a false sense of security, allowing the government to continue funding itself despite increasingly unsustainable debt dynamics.

7.2.4 Conclusions from the Country Experiences

What lessons can be drawn from the experience of these three countries? In each case, the experience highlights the power of a rule-based system to quickly change perceptions and economic behavior, enabling the government to reap the benefits of its stabilization program. In all three cases, the exchange rate anchor quickly stabilized inflation, leading to a rapid decline in interest rates and an initial resumption of economic growth.

What, then, explains the different outcomes? The explanation must be sought in the initial conditions, preparedness, political mandate, and willingness to tackle deep-rooted structural problems even—indeed especially—following the stabilization honeymoon.

In Bulgaria, a year of high inflation in a largely nonindexed economy had sufficed to place fiscal accounts on a sustainable path and to improve the solvency of the banking system. The new government, acting with a clear mandate, was thus able to implement steps that would have been all but impossible a year earlier.

In contrast, Turkey's banking sector weaknesses were far from resolved at the outset of its stabilization program. Equally important, while real interest rates fell considerably, Turkey's long history of high inflation had generated a much greater degree of direct and indirect indexation: In contrast to Bulgaria, Turkey could not wipe the slate clean with a single burst of high inflation. Weaknesses in the financial sector soon became a testing ground for the authorities' commitment to the rule-based system. Nor was there much of a political consensus. Infighting delayed, or outright prevented, several crucial structural reforms aimed at improving financial sector supervision. Perhaps most important, when it came down to the crunch, the coalition government was unable to tighten fiscal policy.

In Argentina's case, the lessons are more complex. The initial adoption of the currency board was undoubtedly a success, leading to sharply lower inflation and a resurgence of economic growth. Furthermore, fiscal spending was relatively restrained in the initial years. The eventual downfall of the currency board reflected both deliberate policy choices, and—in the shape of the Asian and Brazilian crisis—bad luck. The initial success, coupled with domestic politics, fostered capital inflows and reduced the perceived urgency of further structural reforms, most notably those of the labor market. The success over the first years also did not pervent the reemergence of fiscal profligacy, notably at the provincial level.

The Argentine and Turkish experiences provide a useful reminder that pegging the exchange rate in a disinflation program is not a "magic bullet" if insufficient attention is paid to accompanying fiscal and structural reforms. But by the same token, Bulgaria's experience shows that a carefully implemented exchange rate–based stabilization can achieve durable disinflation without succumbing to the ERBS syndrome.

Exits and Crises

Traditionally, concerns about an eventual exit played little or no role in the choice of the exchange rate regime. The classic gold standard, the interwar gold exchange standard, and the Bretton Woods system were all perceived, and in the latter case, conceived as semipermanent fixtures of the world monetary order.

The collapse of the Bretton Woods system introduced the possibility of regime choice, thereby also raising the issue of regime exit, in two ways. The first relates to voluntary exits: Governments gained the ability to use different regimes at different times for achieving specific, and often temporary, objectives (such as disinflation in exchange rate–based stabilizations). The second type of transition is more traumatic: Even when there is no intention to exit, growing international capital mobility may make some types of regimes more vulnerable to forced exits. To the extent that such exits are economically (and perhaps politically or socially) disruptive, they may have an important bearing on the cost-benefit calculus of adopting such regimes.

The two types of transition carry starkly different implications. A voluntary exit replaces one nominal anchor (e.g., the exchange rate) by another (e.g., an inflation target) that is believed to offer superior performance (or to fulfill other objectives). If the process is fully prepared and well managed, the market should have ample time to incorporate the regime shift into expectations and asset prices, and there is no reason why the transition should not proceed smoothly.

By contrast, an exit occurring in the aftermath of a speculative attack damages the reputation of the central bank and, in the short run, may leave economic policy without any nominal anchor. This is likely to result in a period of volatile asset prices, unstable expectations, and higher risk premia—until the nature and credibility of the successor regime have been established.

This chapter first reviews the trends in regime shifts over the post-Bretton Woods period and presents a typology of regime changes. It then takes up four issues related to voluntary and forced exits from exchange rate regimes. First, what operational considerations need to be taken into account in planning a smooth transition to a new exchange regime? Second, why are voluntary exits so often delayed, sometimes until a speculative attack forces the issue? Third, are pegged exchange rate systems particularly susceptible to crisis so that the risk of a "forced" exit must be considered an integral part of the decision to adopt a peg? Finally, are crises under pegged regimes particularly costly?

8.1   Regime Transitions: Stylized Facts

For the six-way regime classification, on average about one in ten countries exited its exchange rate regime in any given year of the sample period (1975–1999). To some extent, this reflects the underlying secular trends in the international monetary system documented in chapter four. Figure 8.1 reports the frequency distributions of exchange rate regimes for the six-way de jure classification.

Over this period, the proportion of single currency pegs declined steadily, from about half of the total number of observations in 1975 to less than 15 percent by 1999. Basket pegs also lost popularity, falling from about 20 percent to 10 percent of all regimes. The big net winners were pure floats, and floats with discretionary intervention, which rose from a negligible number in the early years of the sample period to nearly 50 percent of all countries by the end.

Trends in the evolution of the six-way de jure classification thus provide some support for the "hollowing out" hypothesis (Eichengreen 1994), which predicts that countries will gravitate to extreme regimes at either end of the spectrum. As figure 8.1 shows, the share of the two most extreme regimes—pure floats and hard pegs—has indeed increased steadily, from 5 percent of all observations in the early 1970s to more than 40 percent at the end of the sample.[1]

These secular trends do not provide the full story, however. There have also been a significant number of transitions between floating and intermediate regimes, while numerous countries adopted new pegs. Table 8.1 reports the transition matrix of exits from, and entries

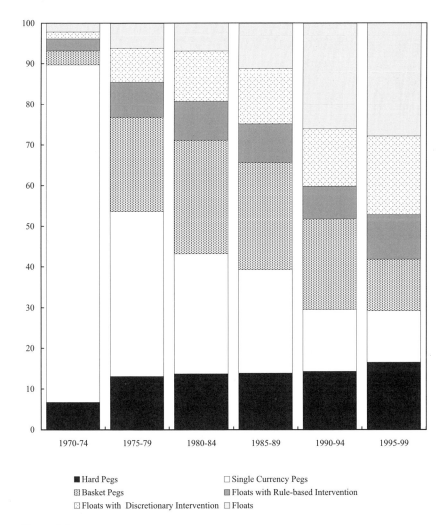

Figure 8.1
Distribution of exchange rate regimes, 1970–1999 (detailed de jure classification)
Source: IMF, *Annual Report on Exchange Arrangements and Exchange Restrictions* (various issues).

Table 8.1
Transition matrix of de jure regimes, 1975–1999[1]

Original regime		New regime						Total exits	Total exits in percentage of observations[2]
		Hard peg (1)	Single currency peg (2)	Basket peg (3)	Float with rule-based intervention (4)	Float with discretionary intervention (5)	Float (6)		
Hard peg	(1)	—	0	0	0	0	0	0	0.0
Single currency peg	(2)	6	—	39	10	27	19	101	11.5
Basket peg	(3)	0	10	—	6	27	20	63	7.7
Float with rule-based intervention	(4)	11	3	6	—	10	12	42	12.2
Float with discretionary intervention	(5)	2	17	10	20	—	30	79	15.6
Float	(6)	3	5	2	9	35	—	54	9.0
Total entries		22	35	57	45	99	81	339	9.2
Net entries		22	−66	−6	3	20	27	—	—

[1] Number of entries and exits from each regime, six-way de jure classification.
[2] Total number of exits as a percentage of all observations of the original regime.

to, each regime during the period 1975–1999. With the exception of hard pegs, for which there are no recorded exits during the sample period (Argentina's exit in 2002 falls outside the sample), movements are not unidirectional. Floats with rule-based intervention, and floats with discretionary intervention have the largest proportion of "gross" transitions. In terms of net gains and losses, pure floats, floats with discretionary intervention and hard pegs have the largest net gains, at the expense of single currency and basket pegs.

One argument against traditional pegged exchange rate regimes stems from doubts about their durability under high capital mobility (Fischer 2001). Has greater capital mobility resulted in more countries exiting pegged exchange rate regimes?

Tables 8.2a and 8.2b give the corresponding transition matrices as table 8.1, but split into countries with and without capital controls. The result is surprising but unambiguous: The exit rate from traditional pegs is twice as high in countries *with* capital controls than in countries without. (Nor does this reflect countries imposing capital controls in the midst of a crisis: Classifying countries according to the lag of the capital controls index yields virtually identical results.) Indeed, except for basket pegs, the exit rate is uniformly lower for countries with full capital mobility. There are, of course, many other factors influencing exits, some of them correlated with the choice to impose or eschew capital controls.[2]

8.2 A Transition Classification

The large number of regimes implies an even larger number of possible transitions. Some of these are easily managed; others require both extensive legal and institutional changes and the coordination of multiple institutions and constituencies.

Table 8.3 discusses the different levels of complexity of well-managed transitions for a four-way classification (hard pegs, pegs, intermediate regimes, and floats). Depending on the original and the proposed regime, legal, institutional, regulatory and/or policy implementation changes may be needed for a smooth change from one regime to another.

In terms of difficulty, transitions between variants of intermediate regimes and floating regimes are the least complex, needing little adjustment beyond a reorientation of the intervention rules. Shifts from intermediate and floating rate systems to adjustable pegs are

Table 8.2a
Transition matrix of de jure regimes, 1975–1999[1] (countries without capital controls)

Original regime		New regime						Total exits	Total exits in percentage of observations[2]
		Hard peg (1)	Single currency peg (2)	Basket peg (3)	Float with rule-based intervention (4)	Float with discretionary intervention (5)	Float (6)	Total exits	
Hard peg	(1)	—	0	0	0	0	0	0	0.0
Single currency peg	(2)	0	—	4	1	5	1	11	6.1
Basket peg	(3)	0	0	—	1	4	4	9	8.5
Float with rule-based intervention	(4)	11	0	0	—	2	2	15	9.3
Float with discretionary intervention	(5)	0	4	1	4	—	3	12	12.5
Float	(6)	2	0	1	5	6	—	14	5.8
Total entries		13	4	6	11	17	10	61	6.8
Net entries		13	−7	−3	−4	5	−4	—	—

[1] Number of entries and exits from each regime, six-way de jure classification.
[2] Total number of exits as a percentage of all observations of the original regime.

Table 8.2b
Transition matrix of de jure regimes, 1975–1999[1] (countries with capital controls)

Original regime		New regime						Total exits	Total exits in percentage of observations[2]
		Hard peg (1)	Single currency peg (2)	Basket peg (3)	Float with rule-based intervention (4)	Float with discretionary intervention (5)	Float (6)	Total exits	
Hard peg	(1)	—	0	0	0	0	0	0	0.0
Single currency peg	(2)	5	—	31	9	22	18	85	12.5
Basket peg	(3)	0	10	—	5	21	16	52	7.7
Float with rule-based intervention	(4)	0	3	6	—	8	10	27	14.7
Float with discretionary intervention	(5)	2	13	8	16	—	27	66	16.3
Float	(6)	1	5	1	4	29	—	40	11.3
Total entries		8	31	46	34	80	71	270	10.1
Net entries		8	−54	−6	7	14	31	—	—

[1] Number of entries and exits from each regime, six-way de jure classification.
[2] Total number of exits as a percentage of all observations of the original regime.

Table 8.3
Issues and complications in switching between exchange rate regimes

Current regime	Proposed regime			
	Hard peg	Peg	Intermediate regime	Float
Hard peg	May imply legal and technical changes if the new anchor or parity is not consistent with the current law. Otherwise a moderately complex transition, as the implementation framework remains unchanged.	Requires a legal change to abolish the hard peg. May require creation of a full-fledged central bank.	Requires a legal change to abolish the hard peg. May require the creation of a full-fledged central bank and technical preparations, including measures to introduce or strengthen foreign exchange markets and regulatory framework for hedging instruments.	Same as for switch from hard peg to an intermediate regime.
Peg	Requires legal change to introduce a hard peg and requires the reorganization of the central bank to take account of the legal limits on activity and on reserve management. No major technical changes in financial policy implementation.	Requires a change of the base currency for the peg and/or a change in the parity. Implementation framework for financial policies stays the same.	Requires technical preparations for the central bank to operate the different monetary regime. May require measures to introduce or strengthen foreign exchange markets and a regulatory framework to allow for the development of hedging instruments.	Same as for switch from peg to an intermediate regime.

Intermediate regime	Requires legal change to introduce a hard peg and requires the reorganization of the central bank to take account of the legal limits on activity and on reserve management.	Reduces need for active intervention, though technical framework would be retained. Unlikely to require a change of the market framework.	Adjustment in operating principles. No technical changes inside the central bank and/or the market framework needed.	Reduced role of the central bank in the foreign exchange market. No need for technical changes.
Float	Same as for a switch from an intermediate regime to a hard peg.	Same as for a switch from an intermediate regime to a peg.	Adjustment in the operating framework for financial polices, with a more pronounced central bank presence in the foreign exchange market. No major changes in implementation framework.	—

only slightly more involved, especially if the new framework retains a role for the existing foreign exchange markets.

The most demanding transitions are those between the extremes. The adoption of hard pegs typically requires changes to the central bank law (and thus parliamentary approval) in addition to extensive changes to reserve management, and perhaps accompanying measures, such as the development of a fiscally based lender of last resort. Managing the reverse transition is yet more daunting. Quite aside from the legal requirements of reestablishing central bank autonomy (indeed, in extreme cases, reestablishing a central bank), financial markets and supervisory knowledge for dealing with exchange rate risk are likely to have atrophied.

Correlating observed exits with the complexity ratings yields a clear pattern: While low-complexity transitions between floating and intermediate regimes have been very frequent, not a single exit from a hard peg has occurred during the sample period. The willingness of the Argentinean government to tolerate persistent deflation and recession and to adopt far-reaching convertibility restrictions in its ultimately futile attempt to preserve the currency board provides a vivid illustration of the perceived difficulties (and costs) of gracefully exiting a hard peg.

Against this empirical and conceptual background, we now turn to a closer examination of both voluntary and forced exists.

8.3   Voluntary Exits

The theory outlined in chapter 3 relates the optimal exchange rate regime to the structural characteristics of the economy, the stochastic environment, and the credibility of the monetary authorities, among other factors. As these determinants vary over time, so does the optimal exchange rate regime, though actual voluntary transitions will presumably only occur once the expected welfare difference between the current and the optimal regime exceeds the transition costs.

At first sight, it would seem a simple and straightforward exercise to decide upon, and then communicate a welfare-enhancing change of regime. In practice, switching between regimes encounters several hurdles, most notably the question of timing, to which we now turn.

8.3.1   Timing of Exits
As an empirical matter, countries often seem reluctant to exit their existing regime, particularly when it is a peg (table 8.1). In part, this

may reflect general satisfaction with the performance of the regime. Yet, it is often argued that regimes (especially fixed exchange rates regimes adopted as part of an exchange rate–based stabilization program) endure well beyond the point at which not only their optimality, but their very sustainability has come into doubt.[3] As a result, exits from pegs often end up being involuntary. What explains this "fear of exit"?

A first answer might be sought in the political economy of risk taking. While it is easy to recommend in the abstract that exits should occur in good times, in practice it requires a great deal of prescience and political courage for a government to exit a system perceived to be performing well. The very act of preparing for an exit might precipitate a crisis (or at least instability), while a successful exit potentially avoids a future crisis that no one can be sure would have even occurred. At best, the government receives no credit; at worst, it risks receiving the blame if the transition goes wrong.

For exchange rate–based stabilization programs, there is also the concern that the credibility of the anti-inflationary stance might be compromised by exiting the regime. In particular, there is a fear that wage and price setters interpret the exit decision as a shift in the inflation preferences of the monetary authorities. It is not evident that this concern is valid.[4] Even if it were, any such costs must be viewed in relation to the costs of continuing the peg. Specifically, if—following a successful stabilization—the real exchange rate has become overvalued, any reputation costs of an exit (a devaluation or a shift to a more flexible regime) must be weighed against the cost of continuing a regime perceived to be fragile (particularly since most overvaluations are resolved by an eventual adjustment of the nominal exchange rate rather than through lower inflation (Goldfajn and Valdés 1999).

In practice, pinning down the correct moment to exit is a very difficult endeavor, as illustrated by the experiences of Argentina and Turkey. In the case of Argentina, some observers have argued that the currency board should have been shed in 1994, as soon as the inflation rate reached single digits. In the light of repeated failed stabilization programs during the 1980s, a switch to more discretionary monetary policy at such an early stage (and against the backdrop of persisting fiscal imbalances) could have, however, easily risked rekindling inflationary expectations.

The window of opportunity was, in any case, brief. By December 1994, Argentina was suffering from the contagion effects of the Mexican crisis, leading to a subsequent withdrawal of deposits and loss of reserves in the first quarter of 1995. A second brief window of opportunity opened in 1996, but by 1997, emerging market countries were in the throes of the contagion from East Asia, followed by the Russian and Brazilian crisis in 1998 and 1999. Thus, even if the government had contemplated such a strategy, given the time-consuming prerequisites for an exit from a currency board, including the crucial challenge of communicating the shift to the markets, there simply were not many opportunities for Argentina to achieve a graceful exit without at least some risk of undermining credibility and reigniting inflationary expectations.

In contrast to Argentina, Turkey never conceived or marketed its "hard" crawling peg as a permanent regime. Rather than postponing the exit decision, with the risk that it would be interpreted as a negative surprise, the 1999 Turkish stabilization program boldly confronted the issue by preannouncing the intention to gradually exit the peg and adopt a more flexible regime. While the counterfactual is unknown, it is clear that against a track record of three decades of accelerating inflation, the decision to preannounce the exit risked reducing the credibility of the stabilization effort, making a speculative attack more likely.

8.3.2 Exit Strategies

Are graceful exits impossible? While admittedly rare, several countries have managed to leave pegs without triggering a crisis.[5] These include Chile, with a variety of transitions toward successively more flexible regimes; Israel, with a successful shift from a dollar peg to a basket peg in 1986; and Poland, achieving increasing flexibility in several steps throughout the 1990s.

In light of the possible costs of exchange rate crises, the characteristics and prerequisites of successful exit strategies have recently received increasing interest, yielding a number of findings and recommendations.[6] First, smooth exits require resilience of the financial system to exchange rate changes, fostered through the application of prudential controls on open positions, through well-developed risk-management practices of financial firms, and through the availability of hedging instruments. Second, exits should ideally occur from a position of strength (with appreciation pressures) rather than at a time when the regime is already considered by the markets to be fragile and ripe for speculative attack (Fischer 2001). Third, smooth exits that did occur have all been carefully thought out in advance, with plenty of foreign exchange reserves on hand, and extensive contingency planning—including, in extremis, the possibility of imposing temporary capital controls.

In sum, successful exits from pegged exchange rates are not impossible, but a smooth transition requires careful preparation, a well thought out communications strategy, opportune timing, and not least, one suspects, a healthy dose of good luck. In light of these acknowledged problems of exiting a fixed exchange rate regime, research is also on going on whether it may be possible to reap some of the credibility benefits of a rule-based system while avoiding the rigidities. One such proposal—a "floating currency board" is described in box 8.1.

8.4   Exchange Rate Regimes, Crises, and Exits

The United Kingdom (1992), Mexico (1994), Thailand (1997), Russia (1998), Brazil (1999), Turkey (2000)—just within the last decade, a lengthy list of pegged exchange rate regimes have suffered ignominious, and often spectacular, collapses.[7] These crises have led to a perception that fixed exchange rate regimes are inherently fragile and prone to collapse. Indeed, it has become fashionable to argue that traditional pegs (as opposed to hard pegs) might no longer be viable in a world with high capital mobility; following the collapse of Argentina's currency board, even hard pegs have come into question.

Of course, even if it were the case that pegged exchange rates are more susceptible to crisis, or that such crises imply higher output costs, it would not necessarily follow that the initial decision to peg the exchange rate was flawed. The regime must be assessed over its entire duration. In many instances (including some of the cases mentioned above), pegged exchange rates have been instrumental in achieving macroeconomic stability after years, and sometimes after decades, of high inflation and economic chaos.

Nonetheless, a marked susceptibility to crises would certainly be an important consideration in any decision to adopt a peg, ultimately altering the cost-benefit calculus of regime choice. In this section, therefore, we look at the empirical record, focusing on three

Box 8.1
Can a Currency Board Float?

A currency board is traditionally defined as a fixed exchange rate regime in which the central bank is committed to buying or selling the domestic currency at the announced parity while always maintaining sufficient foreign exchange reserves to fully cover its monetary liabilities (or, more generally, a wider monetary aggregate). The key advantages of such a regime are the stability of the nominal exchange rate and the credibility that derives from the stricture on central bank credit creation—considerations that may be of particular importance in countries emerging from high inflation. But currency boards also have drawbacks, especially over the longer run. Unless wages and prices are sufficiently flexible, the constraint on the nominal exchange rate can lead to real exchange rate misalignments that undermine competitiveness and, ultimately, the existence of the exchange rate regime itself as speculators come to realize that the parity cannot be maintained.

Against this background, it is worth asking whether it would be possible to design a system that combines the credibility of the currency board—specifically the rule that ties money growth to the increase in foreign exchange reserves—with the flexibility of a floating regime. Such a "floating currency board" would have the following features:

• The central bank would not commit to defend a particular value of the nominal exchange rate and thus would not be obliged to intervene in the foreign exchange markets. The exchange rate would largely be determined by private supply and demand, with the central bank intervening at its discretion. In this respect, therefore, the regime would resemble a floating exchange rate.

• At the same time, the central bank would commit itself to maintaining sufficient foreign exchange reserves to cover all central bank liabilities (or, indeed, a wider monetary aggregate) at a given accounting exchange rate—the "coverage" exchange rate—which could either be constant or could follow a preannounced crawl. In terms of the coverage requirement, the regime would resemble a currency board.

• Under the regime, foreign exchange interventions by the central bank would be undertaken at the market exchange rate but booked on the monetary accounts at the coverage exchange rate.[8] This would allow—but not require—the central bank to intervene in the markets in a "stabilizing" manner, that is, to bring the market exchange rate closer to the coverage exchange rate.[9]

What would be the advantages of such a regime? Relative to a currency board:

• The country would give not up the exchange rate as a future adjustment tool.

Box 8.1
(continued)

> • The central bank would not be committed to defending a particular value of the exchange rate that could serve as a focal point for speculative attacks.
>
> • There would continue to be foreign exchange markets—indeed, the exchange rate would float—so that the market structure and risk management skills would not atrophy. More generally, the moral hazard of excessive foreign currency risk exposure (as arguably happened in Thailand prior to the 1997 crisis) would be reduced because of nominal exchange rate volatility.
>
> Relative to a free float:
>
> • Holders of domestic currency would have the assurance that the central bank would not "print money"—that is, undertake massive liquidity expansions (which could validate pessimistic expectations about the exchange rate) either to finance the budget—directly or indirectly through the banking system—or to provide liquidity to the financial system in the event of a banking crisis.[10]
>
> Such a hybrid regime, therefore, might be particularly well suited in a country attempting to disinflate or, having achieved disinflation, trying to wean itself from a more rigid pegged exchange rate regime.

related questions. First, are fixed exchange rate regimes indeed more susceptible to severe exchange rate pressures and crises? Second, are currency crises under fixed exchange rates particularly costly? Third, does the incidence of macroeconomic crises, more broadly construed, differ across exchange rate regimes?

8.4.1 The Probability of Currency Crises

We begin with the simplest question: Are pegged regimes more susceptible to currency crises than floating regimes? This certainly appears to be a widely held perception, yet it may be just that: The particularly dramatic and discrete nature of such collapses naturally draws attention. Indeed, one key difference between pegged regimes and floating regimes is that a currency crisis is likely to lead to an exit from the peg, whereas the floating exchange rate can—and typically does—continue, albeit with a faster pace of depreciation. As such, a currency crisis under a pegged regime is inherently more visible.[11]

To address the relative incidence of crises under alternative regimes, we use the classification provided by Glick and Hutchinson

Table 8.4
Occurrence of currency crises[1]

	De jure classification[2]	Consensus classification[2]
All countries		
All regimes	5.2	2.3
Pegged regimes	4.8	1.5
Intermediate regimes	5.1	9.0
Floating regimes	6.9	5.5
Upper- and upper-middle-income countries		
All regimes	5.4	2.4
Pegged regimes	4.5	1.1
Intermediate regimes	6.3	11.7
Floating regimes	6.6	0.0
Lower- and lower-middle-income countries		
All regimes	5.1	2.3
Pegged regimes	5.0	1.7
Intermediate regimes	3.6	3.4
Floating regimes	7.2	7.7

Asterisks denote differences from the pegged regime proportion that are significant at the 5 percent (*) and 1 percent (**) significance levels, respectively.
[1] Currency crises defined by Glick and Hutchison (2001).
[2] Percentage of observations with a currency crisis.

(2001). The Glick and Hutchison index measures exchange market pressure by combining monthly changes in the real exchange rate and in the level of foreign exchange reserves. A crisis is defined as a "large" deviation from the mean, where large is considered to be any deviation greater than two (country-specific) standard deviations. Since the Glick and Hutchinson index uses movements in the (real) exchange rate as well as reserve changes, it allows for currency crises under both pegged and floating exchange rates.

Table 8.4 summarizes the distribution of crises across regimes. The results are perhaps surprising: Currency crises are more prevalent under de jure floating regimes than under de jure pegged regimes, with the same pattern holding for lower and higher income countries.

8.4.2 The Cost of Currency Crises

What matters, of course, is not just the likelihood of crises, but also their costs: Even if currency crises are more common under floating regimes, they might well be less costly. Measuring the full costs of

Table 8.5
Output costs of currency crises[1]

	Per capita GDP (percent change)[2]	Per capita GDP growth		
		Precrisis[3]	Postcrisis[4]	Change
All countries				
All regimes	2.0	1.2	0.6	−0.6
Pegged regimes	1.2	1.1	0.1	−1.1
Intermediate regimes	3.3	2.1	1.0	−1.0
Floating regimes	3.0	0.4	1.6	1.2
Upper- and upper-middle-income countries				
All regimes	2.9	1.6	1.0	−0.6
Pegged regimes	2.7	1.8	0.7	−1.1
Intermediate regimes	2.6	1.8	0.9	−0.9
Floating regimes	3.8	1.1	1.7	0.6
Lower- and lower-middle-income countries				
All regimes	1.4	0.8	0.3	−0.5
Pegged regimes	0.5	0.8	−0.2	−1.1
Intermediate regimes	4.9	2.7	1.3	−1.4
Floating regimes	2.3	−0.3	1.4	1.7

[1] De jure classificantion of regimes; currency crises as defined by Glick and Hutchison (2001).
[2] Percentage change between per capita GDP averaged over years $(t-1, t-2, t-3)$ and years $(t, t+1, t+2)$.
[3] Average of years $t-3$, $t-2$, and $t-1$.
[4] Average of years t, $t+1$, $t+2$.

a crisis, which could include political and social costs in addition to purely economic disruptions, is nearly impossible for an extensive sample of countries. We therefore focus solely on the output costs, measured by the difference in real per capita GDP growth in the three years before and the three years following the crisis. The results are reported in table 8.5.

Under all regimes, the level of per capita GDP is higher three years after the crisis compared to three years before the crisis: On average, crises do not push growth rates into negative territory. Yet both pegged and intermediate regimes experience a substantial decline in growth: In the three years following the crisis, per capita growth is about 1 percentage point lower than in the three years preceding the crisis. For floating rates, the opposite holds, growth *increases* from less than one-half of 1 percent before the crisis, to 1.5 percent per year afterward.[12]

Of course, not all of the costs of a crisis necessarily arise during or after the crisis. If the government attempts (though ultimately fails) to defend a peg over a prolonged period by deflationary measures (Argentina provides an example), then arguably some of the costs of the crisis under a peg are incurred in advance of the collapse. To assess this possibility, Figure 8.2 plots the average growth rate of crisis countries under pegged and floating regimes in the precrisis and postcrisis periods.

The differences across regimes are striking. Growth under pegged regimes indeed peaks two years before the crisis, and continues to slump into the first postcrisis year before stabilizing at around zero. Growth under intermediate regimes displays the same precrisis slump; however, the nadir is reached in the crisis year, followed by a rapid increase in the growth rate over the subsequent years. In sharp contrast, growth under floating regimes bottoms two years before the crisis, and rises steadily through the crisis and postcrisis years.

In effect, a "currency crisis" under a floating regime is thus not much of a crisis. To some degree, this is not surprising: Currency crises under floating rates are simply sharp depreciations, typically associated with rapid credit expansions. Such monetary loosening is likely to have a stimulative effect on the economy, at least over the short run. Moreover, since the exchange rate is not fixed, even a sharp depreciation is unlikely to be as traumatic as a large devaluation under a pegged regime (after all, it is precisely the cost of abandoning the peg that gives rise to its credibility benefits).

This suggests that a fairer comparison of performance under alternative regimes should consider "macroeconomic" crises more generally—that is, any situation in which there is a sharp reversal of growth, regardless of whether it is accompanied by a currency crisis as well.

8.4.3   Growth Crises

We define growth crises according to three thresholds on the decline in real GDP growth. A *mild* crisis occurs in year t if real per capita GDP growth, averaged over years t to $t + 2$, is negative, and is at least one percentage point lower than the average growth rate in years $t - 3$ to $t - 1$. *Moderate* and *severe* output crises are defined analogously with thresholds of 3 and 5 percentage points, respectively.

Table 8.6 reports the likelihood of the three types of output crisis under the alternative exchange rate regimes, alongside the average

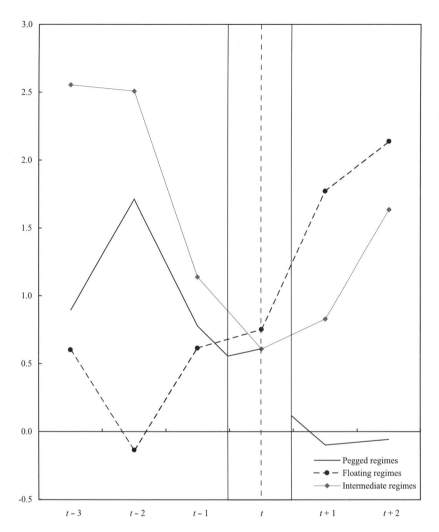

Figure 8.2
Output dynamics during currency crises, real per capita GDP growth (in percent per year)

Table 8.6
Declines of per capita GDP growth rates across exchange rate regimes

	Growth declines of at least 1 percentage point				Growth declines of at least 3 percentage points				Growth declines of at least 5 percentage points			
	Per capita GDP growth (in percent per year)			Proportion of observations (in percent)[3]	Per capita GDP growth (in percent per year)			Proportion of observations (in percent)[3]	Per capital GDP growth (in percent per year)			Proportion of observations (in percent)[3]
	Pre-crisis[1]	Post-crisis[2]	Change		Pre-crisis[1]	Post-crisis[2]	Change		Pre-crisis[1]	Post-crisis[2]	Change	
All countries												
All regimes[4]	1.9	−3.2	−5.1	19.5	2.8	−3.5	−6.3	13.7	3.8	−4.4	−8.3	7.3
Pegged regimes	2.0	−3.3	−5.3	24.4	2.9	−3.6	−6.5	17.6	4.1	−4.3	−8.3	10.0
Intermediate regimes	2.3	−2.2	−4.5	8.7*	3.0	−2.5	−5.5	6.2*	4.1	−3.5	−7.6	2.5*
Float regimes	1.0	−3.2	−4.2	15.8*	1.6	−4.1	−5.7	9.1*	1.1	−7.1	−8.2	3.7*
Upper- and upper-middle-income-countries												
All regimes	2.7	−2.7	−5.5	13.5	3.7	−3.1	−6.8	9.8	5.8	−4.2	−10.0	4.5
Pegged regimes	3.0	−3.3	−6.3	16.9	3.9	−3.6	−7.5	13.1	6.0	−4.2	−10.3	7.4
Intermediate regimes	2.5	−2.1	−4.6	8.8*	3.2	−2.4	−5.6	6.3*	4.5	−4.0	−8.6	2.2*
Float regimes	2.0	−1.1	−3.1	11.7*	2.8	−1.1	−4.0	6.1*	—	—	—	—
Lower- and lower-middle-income countries												
All regimes	1.6	−3.3	−4.9	23.8	2.4	−3.7	−6.1	16.5	3.1	−4.5	−7.7	9.4
Pegged regimes	1.7	−3.3	−4.9	28.5	2.5	−3.6	−6.1	20.1	3.4	−4.3	−7.7	11.5
Intermediate regimes	2.0	−2.3	−4.4	8.5*	2.6	−2.6	−5.3	6.0*	3.6	−3.0	−6.6	2.8*
Float regimes	0.4	−4.4	−4.8	19.6*	1.0	−5.5	−6.5	12.0*	1.1	−7.1	−8.2	7.2

[1] Average of years $t - 3$, $t - 2$, and $t - 1$.
[2] Average of years t, $t + 1$, $t + 2$.
[3] Asterisks denote differences in proportions from the pegged regime proportion significant at the 5 percent (*) and 1 percent (**) levels, respectively.
[4] De jure classification of regimes.

Box 8.2
Exchange Rate Regimes and Banking Crises

Do fixed exchange rate regimes cause banking crises? There is a widespread perception of a causal link, based in part on the occurrence of twin crises—a banking crisis and a currency crisis in close succession (Kaminsky and Reinhart (1999)). Such a link might occur either because pegged exchange rate regimes make fragility more likely—for example, by promoting excessive risk taking in the form of unhedged foreign currency exposures—or because they limit the ability of central banks to respond to such fragilities by lender of last resort operations.

In practice, the link is less clear-cut. Excessive borrowing implies some market imperfection that can be addressed directly through prudential measures. The absence of lender of last resort (LLOR) functions also implies less risk of moral hazard. Furthermore, LLOR functions can be shifted to the fiscal authorities (and are also limited under floating rates, reflecting their inflationary impact).

To examine empirically whether banking crises are more likely under pegged exchange rate regimes, we use a large database of banking crises to correlate the year of the *occurrence* (or all years of the *duration*) of a banking crisis to the prevailing exchange rate regime.[14] The results, are striking: Banking crises were actually more prevalent under floating and intermediate regimes than under pegged exchange rates, the difference is statistically significant.[15] The same pattern holds true for high- and low-income countries.

Occurrence and Duration of Banking Crises[16]

	Occurrence	Duration
Pegged regimes	2.5	9.6
Intermediate regimes	3.8	10.6
Floating regimes	5.7	14.9

If banking crises are not more frequent under pegged regimes, are they more costly? The fiscal costs of resolving the banking crisis—the preferred cost measure—are not available on a consistent basis for our large data set. We instead use a proxy, the change in the per capita GDP growth rate around the years of the banking crisis. Against this yardstick, fixed exchange rates do not seem to cause the most severe crises. In fact, the decline in growth rates is the smallest for the countries with pegged exchange rates. While the precrisis growth rate was also the lowest for the pegged exchange rate countries, this may be symptomatic of more pervasive economic problems in such countries, which would further suggest that the pegged exchange rate regime was not to blame for the banking crisis.

Box 8.2
(continued)

Growth Effects of Banking Crises

Per capita real GDP growth (in percent per year)

	Pre-crisis	Post-crisis
Pegged regimes	0.0	−0.3
Intermediate regimes	2.5	1.8
Floating regimes	1.6	1.0

In sum, there is little support for the view that banking crises are systematically caused by the exchange rate regime. Crises are at least as likely and equally costly under floating exchange rates than under fixed exchange rates. Twin crises are more likely to have been caused by the same underlying policy mistakes—for example, excessively expansionary policies eroding the credibility of the peg while leading to a lending boom and the associated decline in loan quality.

---

decline in per capita GDP growth. Across the three definitions of a macroeconomic crisis, the results suggest that the probability of a crisis in countries operating under pegged exchange rate regimes is some 5 to 10 percent higher than the corresponding probability in countries operating under floating regimes; the differences are statistically significant. Moreover, pegged exchange rates generally fare worse than floating regimes in terms of the swing in real GDP growth. Intermediate regimes perform best, enjoying both a lower probability of crises and smaller growth swings than either pegged or floating regimes.

What about other types of crisis? It is sometimes argued, particularly in the aftermath of the 1997 East Asian crises, that fixed exchange rates encourage excessive exposure to foreign exchange risk, while limiting the central bank's ability to act as lender of last resort.[13] A close look at the evidence (see box 8.1), however, does not support this view: Banking crises are neither more frequent nor more severe under pegged exchange rates.

8.5 Conclusions

Fundamentally, exchange rate regimes, as most institutional arrangements, are not "forever." The perception of (near) permanence is, however, an integral part of the credibility that supports the system, especially in the case of fixed exchange rate regimes. Faced with this dilemma, "fear of exit" may lead policy makers to delay necessary adjustments, ultimately contributing to crises rather than helping to avoid them. Defining and implementing a successful exit strategy is possible, but hardly trivial. It requires careful planning and proper timing, and even then will, to some extent, depend on luck in the form of a period without major economic shocks.

Should the risk of a crisis, and—for pegged exchange rate regimes—of a forced exit, be an independent consideration in the choice of an exchange rate regime? We conclude that concerns about the susceptibility of pegged regimes to currency crises are at least partly justified. Although, statistically, currency crises are more likely under floating regimes, their impact is more severe under pegged and intermediate regimes. On the other hand, in terms of macroeconomic crises more generally, pegged regimes fare only somewhat worse than floats, and in terms of banking crises, they actually fare better.

9   Conclusions

Does the choice of exchange rate regime matter? Experience over the past thirty years suggests that it does. Countries choose their exchange rate regime for a variety of reasons, some of which have little to do with economic considerations. However, if the choice of exchange rate regime is to have any rational economic basis, then a first requirement must surely be to understand the properties of alternative regimes. Our analysis, based on a comprehensive dataset of IMF member countries, suggests a number of conclusions.

First, floating exchange rates do not necessarily lead to greater volatility of the real exchange rate. This is particularly true at longer horizons and for developing countries, where capital flows may be of less importance.

Second, pegged exchange rate regimes are associated with significantly better inflation performance. This is of less relevance for the major industrialized countries, which tend to have strong institutional frameworks and good inflation performance anyway, but it is an important benefit for the majority of developing and emerging market countries where policy credibility may be lower.

Third, this anti-inflationary benefit carries over to explicit disinflation programs. We find no evidence that exchange rate–based stabilizations are more prone to failure than money-based programs or that they are more costly, whether they succeed or fail.

Fourth, there is weak evidence that pegged (and, especially, intermediate) regimes are associated with better growth performance, though this link may largely reflect country specific factors and the likelihood that countries with strong growth performance are better able to sustain stable exchange rates.

Fifth, output volatility tends to be greater under pegged exchange rate regimes.

Finally, pegged exchange rate regimes are associated with a somewhat greater likelihood of growth crises, but not of banking crises.

These conclusions point to some important trade-offs in the choice of the exchange rate regime. For most countries, pegging the exchange rate promises to impose policy discipline, engendering confidence in the currency. The potential confidence gain must be weighed against a greater risk of macroeconomic crisis. Our results suggest, however, that the importance of crises—their publicity attracting drama notwithstanding—should not be exaggerated. Crises have happened under all exchange rate regimes, the difference between pegged and floating rates in this regard is only a matter of degree. Perhaps the more important lesson is that no exchange rate regime can substitute for sound macroeconomic management, and that graceful exits and smooth transitions require a great deal of prior thought and careful planning.

Writing a few years ago, we noted that "no regime is likely to serve all countries at all times."[1] This remains true. But countries must nonetheless decide upon some regime at any given point in time. We hope this book goes some way toward making that an informed decision.

Appendix

This appendix provides a brief description of the data used for our empirical analysis. The dataset is annual, covering the period 1970–1999. Table A.1 lists the countries included the sample. The dataset consists of three main elements: (1) exchange rate regime classifications, (2) key macroeconomic variables, (3) other variables.

Exchange Rate Regime Classification

Our de jure exchange rate regime classification is based on the annual issues of the International Monetary Fund's *Annual Report on Exchange Arrangements and Exchange Restrictions*.

As discussed in chapter 4, the consensus classification uses the intersection of the de jure classification and a de facto classification. To construct the de facto classification, we compute the z score given by $z = \sqrt{\mu_{\Delta e}^2 + \sigma_{\Delta e}^2}$, where $\mu_{\Delta e}$ is the average monthly rate of change of the nominal exchange rate during the year, and $\sigma_{\Delta e}^2$ is the variance of those monthly changes. For each country in the sample, we compute this measure separately against each of the G-7 currencies, the ECU and the SDR, and then select the reference currency yielding the smallest z score. (For the small set of countries reporting a de jure peg vis-à-vis a currency not in this group, we added the currency in question (the South African rand, the Indian rupee, the Spanish peseta, the Australian dollar, and the Portuguese escudo) to the search for that particular country.) For each year, countries are ranked according to this z score, then mapped into pegged, intermediate, and floating regimes with the same proportional distribution as the de jure classification for that year.

Table A.1
Country sample

Country	IFS country code	First-year in exchange rate regime	First-year in basic statistics	First-year in inflation regression	First-year in growth regression
United States	111	1970	1972	1972	1972
United Kingdom	112	1970	1972	1972	1972
Austria	122	1970	1972	1972	1977
Belgium	124	1970	1972	—	—
Denmark	128	1970	1978	1978	1978
France	132	1970	1972	1972	1972
Germany	134	1970	1972	1972	1972
Italy	136	1970	1972	1972	1978
Luxembourg	137	1970	—	—	—
Netherlands	138	1970	1986	1986	1986
Norway	142	1970	1972	1972	1977
Sweden	144	1970	1972	1972	1977
Switzerland	146	1970	1972	1972	1984
Canada	156	1970	1972	1972	1972
Japan	158	1970	1972	1972	1972
Finland	172	1970	1972	1972	1977
Greece	174	1970	1972	1972	1977
Iceland	176	1970	1975	1975	1975
Ireland	178	1970	1972	1972	1977
Malta	181	1970	1972	1972	1972
Portugal	182	1970	1976	1976	1981
Spain	184	1970	1972	1972	1981
Turkey	186	1970	1972	1972	1989
Australia	193	1970	1972	1972	1972
New Zealand	196	1970	1976	1976	1981
South Africa	199	1970	1972	—	—
Argentina	213	1970	1972	1972	1972
Bolivia	218	1970	1980	1980	1983
Brazil	223	1970	1977	1977	1981
Chile	228	1970	1972	1972	1982
Colombia	233	1975	1976	1976	1983
Costa Rica	238	1970	1972	1972	1972
Dominican Republic	243	1970	1972	1972	1982
Ecuador	248	1970	1972	1972	1972
El Salvador	253	1970	1972	—	1984
Guatemala	258	1970	1972	1972	1986
Haiti	263	1970	1972	1975	1972
Honduras	268	1970	1972	1972	1972
Mexico	273	1970	1972	1972	1972
Nicaragua	278	1970	1978	—	1978
Panama	283	1970	1972	1972	1972
Paraguay	288	1970	1972	—	1972
Peru	293	1970	1976	1976	1976

Table A.1
(continued)

Country	IFS country code	First-year in exchange rate regime	First-year in basic statistics	First-year in inflation regression	First-year in growth regression
Uruguay	298	1970	1972	1972	1987
Venezuela	299	1970	1972	1972	1972
Antigua & Barbuda	311	1970	1977	1985	—
Bahamas, The	313	1970	—	—	—
Barbados	316	1970	1977	1977	1977
Dominica	321	1970	1972	1981	1982
Grenada	328	1970	1972	1980	—
Guyana	336	1970	1993	1993	1993
Belize	339	1977	1978	1985	—
Jamaica	343	1970	1972	1972	1972
Netherlands Antilles	353	1970	—	—	—
St. Lucia	362	1970	1972	1985	—
S. Vincent & Grenadines	364	1970	1972	1980	—
Suriname	366	1970	1972	1972	—
Trinidad & Tobago	369	1970	1972	1972	1983
Bahrain	419	1970	1975	1975	1983
Cyprus	423	1970	1972	1972	1972
Iran, I.R. of	429	1970	1972	1985	1985
Iraq	433	1970	—	—	—
Israel	436	1970	1980	1980	1982
Jordan	439	1970	1972	1972	1972
Kuwait	443	1970	1985	1985	1985
Lebanon	446	1970	1990	1990	—
Oman	449	1970	1972	—	—
Qatar	453	1970	1983	1991	—
Syrian Arab Republic	463	1970	1973	1973	1973
United Arab Emirates	466	1970	1978	—	—
Egypt	469	1970	1972	1972	1975
Afghanistan, I.S. of	512	1970	—	—	—
Bangladesh	513	1972	1973	—	1977
Myanmar	518	1970	1972	—	1983
Sri Lanka	524	1970	1972	1972	1972
China, People's Republic: Hong Kong	532	1970	1982	1990	1982
India	534	1970	1977	1977	1977
Indonesia	536	1970	1972	1972	1976
Korea	542	1970	1972	1972	1972
Lao People's Dem. Rep	544	1970	1984	—	—
Malaysia	548	1970	1972	1972	1986
Maldives	556	1978	1975	—	—
Nepal	558	1974	1972	1985	1985
Pakistan	564	1970	—	1972	1972

Table A.1
(continued)

Country	IFS country code	First-year in exchange rate regime	First-year in basic statistics	First-year in inflation regression	First-year in growth regression
Philippines	566	1970	1972	1972	1972
Singapore	576	1970	1983	1983	1983
Thailand	578	1970	—	—	—
Vietnam	582	1983	1990	—	1990
Djibouti	611	1970	1990	1990	—
Algeria	612	1973	1975	1975	1975
Botswana	616	1970	1974	—	—
Burundi	618	1970	1980	—	1990
Cameroon	622	1970	1980	—	1981
Cape Verde	624	1970	1972	1975	—
Central African Republic	626	1970	1972	—	1982
Chad	628	1970	1981	—	—
Comoros	632	1976	1987	1987	—
Congo, Republic of	634	1970	1972	—	1981
Congo, Democratic Republic of	636	1970	1977	1977	—
Benin	638	1970	1972	—	1981
Equatorial Guinea	642	1970	1972	—	—
Ethiopia	644	1970	1973	1973	1995
Gabon	646	1970	1972	—	—
Gambia, The	648	1970	1980	1980	1984
Ghana	652	1970	1972	1972	1981
Guinea-Bissau	654	1977	1981	—	—
Guinea	656	1970	1972	—	—
Cote D'Ivoire	662	1970	1972	—	—
Kenya	664	1970	1972	1972	1981
Lesotho	666	1970	1972	—	1972
Liberia	668	1970	1972	—	—
Libya	672	1970	1977	1977	1977
Madagascar	674	1970	1980	—	—
Malawi	676	1970	1972	1972	1981
Mali	678	1970	1980	—	1981
Mauritania	682	1970	1972	—	1990
Mauritius	684	1970	1972	1972	1979
Morocco	686	1970	1972	1972	—
Mozambique	688	1984	1985	—	1985
Niger	692	1970	1972	—	1981
Nigeria	694	1970	1972	1972	—
Zimbabwe	698	1980	1981	1985	1985
Rwanda	714	1970	1972	1972	1981
São Tomé & Príncipe	716	1978	1982	—	—
Seychelles	718	1976	1977	1977	1985

Table A.1
(continued)

Country	IFS country code	First-year in exchange rate regime	First-year in basic statistics	First-year in inflation regression	First-year in growth regression
Senegal	722	1970	1972	—	1981
Sierra Leone	724	1970	1972	—	1981
Somalia	726	1970	—	—	—
Sudan	732	1970	1978	—	1978
Swaziland	734	1970	1982	—	—
Tanzania	738	1970	1972	1972	—
Togo	742	1970	1972	—	1981
Tunisia	744	1970	1972	—	1972
Uganda	746	1970	1976	1976	1984
Burkina Faso	748	1970	1973	—	—
Zambia	754	1970	1977	1977	1981
Solomon Islands	813	1979	1980	—	—
Fiji	819	1970	1972	1972	1972
Vanuatu	846	1981	—	—	—
Papua New Guinea	853	1975	1976	1976	—
Samoa	862	1970	—	—	—
Tonga	866	1985	1987	1987	—
Armenia	911	1993	—	—	—
Azerbaijan	912	1995	—	—	—
Belarus	913	1996	1997	1997	—
Albania	914	1992	1994	—	—
Georgia	915	1995	—	—	—
Kazakhstan	916	1995	—	—	—
Kyrgyz Republic	917	1993	—	—	—
Bulgaria	918	1991	1992	—	1992
Moldova	921	1994	—	—	—
Russia	922	1992	1993	1996	1996
Tajikistan	923	1995	—	—	—
China, People's Republic: Mainland	924	1970	1972	1982	1982
Turkmenistan	925	1994	—	—	—
Ukraine	926	1993	1996	1996	—
Czech Republic	935	1993	1994	1995	1995
Slovak Republic	936	1993	1994	1995	—
Estonia	939	1992	1993	1995	—
Latvia	941	1992	1993	1996	—
Hungary	944	1981	1982	1982	—
Lithuania	946	1993	1995	1995	—
Slovenia	961	1992	1993	1995	—
Poland	964	1991	1993	1993	1993
Romania	968	1970	1972	1972	1972
Total number of countries	—	165	147	106	103

Dash indicates that the country was omitted due to lack of data.

Macroeconomic Variables

Data on most macroeconomic variables are taken from the IMF's *World Economic Outlook* database, an annual database covering virtually every IMF member country. A few series are taken from the *International Financial Statistics* database. Variables used in the analysis are listed in table A.2; basic statistics on the main macroeconomic variables are reported in tables A.3 and A.4, for the de jure and consensus classifications, respectively.

Other Variables

Other variables used in our analysis include:

• The central bank turnover rate, which is the number of central bank governors per five-year period, based on a questionnaire sent to central banks, updating the database of Steven Webb (World Bank).

• Average years of schooling of total population aged twenty-five years or older, taken from the Barro-Lee dataset. Available online at ⟨www.worldbank.org/research/growth/ddbarle2.htm⟩.

• Indexes of current account and capital account restrictions, taken from the IMF's *Annual Report on Exchange Arrangements and Exchange Restrictions*.

• Nominal and real effective exchange rate indexes, taken from the IMF's *Information Notice System*.

• Export concentration ratios, calculated from the IMF's *Direction of Trade Statistics* database.

• Currency and banking crises, taken from Glick and Hutchison (2001), augmented by Alexander et al. (1997).

Table A.2
Data sources

Name	Variable	Source[1]	Units[2]	Mean[3]	Median	Min	Max	Nobs
NAM	IFS code	IFS	—	—	—	111.00	968.00	2855
YRS	Year	—	—	—	—	1972.00	1999.00	2855
NGDP	Nominal GDP	WEO	Billions, national currency	—	—	—	—	2855
NGDP_R	Real GDP	WEO	Billions, national currency, constant prices	—	—	—	—	2855
NGDPD	Nominal GDP	WEO	Billions, U.S. dollars	137.26	7.37	0.02	9299.00	2855
NCP_R	Private Consumption Expenditure	WEO	Billions, national currency, constant prices	—	—	—	—	2099
TT	Terms of Trade	WEO	Index	107.864	100.000	4.230	992.520	2855
CPIG	Consumer Price Index growth (average of period)	WEO	Percent per year, (decimal fraction)	0.168	0.085	-0.029	9.119	2855
GDPG	Real GDP growth	WEO	Percent per year, (decimal fraction)	0.035	0.037	-0.170	0.189	2855
GDPPCG	Per capita Real GDP growth	WEO	Percent per year, (decimal fraction)	0.015	0.018	-0.177	0.167	2855
BMG	Broad Money growth	WEO	Percent per year, (decimal fraction)	0.218	0.154	-0.110	5.542	2855
IRATE	Nominal Interest Rate	IFS	Percent per year, (decimal fraction)	0.141	0.090	0.001	11.610	2225
XGDP	Exports of Goods and Services (percent of GDP)	WEO	Decimal fraction	0.341	0.291	0.005	1.856	2855

Table A.2
(continued)

Name	Variable	Source[1]	Units[2]	Mean[3]	Median	Min	Max	Nobs
MGDP	Imports of Goods and Services (percent of GDP)	WEO	Decimal fraction	0.403	0.330	0.011	1.772	2855
XG	Exports of Goods and Services, volume growth	WEO	Decimal fraction	0.061	0.057	−0.558	2.688	2242
MG	Imports of Goods and Services, volume growth	WEO	Decimal fraction	0.059	0.052	−0.674	2.206	2855
MGM3	Imports of Goods and Services, volume growth, 3-year backward average	WEO	Decimal fraction	0.058	0.052	−0.486	1.495	2855
POP	Population	WEO	Millions	34.409	6.555	0.061	1253.000	2855
POPG	Population growth	WEO	Decimal fraction	0.020	0.021	−0.135	0.165	2855
CGGDP	Central Government Balance (percent of GDP)	WEO	Decimal fraction	−0.043	−0.036	−0.450	0.195	2855
CGGDPM3	Central Government Balance (percent of GDP), 3-year backward average	WEO	Decimal fraction	−0.044	−0.037	−0.265	0.169	2855
TAXGDP	General Government Revenue (percent of GDP)	WEO	Decimal fraction	0.288	0.276	0.007	0.806	2370
TAXGDPM3	General Government Revenue (percent of GDP), 3-year backward average	WEO	Decimal fraction	0.286	0.273	0.007	0.936	2370
GAP	Ratio of Per Capita GDP to US Per Capita GDP in 1970 (international prices)	WEO	Number	0.331	0.162	0.029	3.959	2855
IGDP	Gross Fixed Investment (percent of GDP)	WEO	Decimal fraction	0.218	0.211	0.022	0.529	2855

Code	Description	Source	Units					
CAGDP	Current Account (percent of GDP)	WEO	Decimal fraction	-0.037	-0.029	-0.528	0.291	2242
TTG	Terms of Trade growth	WEO	Percent per year, (decimal fraction)	0.007	0.000	-0.338	0.628	2855
TTGM3	Terms of Trade growth, 3-year backward average	WEO	Percent per year, (decimal fraction)	0.010	0.001	-0.377	1.743	2854
TTGS3	Terms of Trade growth, 3-year centered standard deviation	WEO	Percent per year, (decimal fraction)	0.103	0.063	0.000	3.715	2853
POPGM3	Population growth, 3-year backward average	WEO	Percent per year, (decimal fraction)	0.020	0.022	-0.063	0.160	2855
GDPPCGS3	Per capita Real GDP growth, 3-year centered standard deviation	WEO	Percent per year, (decimal fraction)	0.031	0.023	0.000	0.465	2855
IGDPM3	Gross Fixed Investment (percent of GDP), 3-year backward average	WEO	Decimal fraction	0.219	0.212	0.000	0.978	2852
IGDPS3	Gross Fixed Investment (percent of GDP), 3-year centered standard deviation	WEO	Decimal fraction	0.019	0.013	0.000	0.347	2846
NCPRG	Private Consumption Expenditure growth, constant prices	WEO	Percent per year, (decimal fraction)	0.033	0.031	-0.210	0.356	1936
NCPRGS3	Private Consumption Expenditure growth, constant prices, 3-year centered standard deviation	WEO	Percent per year, (decimal fraction)	0.047	0.029	0.000	0.467	1936
NCGDP	Private Consumption Expenditure (percent of GDP)	WEO	Decimal fraction	0.663	0.644	0.089	1.420	1936

Table A.2
(continued)

Name	Variable	Source[1]	Units[2]	Mean[3]	Median	Min	Max	Nobs
NCGDPS3	Private Consumption Expenditure (percent of GDP), 3-year centered standard deviation	WEO	Decimal fraction	0.023	0.014	0.000	0.388	1936
GDPGS3	Real GDP growth, constant prices, 3-year centered standard deviation	WEO	Percent per year, (decimal fraction)	0.030	0.022	0.000	0.554	2855
CPIGX	Consumer Price Inflation, scaled, $\pi/(1+\pi)$, average of period	WEO	Percent per year, (decimal fraction)	0.110	0.078	−0.030	0.901	2855
BMGX	Broad Money growth, scaled, $\mu/(1+\mu)$, average of period	WEO	Percent per year, (decimal fraction)	0.150	0.133	−0.124	0.847	2855
AVGYRSCH	Average number of years of schooling of total population age 25 and older	Barro-Lee	Years	5.011	4.570	0.140	12.180	2236
CBTURN5	Central Bank Governor Turnover Rate (per 5 years)	Authors	Decimal fraction	0.229	0.200	0.000	1.400	2105
CURCON	Current Account Restrictions	AREAR	Dummy variable	1277	—	0.00	1.00	2764
KAPCON	Capital Account Restrictions	AREAR	Dummy variable	2070	—	0.00	1.00	2768
XPORT3	Share of total exports to 3 largest trading partners	DOTS	Percent	53.742	51.300	2.470	97.930	2620
DIST1	Squared distance weighted dollar GDP of other countries	Authors	US dollars	7026	5461	557	55695	2855
DNEERM	Nominal Effective Exchange Rate, average monthly growth, end period	INS	Percent per month (decimal fraction)	−0.003	0.000	−0.143	0.110	2331

DREERM	Real Effective Exchange Rate, average monthly growth, end period	INS	Percent per month (decimal fraction)	0.001	0.001	−0.061	0.258	2192
DNEERS	Nominal Effective Exchange Rate, standard deviation of monthly growth, end period	INS	Percent per month (decimal fraction)	0.019	0.012	0.000	0.588	2330
DREERS	Real Effective Exchange Rate, standard deviation of monthly growth, end period	INS	Percent per month (decimal fraction)	0.023	0.015	0.002	0.533	2191
DNEERZ	Nominal Effective Exchange Rate, sum of absolute average and standard deviation of monthly growth	INS	Percent per month (decimal fraction)	0.022	0.013	0.000	0.598	2330
DREERZ	Real Effective Exchange Rate, sum of absolute average and standard deviation of monthly growth	INS	Percent per month (decimal fraction)	0.025	0.017	0.002	0.540	2191
NEER1M	Nominal Effective Exchange Rate, 1-month absolute change, average for year	INS	Percent per month (decimal fraction)	0.015	0.010	0.001	0.132	2132
REER1M	Real Effective Exchange Rate, 1-month absolute change, average for year	INS	Percent per month (decimal fraction)	0.017	0.013	0.002	0.172	2132
NEER60M	Nominal Effective Exchange Rate, 60-month absolute change, average for year	INS	Percent per month (decimal fraction)	0.009	0.004	0.000	0.351	1684
REER60M	Real Effective Exchange Rate, 60-month absolute change, average for year	INS	Percent per month (decimal fraction)	0.004	0.002	0.000	0.154	1643

Table A.2
(continued)

Name	Variable	Source[1]	Units[2]	Mean[3]	Median	Min	Max	Nobs
RELP1M	Relative CPI (trading partner / home country) 1-month absolute change, average for year	INS	Percent per month (decimal fraction)	0.011	0.007	0.000	0.165	2132
RELP60M	Relative CPI (trading partner / home country) 60-month absolute change, average for year	INS	Percent per month (decimal fraction)	0.008	0.003	0.000	0.304	1647
RGDPDVS3	Deviation of Real GDP from HP-filtered trend, 3-year standard deviation	WEO	Percent (decimal fraction)	0.025	0.019	0.000	0.256	2851
DISA	Initial inflation below 20 percent per year, at least 5 percentage point decline over 2 years	Authors	Dummy variable	295.0	—	0.00	1.00	2775
DISB	Initial inflation below 50 percent per year, at least 10 percentage point decline over 2 years	Authors	Dummy variable	235.0	—	0.00	1.00	2775
DISC	Initial inflation above 50 percent per year, at least 20 percentage point decline over 2 years	Authors	Dummy variable	111.0	—	0.00	1.00	2775
BNKSTRT	Banking crisis start year	Glick and Hutchison; authors	Dummy variable	93.0	—	0.00	1.00	2855

BNKDUR	Banking crisis duration	Glick and Hutchison; authors	Dummy variable	437.0	—	0.00	1.00	2855
CURSTRT	Currency crisis start year	Glick and Hutchison	Dummy variable	133.0	—	0.00	1.00	2855
CURDUR	Currency crisis duration	Glick and Hutchison	Dummy variable	195.0	—	0.00	1.00	2855
DEVALG	Nominal Exchange Rate, national currency per reference currency, average growth	IFS	Percent per month (decimal fraction)	0.110	0.003	−0.324	24.021	2855
UIC	Upper-income countries	World Bank	Dummy variable	638.0	0.00	0.00	1.00	2855
UMIC	Upper-middle-income countries	World Bank	Dummy variable	543.0	0.00	0.00	1.00	2855
LMIC	Lower-middle-income countries	World Bank	Dummy variable	760.0	0.00	0.00	1.00	2855
LIC	Lower-income countries	World Bank	Dummy variable	914.0	0.00	0.00	1.00	2855

[1] Data are derived from the following sources: WEO—*World Economic Outlook* database, IMF; IFS—*International Financial Statistics*, IMF; INS—*Information Notice System*, IMF; DOTS–Direction of Trade Statistics, IMF.

[2] Percentages are expressed as decimal fractions; for example, 10 percent is 0.10.

[3] In the case of dummy variables, the sum is given instead of the mean.

Table A.3
Basic statistics, de jure classification of exchange rate regimes (in percent per year, unless otherwise specified)

	Num-ber of obser-vations	Inflation			Broad money growth		
		π Mean	π Median	$\pi/(1+\pi)$ Mean	μ Mean	μ Median	$\mu/(1+\mu)$ Mean
All countries							
All regimes	2855	16.8	8.5	11.0	21.8	15.4	15.0
Pegged regimes	1807	13.3	8.0	9.6	17.7	14.4	13.4
Intermediate regimes	606	22.0	9.6	13.9	29.3	18.3	18.6
Floating regimes	442	24.3	9.0	13.1	28.1	15.5	16.9
Upper- and upper-middle-income countries							
All regimes	1181	13.6	6.2	9.0	19.8	12.2	13.4
Pegged regimes	633	10.2	6.4	7.8	16.4	13.2	12.6
Intermediate regimes	336	21.9	6.9	12.4	28.3	12.3	16.5
Floating regimes	212	10.7	4.4	7.1	16.4	9.1	10.7
Lower- and lower-middle-income countries							
All regimes	1674	19.1	10.1	12.5	23.2	17.4	16.2
Pegged regimes	1174	14.9	9.1	10.6	18.4	15.1	13.8
Intermediate regimes	270	22.2	12.2	15.8	30.6	22.8	21.2
Floating regimes	230	36.9	15.0	18.6	39.0	22.9	22.6
Countries without current account restrictions							
All regimes	1487	10.7	6.1	8.1	17.1	11.9	12.8
Pegged regimes	844	8.0	6.1	6.9	14.7	12.0	11.8
Intermediate regimes	320	13.1	5.9	9.6	19.8	11.2	14.2
Floating regimes	323	15.3	6.9	10.1	20.7	12.5	14.0
Countries without capital account restrictions							
All regimes	698	9.3	4.2	7.0	15.8	10.6	12.1
Pegged regimes	305	7.1	4.4	6.0	14.8	13.1	11.9
Intermediate regimes	184	11.8	3.5	8.5	18.1	9.5	13.2
Floating regimes	209	10.2	4.2	7.1	15.4	9.1	11.4
Very open economies							
All regimes	1063	10.7	6.7	8.3	17.3	13.6	13.1
Pegged regimes	808	8.5	6.4	7.3	14.7	13.0	11.9
Intermediate regimes	161	11.6	6.3	8.9	19.5	14.9	14.6
Floating regimes	94	27.5	10.8	16.0	35.7	19.7	20.3
Low central bank turnover rate							
All regimes	707	12.2	6.3	8.4	18.4	13.1	13.2
Pegged regimes	354	7.8	6.2	6.9	14.6	13.2	12.1
Intermediate regimes	190	13.4	6.1	9.9	19.3	14.0	14.3
Floating regimes	163	20.3	6.9	10.1	25.5	12.1	14.1

Interest rate				Real GDP growth				
Nominal		Real			Std. dev.	HP-filter Std. dev.	Per capita Mean	Per capita Median
Mean	Median	Mean	Median	Mean				
14.1	9.0	0.2	1.9	3.5	3.0	2.5	1.5	1.8
8.6	7.3	−0.7	0.7	3.5	3.4	2.8	1.2	1.5
23.9	12.4	1.6	2.9	3.8	2.1	1.9	2.4	2.4
16.8	12.3	1.1	3.2	2.9	2.3	2.0	1.2	1.8
15.2	8.0	1.8	2.7	3.5	2.6	2.2	2.1	2.4
8.8	7.0	1.0	1.9	3.9	3.2	2.6	2.1	2.5
27.3	11.2	2.9	3.0	3.2	2.0	1.8	2.5	2.6
11.0	8.0	2.2	3.1	2.6	1.7	1.6	1.7	2.2
13.1	10.0	−1.2	0.9	3.4	3.2	2.7	1.0	1.3
8.5	7.5	−1.9	−0.3	3.3	3.5	2.9	0.8	1.0
19.1	14.3	−0.3	2.4	4.4	2.1	2.0	2.4	2.4
22.8	16.8	0.0	3.2	3.1	2.9	2.5	0.7	1.5
12.0	8.5	2.1	3.0	3.4	2.8	2.4	1.6	1.9
8.7	7.4	1.6	2.6	3.6	3.4	2.8	1.3	1.6
16.2	10.5	3.2	3.5	3.5	1.9	1.8	2.6	2.6
14.4	10.2	2.1	3.2	2.8	2.3	2.0	1.4	1.9
10.8	7.5	2.6	3.4	3.5	2.8	2.4	1.7	2.1
8.2	7.0	2.5	3.9	3.9	3.8	3.1	1.1	1.5
13.3	8.0	2.2	2.9	3.6	2.1	1.9	2.6	2.4
11.0	8.4	2.9	3.7	2.7	1.9	1.7	1.6	2.2
10.1	7.4	0.7	2.2	3.8	3.3	2.7	1.8	2.1
7.7	7.0	0.5	1.6	3.9	3.5	2.9	1.8	2.0
11.9	9.5	1.2	3.0	4.0	2.0	2.2	2.9	3.3
23.3	15.0	0.8	3.6	2.4	3.1	2.3	0.5	1.5
11.0	8.5	1.3	2.8	3.6	2.4	2.2	2.0	2.2
7.6	6.6	0.5	1.0	4.1	2.9	2.4	2.2	2.1
14.4	10.9	2.0	3.3	3.7	1.7	1.9	2.5	2.6
12.9	10.9	1.8	3.7	2.6	2.2	2.0	0.9	1.8

Table A.3
(continued)

	Gov. balance (in percent of GDP)		Gross fixed invest-ment (in per-cent of GDP)	Current account (in per-cent of GDP)	Private saving (in per-cent of GDP)	Public saving (in per-cent of GDP)
	Mean	Median	Mean	Mean	Mean	Mean
All countries						
All regimes	−4.3	−3.6	21.8	−3.7	15.9	3.0
Pegged regimes	−4.7	−3.9	22.0	−4.6	14.6	3.7
Intermediate regimes	−3.8	−3.3	22.5	−1.9	19.3	2.2
Floating regimes	−3.7	−2.8	20.0	−3.2	15.3	1.9
Upper- and upper-middle-income countries						
All regimes	−3.3	−2.8	23.6	−1.8	19.3	2.9
Pegged regimes	−3.1	−2.8	25.0	−2.7	18.0	4.8
Intermediate regimes	−3.4	−3.0	22.4	−0.6	21.3	1.1
Floating regimes	−3.6	−2.5	21.4	−1.3	19.4	1.0
Lower- and lower-middle-income countries						
All regimes	−5.1	−4.1	20.5	−5.3	12.9	3.2
Pegged regimes	−5.5	−4.5	20.3	−5.8	12.2	3.1
Intermediate regimes	−4.1	−3.6	22.6	−3.6	16.6	3.7
Floating regimes	−3.7	−3.0	18.7	−5.2	10.9	2.9
Countries without current account restrictions						
All regimes	−3.6	−2.9	22.2	−3.0	16.5	3.2
Pegged regimes	−3.7	−3.0	22.7	−4.3	14.6	4.8
Intermediate regimes	−3.3	−2.9	22.7	−0.6	20.9	1.6
Floating regimes	−3.5	−2.5	20.3	−2.6	16.1	1.9
Countries without capital account restrictions						
All regimes	−3.2	−2.8	22.3	−1.9	18.0	2.4
Pegged regimes	−3.7	−3.3	23.6	−3.8	15.5	3.9
Intermediate regimes	−2.3	−2.8	21.9	0.9	22.1	1.7
Floating regimes	−3.2	−2.4	20.8	−2.4	17.1	1.5
Very open economies						
All regimes	−4.5	−3.7	25.3	−3.9	17.3	4.1
Pegged regimes	−4.8	−3.9	25.8	−4.6	16.6	4.8
Intermediate regimes	−3.3	−3.2	24.2	−0.5	21.6	2.1
Floating regimes	−3.8	−1.8	22.7	−5.7	14.0	3.2
Low central bank turnover rate						
All regimes	−3.3	−3.0	22.7	−3.1	17.7	3.0
Pegged regimes	−3.0	−3.0	23.6	−4.3	16.9	4.7
Intermediate regimes	−3.5	−3.1	23.2	−0.8	20.6	2.1
Floating regimes	−3.9	−2.9	20.1	−4.0	15.7	1.0

Export growth Mean	Trade openness (in percent of GDP) Mean	Private consumption			Nominal effective exchange rate absolute change		Real effective exchange rate absolute change	
		Growth Mean	Volatility (std. dev.) Real	Percent of GDP	1 Month	12 Month	1 Month	12 Month
6.1	70.4	3.3	4.7	2.3	19.4	11.5	21.7	8.4
4.9	76.0	3.3	5.9	2.8	16.3	9.0	21.7	8.2
8.4	70.3	3.3	3.0	1.6	20.7	13.8	18.5	7.6
7.0	56.4	3.3	3.8	2.0	27.5	16.5	26.4	9.9
6.0	79.5	3.2	3.4	1.6	15.4	8.6	14.8	5.7
5.2	95.2	3.8	4.8	2.1	12.0	6.1	13.9	5.3
7.0	79.1	3.0	2.6	1.1	17.3	11.9	13.3	5.4
6.2	51.9	2.5	2.0	1.5	33.3	22.3	33.0	12.2
6.3	62.5	3.3	5.8	3.0	22.5	13.7	27.2	10.4
4.6	64.8	2.9	6.6	3.3	19.0	10.7	26.5	10.0
10.3	56.5	3.8	3.6	2.4	24.6	16.0	24.7	10.1
7.8	61.2	4.1	5.7	2.6	33.3	22.3	33.0	12.2
6.1	78.0	3.4	4.2	2.1	15.9	8.8	17.2	6.6
5.0	88.0	3.7	5.5	2.7	12.6	6.8	16.4	6.1
7.2	83.5	3.4	2.6	1.4	14.1	7.8	13.4	5.1
7.4	56.4	2.9	3.3	1.9	25.1	14.0	23.1	9.1
6.3	85.8	3.1	3.6	1.7	16.8	8.6	16.8	6.3
5.3	124.2	3.7	7.4	2.9	15.4	7.7	16.3	6.1
7.3	100.2	3.4	2.6	1.3	13.9	7.0	13.7	5.1
6.4	53.1	2.6	2.1	1.2	21.0	10.9	20.1	7.4
6.5	118.4	3.7	6.1	3.0	15.4	8.4	17.4	6.3
5.6	119.9	3.9	7.1	3.3	13.1	6.6	16.5	5.9
9.0	125.1	3.6	3.0	2.0	14.2	8.3	14.6	5.8
8.4	97.5	3.3	7.1	3.2	34.7	21.5	28.6	9.8
5.7	78.4	3.5	3.9	2.1	15.1	7.6	16.8	6.3
5.0	86.2	4.0	5.4	2.6	12.1	5.6	15.0	5.1
6.3	87.3	3.1	2.5	1.5	14.3	8.6	14.0	5.9
6.3	55.8	3.3	3.2	2.1	21.7	10.1	23.9	8.9

Table A.4
Basic statistics, concensus classification of exchange rate regimes (in percent per year, unless otherwise specified)

	Number of observations	Inflation			Broad money growth		
		π Mean	π Median	$\pi/(1+\pi)$ Mean	μ Mean	μ Median	$\mu/(1+\mu)$ Mean
All countries							
All regimes	1483	14.2	7.3	9.6	19.5	14.5	13.9
Pegged regimes	1280	9.4	6.9	7.9	15.5	13.7	12.4
Intermediate regimes	103	30.2	11.4	17.2	39.2	18.8	21.5
Floating regimes	100	58.8	21.7	23.0	51.4	26.7	24.7
Upper- and upper-middle-income countries							
All regimes	537	11.5	5.7	8.2	18.9	13.1	13.4
Pegged regimes	442	7.4	5.4	6.4	14.7	13.0	12.0
Intermediate regimes	67	38.4	11.4	19.9	47.9	17.6	23.8
Floating regimes	28	12.8	2.7	8.5	16.2	6.5	11.3
Lower- and lower-middle-income countries							
All regimes	946	15.7	8.7	10.3	19.9	15.6	14.2
Pegged regimes	838	10.5	7.9	8.7	15.9	14.3	12.7
Intermediate regimes	36	14.9	11.9	12.1	22.9	18.9	17.4
Floating regimes	72	76.7	31.2	28.7	65.1	32.5	29.8
Countries without current account restrictions							
All regimes	779	9.9	5.8	7.6	15.8	12.0	12.3
Pegged regimes	663	7.1	5.6	6.3	13.7	11.7	11.3
Intermediate regimes	50	19.9	5.4	12.2	25.0	13.5	16.5
Floating regimes	66	31.0	16.0	18.0	29.5	18.2	19.1
Countries without capital account restrictions							
All regimes	317	9.9	4.2	7.1	16.0	11.6	12.3
Pegged regimes	267	6.3	4.4	5.6	14.0	12.3	11.5
Intermediate regimes	24	17.4	2.3	11.1	20.0	9.4	14.2
Floating regimes	26	39.5	3.8	18.4	33.5	10.2	18.8
Very open economies							
All regimes	651	8.6	6.0	7.2	15.4	13.2	12.3
Pegged regimes	602	7.6	5.7	6.7	14.4	12.8	11.7
Intermediate regimes	27	6.8	5.4	6.1	18.1	17.4	14.9
Floating regimes	22	38.8	26.1	24.2	39.1	30.0	25.0
Low central bank turnover rate							
All regimes	312	14.3	6.0	8.4	21.0	14.1	13.9
Pegged regimes	239	7.2	5.8	6.4	14.8	13.7	12.2
Intermediate regimes	38	13.6	5.6	9.8	19.8	16.4	14.8
Floating regimes	35	63.6	13.6	20.6	65.4	17.2	24.3

| Interest rate | | | | Real GDP growth | | | | |
| Nominal | | Real | | | Std. | HP-filter Std. | Per capita | Per capita |
Mean	Median	Mean	Median	Mean	dev.	dev.	Mean	Median
11.9	7.3	0.3	1.7	3.5	3.4	2.8	1.2	1.6
7.6	7.0	0.4	1.7	3.6	3.5	2.9	1.3	1.6
36.3	14.6	2.8	2.4	4.0	2.3	2.3	2.6	2.7
26.0	18.3	−3.5	1.9	1.0	3.6	2.7	−0.9	0.5
13.4	7.0	1.7	2.6	3.9	3.2	2.6	2.1	2.5
7.1	6.7	1.5	2.6	4.0	3.4	2.8	2.1	2.5
44.9	15.1	3.1	2.1	3.9	2.5	2.2	2.9	3.3
11.8	6.9	1.2	4.0	1.5	2.5	1.7	0.7	1.5
10.9	7.7	−0.7	0.9	3.2	3.5	2.9	0.7	1.0
8.0	7.4	−0.3	0.8	3.4	3.5	3.0	0.9	1.1
16.4	11.0	1.9	3.1	4.2	1.8	2.4	2.1	2.0
32.8	23.3	−5.7	0.4	0.7	4.1	3.1	−1.5	−0.2
10.6	7.3	1.8	3.0	3.4	3.5	2.8	1.1	1.6
8.0	7.0	2.1	3.0	3.6	3.5	2.9	1.2	1.5
20.6	10.8	1.8	3.0	4.4	2.1	2.1	3.3	3.8
22.5	15.6	−0.4	2.5	0.4	4.0	2.9	−1.2	0.6
10.4	7.0	2.2	3.8	3.7	3.7	3.0	1.1	1.5
7.8	7.0	3.1	4.1	3.9	3.8	3.1	1.1	1.5
17.3	5.2	0.6	1.9	4.0	2.1	1.9	3.4	3.2
20.2	7.7	−1.7	3.0	0.5	3.6	3.0	−0.4	1.1
8.5	7.0	1.1	2.5	3.8	3.7	3.0	1.7	2.0
7.5	6.7	1.2	2.4	3.9	3.7	3.0	1.7	1.9
10.6	9.3	3.6	3.1	6.0	1.4	2.6	4.8	4.8
27.4	22.6	−4.9	3.4	−0.7	5.8	3.4	−2.5	−0.3
9.8	7.0	0.4	2.1	3.9	2.9	2.5	2.0	2.0
7.2	6.5	0.9	1.9	4.2	3.0	2.5	2.3	2.1
13.7	10.4	1.1	2.2	4.8	1.8	2.3	3.5	3.6
20.1	17.1	−3.7	3.1	0.5	3.6	2.7	−1.5	0.4

Table A.4
(continued)

	Gov. balance (in percent of GDP)		Gross fixed invest-ment (in per-cent of GDP)	Current account (in per-cent of GDP)	Private saving (in per-cent of GDP)	Public saving (in per-cent of GDP)
	Mean	Median	Mean	Mean	Mean	Mean
All countries						
All regimes	−4.6	−3.8	21.8	−4.4	14.4	3.7
Pegged regimes	−4.8	−3.9	22.1	−4.7	14.3	3.9
Intermediate regimes	−2.4	−2.6	21.7	−2.4	16.9	3.5
Float regimes	−5.0	−3.8	18.3	−3.5	13.3	1.8
Upper- and upper-middle-income countries						
All regimes	−3.5	−2.9	24.7	−2.7	18.2	4.2
Pegged regimes	−3.6	−3.1	25.3	−2.9	17.9	4.7
Intermediate regimes	−1.7	−2.2	21.8	−1.2	19.8	2.4
Float regimes	−5.6	−3.8	21.3	−2.4	19.3	0.8
Lower- and lower-middle-income countries						
All regimes	−5.3	−4.2	20.2	−5.6	11.9	3.4
Pegged regimes	−5.4	−4.3	20.4	−5.8	12.0	3.4
Intermediate regimes	−3.7	−3.5	21.5	−4.5	11.7	5.4
Float regimes	−4.7	−3.8	17.1	−4.1	10.2	2.4
Countries without current account restrictions						
All regimes	−3.7	−2.9	22.3	−4.0	14.8	4.3
Pegged regimes	−3.8	−3.0	22.7	−4.5	14.3	4.8
Intermediate regimes	−1.7	−2.4	22.2	−0.3	20.2	2.9
Float regimes	−4.9	−3.3	18.2	−2.4	14.2	1.4
Countries without capital account restrictions						
All regimes	−3.6	−3.2	23.0	−3.2	16.2	3.2
Pegged regimes	−3.7	−3.7	23.4	−3.9	15.5	3.4
Intermediate regimes	0.2	−2.0	22.4	2.3	21.9	4.4
Float regimes	−5.4	−3.2	19.9	−2.9	16.3	0.8
Very open economies						
All regimes	−4.9	−4.0	25.9	−4.8	16.5	4.3
Pegged regimes	−5.1	−4.2	26.0	−5.1	16.2	4.3
Intermediate regimes	−0.7	−1.7	25.7	0.2	22.1	4.1
Float regimes	−3.9	−2.4	21.6	−4.3	14.2	3.0
Low central bank turnover rate						
All regimes	−3.4	−3.1	23.3	−4.1	16.9	4.1
Pegged regimes	−3.4	−3.2	23.8	−4.8	16.2	4.7
Intermediate regimes	−1.9	−2.3	24.3	−0.6	21.2	3.3
Float regimes	−5.6	−3.8	19.0	−4.3	15.7	1.4

Export growth Mean	Trade openness (in per-cent of GDP) Mean	Private consumption			Nominal effective exchange rate absolute change		Real effective exchange rate absolute change	
		Growth	Volatility (std. dev.)		1 Month	12 Month	1 Month	12 Month
		Mean	Real	Percent of GDP				
5.3	75.1	3.3	5.7	2.8	17.5	9.7	21.5	7.9
4.8	78.2	3.4	6.1	2.9	13.9	6.7	19.3	7.0
7.2	68.9	3.7	3.1	1.9	25.4	17.3	19.5	7.2
8.8	57.2	2.2	5.8	2.8	43.9	29.4	44.9	16.9
5.8	92.5	3.7	4.5	1.9	14.7	7.9	14.8	5.8
5.4	103.0	3.9	5.2	2.0	11.0	5.1	13.2	4.9
7.2	75.0	3.8	3.2	1.4	28.6	20.4	17.8	7.2
7.6	46.8	1.6	2.5	2.4	51.6	36.7	52.8	18.9
4.9	65.0	3.1	6.4	3.3	19.3	10.8	25.9	9.3
4.3	66.0	3.1	6.5	3.4	15.7	7.8	23.2	8.3
7.2	56.8	3.6	2.8	2.8	20.5	12.6	22.3	7.3
9.4	62.0	2.4	7.3	3.0	51.6	36.7	52.8	18.9
5.2	84.9	3.7	5.6	2.7	14.6	7.7	17.5	6.4
4.5	89.3	4.0	6.0	2.8	11.2	5.5	15.1	5.2
7.2	88.6	4.7	2.8	2.1	13.7	7.3	13.9	5.6
9.0	55.7	1.6	5.5	2.7	42.5	24.9	39.7	15.8
4.9	110.5	3.2	6.0	2.3	14.6	7.7	17.5	6.4
4.5	123.9	3.5	7.2	2.8	14.6	7.4	15.5	6.0
8.2	117.2	4.7	2.6	0.8	13.7	5.7	13.0	4.7
5.4	51.7	0.6	3.9	1.5	40.2	26.6	38.8	16.3
5.9	124.9	4.0	7.4	3.5	14.6	7.4	15.5	6.0
5.6	125.4	4.0	7.7	3.6	13.7	5.7	13.0	4.7
9.7	141.1	4.8	2.5	2.5	40.2	26.6	38.8	16.3
8.6	94.6	2.5	10.6	3.8	12.1	5.7	15.6	5.3
5.9	86.3	3.9	5.3	2.4	9.4	4.4	9.3	3.1
5.4	87.7	3.9	5.9	2.7	55.5	33.9	48.2	17.9
6.8	100.7	4.5	2.3	1.1	12.1	5.7	15.6	5.3
7.9	63.4	3.2	5.8	2.8	9.4	4.4	9.3	3.1

Notes

Chapter 1   Introduction

1. See Ghosh et al. (1996, 1997), Ghosh, Gulde, and Wolf (2000), and Gulde (1999). The views expressed in this book are solely those of the authors and should not be interpreted as the views of the IMF, where two of the authors are employed.

Chapter 2   A Short History of the International Monetary System

1. A comprehensive historical account is beyond the scope of this book. Excellent critical histories on which this chapter draws are provided by Hawtrey (1948), Kemmerer (1935), Yeager (1976), Kindleberger (1984), Eichengreen (1996), and Eichengreen and Sussman (2000), among others.

2. The shift itself was more accidental than deliberate. The long shift began in the eighteenth century with the mispricing of silver in terms of gold by Issac Newton (then master of the mint) leading to an incentive for silver exports and shifting England to a de facto gold standard. The transition finally reached critical mass more than a century later after Germany shifted from a silver standard to a gold standard using the gold indemnity it received following the Franco-Prussian war. See Hawtrey (1948), Yeager (1976), Bordo (1999), Bordo and Schwartz (1984), Bayoumi, Eichengreen, and Taylor (1996), Gallarotti (1995), and Eichengreen (1996) for detailed treatments of the classic gold standard. China and some Central American countries were the main exceptions to the shift to the gold standard, retaining silver standards.

3. As Rockoff (1990) observes, *The Wizard of Oz*, perhaps America's favorite children's story, was intended as an allegorical attack on the gold standard.

4. The late nineteenth century was a high point for international monetary conferences, often with widely published essay competitions on monetary issues. See Russell (1898).

5. See Flanders (1989), Bordo and Schwartz (1994), and Eichengreen (1996).

6. Even here, exceptions applied, notably in times of war, though with an implicit understanding that suspensions of convertibility would be temporary, and would always be followed by a resumption at the old parity once the emergency had passed.

7. Confidence crises and the occasional suspension did occur in some of the smaller economies. See Bordo and McDonald (1997) for an exploration of the link between deviations from the rule and credibility.

8. As Yeager (1976) notes, Phineas Fogg, in preparing to travel around the world in eighty days, simply took a bag filled with sterling notes—a choice apparently viewed as quite natural by contemporary French author Jules Verne.

9. Keynes welcomed the idea of divorcing monetary policy from the constraints of the gold standard—but not its inflationary consequences: "Whilst the economists dozed, the academic dream of a hundred years, doffing its cap and gown, clad in paper rags, has crept into the real world by means of the bad fairies—always so much more potent that the good—the wicked Ministers of Finance" (Keynes 1923).

10. The episode also provided the background for Nurkse's (1944) spirited attack against floating rates, a view influential in setting the postwar monetary reform agenda.

11. The threshold amounted to four hundred fine ounces in the case of Britain, giving rise to the term "bullion standard."

12. The degree to which the gold standard contributed to the banking difficulties in several countries, in particular through the adverse balance sheet effects of deflation, remains an issue of debate. See, for example, Bernanke and James (1990).

13. For a diverse set of views by leading monetary economists, see the Festschrift for Irving Fisher (Gayer 1937).

14. Nurkse's (1944) indictment of floating exchange rates is perhaps the best known argument along these lines, though his evidence on the failure of the interwar central banks to "play by the rules" loses some of its power in light of Bloomfield's (1959) finding of a similar pattern under the classic gold standard.

15. As Keynes (1919) put it, perhaps exaggerating slightly: "The inhabitant of London could order by telephone, sipping his morning tea in bed, the various products of the whole earth.... [H]e could at the same moment and by the same means adventure his wealth in the natural resources and new enterprises of any quarter of the world,... he regarded this state of affairs as normal, certain and permanent" (9–10).

16. For evidence on the evolution of capital mobility over time, see Obstfeld and Taylor (1997) and Bordo, Eichengreen, and Kim (1998).

17. See Lutz (1943) for an early comparison of the alternative proposals, Gardner (1956) for an account of the negotiations, Solomon (1982) for a detailed history, and Bordo and Eichengreen (1993) for a retrospective of the Bretton Woods system.

18. While Nurkse's view was widely shared, it was not unanimous. In particular, Gottfried Haberler (1937), in his *Prosperity and Depression*, foreshadowed many of the later arguments in favor of floating rates. Bordo and James (2001) place the two views in historical perspective.

19. Countries were also allowed a one-time devaluation of up to 10 percent without prior consultation with the IMF—an option that the United States was to make use of in 1971.

20. Elasticity pessimism was not universal. The extensive intervention into market mechanisms prompted Milton Friedman (1953), writing for the U.S. Economic Coop-

eration Administration, to advocate abandoning fixed rates rather than convertibility. More flexible regimes, he argued, would ensure automatic adjustment to payments imbalances, allowing countries to reap the gains from trade. His views, however, remained a minority opinion.

21. The return to convertibility was a reluctant concession made in exchange for financial assistance from the United States. The collapse had little to do with price elasticities for U.K. exports: the unilateral return simply created a window of opportunity for holders of sterling balances to obtain scarce dollars, an option they readily availed themselves of.

22. Although 1949 saw a wave of devaluations relative to the dollar, doubts about the efficacy of devaluations remained, as did restrictions on current account convertibility.

23. See Triffin (1957) and Kaplan and Schleiminger (1989). Eichengreen (1993c) provides an assessment of the feasibility of an earlier return to convertibility.

24. In fairness to Keynes, this was precisely the reason why he wanted to create the "bancor." See Balogh (1949) and Kindleberger (1950) for two early analyses.

25. Most adjustments took the form of forced devaluations, implying a U.S. dollar appreciation—further swelling the dollar glut.

26. The Belagio Group (a group of 32 academic economists meeting under the leadership of Fritz Machlup) issued its report "International Monetary Arrangements: The Problem of Choice" in 1964, advocating more flexible exchange rates. See Hahn (1964) and Einzig (1970) for two spirited examples of the debate from opposing camps.

27. In particular, President Johnson's reluctance to raise taxes to finance the Vietnam War, which would have required a vote in Congress and thus, at least implicitly, a vote on the war itself.

28. Furthermore, some central banks—such as the Bundesbank—had been cooperative in agreeing not to convert their dollar balances into gold. A dollar devaluation would ex post vindicate those central banks, including the Banque de France, which had insisted on gold for their dollar balances.

29. Attempts to resuscitate the global system in the form of the Smithsonian agreement fell victim to the reluctance of the United States to subordinate monetary policy to the exchange rate objective and the difficulties in establishing par values in the aftermath of the first oil shock. Institutional preparation for the post–Bretton Woods system began in 1974 with the establishment of the Interim Committee, leading to the de jure acceptance of floating rates in the Second Amendment to the IMF Articles of Agreement in 1978.

30. See James (1996) for an extended history.

31. The United States also participated in largely ill-fated attempts at international macroeconomic policy coordination in the late 1970s, most notably following the London (1978) and Bonn (1979) summits. On the 1985 Plaza Accord and the 1987 Louvre Agreement, see Funabashi (1988), Volcker and Gyohten (1992), and Ghosh and Masson (1994).

32. See Eichengreen and Frieden (2001) for views on the political economy of the process.

33. See De Grauwe (2000).

Chapter 3   The Theory of Exchange Rate Regimes

1. See Nurske (1944), Friedman (1953) and Johnson (1969) for some of the classic discussions. Recent studies include Berger, Jensen, and Schjedlderup (2000), Cooper (1999), Devereux and Engel (1998, 1999), Eichengreen (1994), Flood and Marion (1991), Flood and Rose (1995), Frankel (1999), Gavin et al. (1999), Krugman (1989), Mussa et al. (2000), and Obstfeld (1985, 1995). Studies that focus on developing countries include Argy (1990), Edwards (1989, 1996, 2000), Aghevli, Khan, and Montiel (1991), and Edwards and Savastano (1999). Larrain and Velasco (1999) and Williamson (2000) make the case for floating and intermediate systems, respectively.

2. See Eichengreen (1993a) for an exploration of alternative political economy hypotheses put forward to account for shifts in these norms.

3. Following the Second Amendment to the IMF's Articles of Agreement, Article IV, 2(b) reads: "Under an international monetary system of the kind prevailing on January 1, 1976, exchange arrangements may include (i) the maintenance by a member of a value for its currency in terms of the special drawing right or another denominator, other than gold, selected by the member, or (ii) cooperative arrangements by which members maintain the value of their currencies in relation to the value of the currency or currencies of other members, or (iii) other exchange arrangements of a member's choice." The return to a Bretton Woods–type system is not precluded by the Articles of Agreement, which note that "the Fund may determine, by an eighty-five percent majority of the total voting power, that international economic conditions permit the introduction of a widespread system of exchange arrangements based on stable but adjustable par values" (Article IV, 4b).

4. See, for example, Einzig (1970).

5. See Gavin et al. (1999), Calvo (1999), Calvo and Reinhart (2000a,b), Frankel (1999), Frankel, Schmukler, and Servén (2000b), and Borensztein, Philippon, and Zettelmeyer (2001).

6. See Stein (1962), Fischer (1977), Turnovsky (1976), and Aizenman and Frenkel (1982), among others.

7. Some papers (e.g., Fischer 1977) take the stabilization of real consumption as the objective.

8. There are several possible mechanisms; see Caballero (1991) and, building on Aizenman (1992), Ghosh and Pesenti (1994).

9. For a spirited defense of intermediate regimes, based on these and other considerations, see Williamson (2000).

10. Among the classic studies are McKinnon (1963), Mundell (1961), and Kenen (1969). The classic literature is surveyed in Tower and Willet (1976); a recent treatment focusing more closely on the European case is De Grauwe (2000).

11. As Kenen (1969) pointed out, there is a need for factor mobility between industries, not regions as such, because output in each region is unlikely to be homogenous.

12. See Eichengreen (1990), Blanchard and Katz (1992), and Sala-i-Martin and Sachs (1992). See De Grauwe (2000) for an extensive critical treatment of monetary unification.

13. Eichengreen (1993a) and Frankel and Rose (1998).

14. For the link between trade and the exchange rate regime, see Glick and Wihlborg (1997). To the extent that a pegged exchange rate regime or full monetary union does result in greater trade openness of the economy, the generally well-established link between trade and GDP growth (Edwards 1993b; Frankel and Rose 1999) can be used to take the argument one step further; to wit, countries with pegged exchange rate regimes, a fortiori those that adopt the currency of their major trading partner, should experience higher output growth as well.

15. See Edison and Melvin (1990) and Goldstein (1995) for surveys of this literature; also Bailey and Tavlas (1986), De Grauwe and Bellefroid (1987), and International Monetary Fund (1984). Frankel and Wei (1995) find some evidence of negative effects of exchange rate variability on bilateral trade during the 1960s and 1970s, although not the 1980s. Bacchetta and van Wincoop (2000), using a general equilibrium model, find inconclusive results on the effect of exchange rate stability on trade.

16. These studies include McCallum (1995) and Engel and Rogers (1996, 1998), who find that trade among Canadian provinces is much greater than the corresponding cross-border trade with U.S. states, a finding they attribute to the common currency. On the evidence of common currencies on trade, see Rose (2000). Of course, the choice to adopt a common currency is arguably endogenous to other factors that may also affect trade.

17. For example, the apparent stability of fixed exchange rates does not rule out an expected future step devaluation and is quite consistent with a growing overvaluation hampering export growth (Nilsson and Nilsson 2000), while part of the short-term volatility under floating rates may be hedged through forward and derivative markets.

18. See, for instance, Eichengreen (1992b) and Bayoumi and Eichengreen (1994).

19. Frankel and Rose (1998) find that a positive association between income correlation and trade intensity.

20. As Cukierman (1992) has argued, the particular mechanism of forward-looking wage setters is not essential to the argument. A similar logic applies whenever the central bank has any incentive to create surprise inflation, be it to raise seignorage or to erode the real value of an outstanding stock of nominal debt. De Kock and Grilli (1993) develop a model in which the need to raise seignorage revenue imparts an inflationary bias to the economy; a pegged exchange rate can avoid part of that bias, though the peg may be abandoned at times of exceptional financing needs of the government (e.g., at times of war).

21. See Cukierman, Kiguel, and Liviatan (1992) for an exploration of the link between the strength of commitment and the perceived cost of reneging.

22. The assumption that the rate of monetization depends upon the long-run growth rate of the economy simplifies the model without losing any of its key insights. The assumption that the rate of monetization—rather than the level of money demand—depends on the inflation rate is more unusual but, at least over time spans of twenty to thirty years, seems to be borne out by the data.

23. Recall that we assumed the foreign inflation rate to be constant (and zero).

24. In particular, suppose that the central bank in fact does *not* have an incentive to generate surprise inflation, so that $\bar{y} = 0$. In this case, the Barro-Gordon problem should not arise. Ignoring shocks, output should be at full employment $y = 0$, inflation would be zero, and the central bank would incur no welfare loss, $L = 0$. This outcome may, however, be hard to realize if the central bank cannot persuade the private sector that it is genuinely committed to low inflation—perhaps because of a high inflation past, or because it has just been created and hence lacks a track record. In this case, in forming its expectations the private sector assumes that the central bank will pursue an inflationary policy: $\pi^e = A\theta\bar{y}^e > 0$. The expectation becomes self-fulfilling: given the inflation expectation built into wage demands, the optimal monetary policy from (9) is indeed to pursue a (somewhat) inflationary monetary policy,

$$\pi_{Flt, \bar{y}=0, \bar{y}^e>0} = \frac{A\theta^2(A\theta\bar{y}^e)}{1 + A\theta^2} > 0$$

Output hence falls below full employment,

$$y_{Flt, \bar{y}=0, \bar{y}^e>0} = \frac{-A\theta^2\bar{y}^e}{1 + A\theta^2} < 0$$

and the central bank incurs a welfare loss,

$$L_{Flt, \bar{y}=0, \bar{y}^e>0} = \frac{1}{2}\left\{\frac{A(A\theta^2\bar{y}^e)^2}{(1 + A\theta^2)^2}\right\} > 0$$

The fact that the central bank finds it optimal to have a nonzero inflation rate (after having "promised" zero inflation) is likely to erode its credibility further. On the other hand, being resolute and pursuing a zero inflation policy in the face of imperfect credibility leads to an even greater output decline,

$$y_{\pi=0, \bar{y}=0, \bar{y}^e>0} = -A\theta^2\bar{y}^e < y_{Flt, \bar{y}=0, \bar{y}^e>0} = \frac{-A\theta^2\bar{y}^e}{1 + A\theta^2} < 0$$

25. Klein and Marion (1994) use a trade-off approach to examine the duration of regimes in seventeen countries, and find that both the degree of misalignment, and political and structural factors, are the key determinants.

26. One reason may be that the exchange rate commitment is generally more transparent and can more readily be monitored. Whatever the reasons, it seems clear that a devaluation is politically more traumatic than simply missing a monetary target. In a classic study, Cooper (1971) found that, in 60 percent of cases, a finance minister who presided over a devaluation had lost his job by the following year (and, in 30 percent of cases, the government fell within a year).

27. Our model abstracts from this distinction by focusing on base money. In practice, inflation is likely to respond to much wider money aggregates that are not under perfect control of the monetary authorities.

28. The fiscal limits imposed on members of the European Monetary Union (EMU) under the Growth and Stability Pact illustrate the perceived significance of this concern.

29. See, for instance, Chang and Velasco (2000); there is also a large body of literature on the "twin crises" (currency and banking crises); see Kaminsky and Reinhart (1999), Gupta, Kaminsky, and Reinhart (2002), and Glick and Hutchinson (2001), among others.

30. The literature on balance of payments crises is too large to be covered here; a recent survey is provided by Flood and Marion (1998).

31. For a recent theoretical model of the real effects of a currency crisis, see Aghion, Bacchetta, and Banerjee (2000); for some empirical evidence, see IMF (1998).

Chapter 4   Classifying Exchange Rate Regimes

1. See Calvo and Reinhart (2000a,b) and Haussmann, Panizza, and Stein (2000).

2. See Calvo and Reinhart (2000a,b), Kaminsky and Schmukler (2001), Levy-Yeyati and Sturzenegger (1999), and Poirson (2001).

3. Levy-Yeyati and Sturzenegger (1999) use an endogenous clustering approach combining "similar" observations into groups. Other approaches impose a priori thresholds on a single aggregated de facto score. Neither approach corresponds closely to theoretical concepts (nor does our own de facto classification rule, described in the text).

4. While direct intervention is the more common tool, changes in interest rates or in domestic credit expansion can also be used to affect the exchange rate in the face of shocks and may thus deserve a role in de facto classifications. See Calvo and Reinhart (2000a) for a careful analysis along these lines.

5. See Ghosh (2002) for an analysis of central bank incentives to intervene secretly. Another difficulty with using changes in reserves as a proxy for intervention is that—at typical publication frequencies (monthly or at best weekly)—the data will not capture daily foreign exchange interventions in which the central bank buys foreign exchange on one day and sells the next.

6. In a number of recent exchange rate crises, assumptions of the private sector (and even the IMF) about the true level of usable reserves were later revealed to be spectacularly wrong since the monetary authorities in these countries had engaged in large, off-balance sheet transactions (or had otherwise encumbered their reserves) in the run-up to the crises.

7. While official payments and receipts can be excluded from reserves (Levy-Yeyati and Sturzenegger 1999), other outliers, including bulky trade transactions, are more difficult to allow for.

8. See Ball (1999), Clarida, Gali, and Gertler (2001), Corsetti and Pesenti (2001), Devereux (2000), Hausmann, Panizza, and Stein (2000), Lahiri and Végh (2001), Masson, Savastano, and Sharma (1997), Obstfeld and Rogoff (2000), and Svensson (2000).

9. It is interesting to note in this context that Levy-Yeyati and Sturzenegger (2001a,b), using a de facto measure, find different growth results compared to earlier results of Ghosh et al. (1997a,b) who use the de jure classification, while their results for inflation are more similar.

10. Under the Second Amendment of the IMF's Articles of Agreement, member countries are free to choose their exchange rate regime, but are required to inform the IMF of their choice and to promptly report any changes to their exchange rate arrangements.

11. The appendix provides a more detailed description of the dataset.

12. Intervention frequency is based on assessments on summaries of the implementation of exchange rate regimes contained in annual IMF country documents.

13. The uptick in pegged regimes in 1999 reflects the shift from the EMS system (classified as intermediate) to EMU (classified as a peg).

14. For the G5 countries, we drop their own currency. For the small set of countries reporting a de jure peg vis-à-vis a currency not in this group, we added the currency in question (the South African rand, the Indian rupee, the Spanish peseta, the Australian dollar and the Portuguese escudo) to the search for that particular country. The z-scores are clustered around zero with a long declining right-hand tail peaking at about 1.5 percent per month.

15. As discussed earlier, there is no fully satisfactory way of mapping the continuous score into a discrete classification. Our identification is based on the assumption that the overall frequency distribution of the de jure regimes (given the partial offset between hard floats and soft pegs) is reasonably accurate.

Chapter 5   Facts and Figures

1. Statistics on other macroeconomic variables are provided in the appendix.

2. The appendix provides further details on data sources. While most macroeconomic variables are available for a large set of countries and relatively long time spans, other variables—such as the turnover rate of the central bank governor—are only available on a more limited basis. In chapter 6, we use a subset of observations for which data on *all* of the variables used in the various regressions are available on a consistent basis. This reduces the dataset to 1,762 observations.

3. Evidence of such excess volatility is provided in Ghosh (1998), who terms this phenomenon "the tail wagging the dog."

4. The nominal and real effective exchange rates are calculated by the IMF's Information Notice System, typically from the end of 1979 onward.

5. This restriction forces us to drop the consensus sample for this issue, since there are rather few cases in which the consensus classification remained unchanged over five years, particularly for floating and intermediate regimes.

6. Notice, in particular, that this difference in the drop-off rate across country groups holds only for floating regimes and is not apparent for either pegged or intermediate regimes.

7. The inflation differential at horizon k in year t is the (absolute value of the) percentage change in the consumer price index (CPI) of the home country, relative to the trade-weighted CPIs of its partner countries, over the previous k months (then averaged over the twelve months of year t).

8. In what follows, we refer to this scaled inflation simply as "inflation." This scaled inflation rate incidentally equals the "tax rate" in the standard formula for the inflation tax:

$$ITax = \left(\frac{\pi}{1+\pi}\right)\left(\frac{M}{P}\right)$$

Money growth is scaled analogously.

9. The graph is plotted by calculating the median money growth rate for various subsamples according to the annual money growth rates (i.e., $[0, 2]$, $[2, 5]$, $[5, 7]$, $[7, 10]$, $[10, 15]$, $[15, 20]$, $[20, 30]$, $[30, 40]$, $[40, 50]$, $[50, 70]$, $[70, 100]$ percent per year) and calculating the corresponding median inflation rates.

10. Fatás and Rose (2001) similarly find limited support for fiscal restraint even among extreme regimes (currency unions and dollarized economies), though currency boards do seem to be associated with fiscal restraint.

11. In periods of high inflation, moreover, the computed ex post real interest rate becomes very sensitive to different assumptions about the precise timing and maturity of the instrument.

12. Our income rankings are based on the World Bank's classification of countries as lower- and lower-middle-income countries (referred to as "lower-income countries") and as upper-middle- and upper-income countries. In what follows, upper-middle and upper-income countries are grouped together into a "higher-income" group, unless the difference between them is significant.

13. One potential explanation for the good growth performance under intermediate regimes is the faster growth rate of exports. However, it, too, cannot provide a full explanation of the output growth patterns since export growth was highest under the consensus floating regime—the regime with the worst GDP growth performance.

14. Furthermore, the correlations provide little basis for deriving causal implications. For instance, it may be the case that the floating category of the consensus classification includes countries that are going through economic turmoil—with large exchange rate depreciations being a manifestation of the underlying crisis—so that poor growth performance has little to do with the exchange rate regime itself.

15. See, for example, Baxter and Stockman (1989) and Flood and Marion (1982).

16. Some of the models surveyed in chapter 3 draw a distinction between stabilizing output and stabilizing consumption. In practice, however, these seem to go hand in hand, with greater volatility of consumption growth or the share of consumption in GDP under pegged regimes.

Chapter 6   Inflation, Growth, and the Exchange Rate Regime

1. See Romer (1993) and Lane (1997) for empirical evidence. Bleaney (1999) finds the relationship to be unstable in the 1990s.

2. To control for potential endogeneity, money growth, real GDP growth, and the fiscal balance are instrumented using their lagged values; t-statistics are computed using White heteroskedastic consistent standard errors.

3. The coefficient on money growth is constrained to be equal across regimes. An alternative formulation would allow for a differential impact of money growth on inflation, depending upon the exchange rate regime

$$\pi = \beta_0 + \beta_{Peg}Peg + \beta_{Int}Int + \beta_m^{Peg}Peg \times \Delta m + \beta_m^{Int}Int \times \Delta m + \beta_m^{Flt}Flt \times \Delta m + \cdots + \varepsilon$$

4. We assume that any other determinants of money growth in (2) are uncorrelated with Peg and Int. The standard error of γ_{Peg}, $\mathrm{SE}(\gamma_{Peg})$, is calculated from the variance-covariance matrix of β_{peg} and β_{money}, treating $\overline{\Delta m_{Peg}} - \overline{\Delta m_{Flt}}$ as known, and the reported t-statistic is simply the ratio $\gamma_{Peg}/\mathrm{SE}(\gamma_{Peg})$.

5. Conditional on money growth, the effect of the pegged exchange rate regime is given by β_{Peg}, as before. The unconditional coefficient, however, now becomes $\gamma_{Peg} = \beta_{Peg} + \beta_{Mon}^{Peg}\overline{\Delta m}_{Peg} - \beta_{Mon}^{Flt}\overline{\Delta m}_{Flt}$. Estimating this alternative regression yields $\beta_{Mon}^{Peg} = 0.125$ (t-stat.: 2.89***) and $\beta_{Mon}^{Flt} = 1.00$ (t-stat.: 9.57***); since $\beta_{Mon}^{Peg} < \beta_{Mon}^{Flt}$ the inflation differential in favor of pegged regimes (unconditional on money growth) becomes larger, while the conditional effect, β_{Peg}, remains roughly the same.

6. The consensus sample drops de jure pegs with high exchange rate volatility and de jure floats with low exchange rate volatility. Inasmuch as greater exchange rate volatility is associated with higher average inflation, the consensus sample tends to drop the de jure pegs with the highest and the de jure floats with the lowest inflation rates—thereby widening the estimate inflation differential. Levy-Yeyati and Sturzenegger (2001b), using a de facto classification, find that the inflation advantage of fixed exchange rates derives primarily from durable pegs in low- and moderate-income countries.

7. Optimal regime choice as a function of country characteristics is the subject of a substantial literature of its own. Recent contributions include Berger, Sturm, and de Haan (2000), Edwards (1996), Flood and Marion (1991), Garber and Svensson (1995), Klein and Marion (1994), Obstfeld and Rogoff (1995a,b), Larrain and Velasco (1999), and Poirson (2001), among others.

8. Note that only the coefficients on country size and export concentration are identified, since these variables do not enter the inflation regression. To identify the other coefficients of the semi-reduced form (5) from the estimated fully reduced form (6) would require some additional identifying restrictions.

9. An alternative approach to the issue of regime endogeneity is to compare the performance of countries that switched from floating to pegged regimes: In the three years following the adoption of the peg, median inflation was some 15 percentage points per year lower in countries that switched regimes.

10. While there is a large body of literature claiming a beneficial effect of exchange rate stability for trade, the theoretical link between investment and the exchange rate regime, operating primarily through exchange rate uncertainty, is more ambiguous. See Aizenman (1992), Bell and Campa (1997), Böhm and Funke (2001), Darby et al. (1999), Goldberg (1993), and Wei (1999) for recent analyses.

11. By attributing the entire difference in openness to the exchange rate regime, we might in fact *overestimate* the effect. To allow for other determinants of openness, we estimate a simple gravity model:

$$Open = \alpha_0 + \alpha_{Peg}Peg + \alpha_{Int}Int + \alpha_4 y + \alpha_5 y^* + \varepsilon$$

where y is the country's U.S. dollar value of GDP, and y^* is the (inverse) squared-distance weighted sum of dollar GDPs of all other countries in the world. The coefficient on Peg is very close to the difference in average openness between pegged and floating regimes, while the coefficient on Int is slightly smaller; the "gravity model" coefficients are of the expected signs ($\alpha_4 > 0, \alpha_5 < 0$) and highly significant. Numerically, therefore, using these estimates rather than simple averages makes negligible difference to the implied effect of the exchange rate regime on growth.

12. While the lack of strong results on growth are consistent with the overall tenor of the literature, they provide an interesting contrast to Levy-Yeyati and Sturzenegger (2001b) who, based on a de facto classification, conclude that fixed regimes are

negatively associated with growth for developing, though not for the industrialized, countries.

13. Since country size (population size) is one of the independent variables in the growth regression, it cannot be used as an exclusion restriction.

14. The results are marginally stronger if intermediate regimes are compared to pegs and floats; the coefficient on $\widehat{Int}$ becomes 0.0046 (t-stat.: 1.27) in the de jure classification, and 0.0042 (t-stat.: 1.04) in the consensus classification.

15. In a detailed study, Flood and Rose (1995) find little evidence for a sturdy link between exchange rate regimes and macroeconomic volatility. Rose (1996) examines the issue from a different angle, finding little evidence of regime shifts on volatility.

Chapter 7   Macroeconomic Stabilization and the Exchange Rate Regime

1. See Giavazzi and Giovannini (1989), Kremers (1990), and Rebelo (1993), among others.

2. There is a sizable literature on this topic; comprehensive reviews are undertaken in Marston (1985), Calvo and Végh (1994, 1999), and Rebelo and Végh (1996).

3. The test for the significance of the difference between pegged and floating regimes in the proportion of stabilization attempts that succeed in achieving durable disinflation yields a z-score of 1.18 (p-value 0.12).

4. The results are for inflation in year t_0 (i.e., the first year in which inflation is stabilized), using the de jure classification, and omitting annual dummies to conserve degrees of freedom. Results including years $t_0 - 1$, or the consensus classification (when there are enough observations to undertake the estimation) are generally comparable, and even slightly stronger.

5. Hamann and Prati (2001) further explore the causes underlying this failure of fiscal adjustment—and thus stabilization efforts.

6. A 1996 review of the banking system found that nine out of ten state banks (accounting for more than 80 percent of banking sector assets) had negative capital; while half of the private banks, among them the largest and best known, were technically bankrupt.

7. As a share of GNP, base money declined from over 10 percent in the early 1970s to 6.5 percent by the mid-1980s, and 4.5 percent by 1998. As a result, despite higher inflation rates, seignorage in the 1990s was about the same as it had been in the preceding decade (about 2.5 percent of GNP). In line with the theoretical model of chapter 3, it is worth pointing out that, throughout the period 1975–1998, Turkey maintained some form of floating exchange rate regime.

8. Prior to 1998, there were four major disinflation attempts in Turkey during the 1990s. None of these involved the use of a strong nominal exchange rate anchor.

9. One way of dealing with this problem would have been to progressively reduce the average maturity of the government's outstanding treasury bills. Such a course, however, was deemed too risky, because it could trigger a funding crisis.

10. The absence of a fixed parity, and the decision not to codify the arrangement in the central bank law (as in Bulgaria) but rather publicize it as a commitment under the country's published Letter of Intent to the IMF meant that the exchange rate regime came closer to a traditional (crawling) peg than to a full-fledged currency board arrangement.

11. The IMF-supported program was approved just before Christmas 1999, and the new exchange rate regime began operation in January 2000, by which time yields on treasury bills in the secondary market had already fallen by 25 percentage points.

12. See Kiguel and Liviatan (1991).

13. The government converted all austral denominated debt maturing in 1990 and the bulk of austral denominated time deposits in the banking system into longer term U.S. dollar denominated bonds.

14. Domingo Cavallo, a Harvard-trained economist, argued that the intractability of Argentina's inflation problem reflected the fiscal irresponsibility of its leaders and their proclivity to intervene in the economy. But Cavallo also rejected the pure "monetarist" stabilization programs that had been the vogue of the Southern Cone Latin American countries in the mid-1970s and 1980s, because such programs applied restrictive policies without tackling the root cause of the inflation problem—fiscal ill-discipline. Corrales (1997) provides an excellent account of Cavallo's career and the politics behind the passage of the Convertibility Law.

15. Other supporting measures introduced around the same time included a comprehensive deregulation of the economy (November 1991) and the liberalization of the current and capital accounts of the balance of payments (1992).

16. In particular, part (initially 10 percent, later raised to 20 percent) of the cover of monetary liabilities could be in the form of U.S. dollar denominated short-term Argentinean Government paper, rather than foreign exchange reserves. Moreover, the new central bank charter of 1992 authorized the central bank to purchase government bonds at market prices. Such holdings could account for up to one-third of the money base, subject to a cap on the increase of the central bank's holding of treasury bills of 10 percent per year. The law also allowed the central bank to extend fully collateralized loans to banks for liquidity reasons for up to thirty days and up to the value of the bank's capital. Finally, the Argentine CBA was notable for its reliance on prearranged external credit lines as a partial "privatization" of lender of last resort functions.

17. Nor would it address concerns about the real overvaluation of the currency.

18. The version of the law that was passed by Congress on June 25, 2001, stipulated that the repegging would take place only once the Euro reached parity against the U.S. dollar. The board collapsed before the condition was fulfilled.

19. Percentage increase of the CPI-based trade-weighted real exchange rate between 1991Q1 and the average level in 2001 (*Source:* IMF Information Notice System).

20. Hristov (2002) and Hanke and Schuler (2002) argue that Argentina's real exchange rate was not much overvalued; Sachs and Larrain (1999) argue the opposite; see also Roubini (1998), Powell (2002), and Hausmann and Velasco (2002).

21. For instance, real import growth of goods and services by Argentina's trading partners declined from 5.3 percent in 1998 to −4.4 percent in 1999, although it recovered sharply in 2000 (11 percent) before declining again to 1.8 percent. Between 1991

and 1997, the average growth rate of real imports by Argentina's trading partners was 12.6 percent.

22. A more formal analysis is undertaken by Ghosh (2002), who estimates banking system credit supply and demand functions that explicitly allow for the possibility of credit rationing. In that framework, credit supply is assumed to depend upon banks' lending capacity and the real lending interest rate, while credit demand is assumed to depend upon the real lending interest rate and the level of real GDP. The results suggest that the decline in real credit during the post-1998 period mostly reflected falling credit demand rather than a reduction in credit supply, essentially because of rising interest rates. Accordingly there is little evidence of quantity rationing.

23. As discussed in Thomas (2002), in 1991 the government passed reforms that represented a marginal increase in labor market flexibility by introducing a limited set of fixed term contracts and special training contracts of young workers, but these contracts could only be invoked by agreement with the industry union, and in practice there were few such cases. In 1995, the government, business, and labor union (CGT) agreed to facilitate temporary hiring and more flexible working time for small and medium-sized companies and to cap severance payments. The payroll tax on employers was reduced by 6 percentage points, and a special regime established for small firms that allowed them to avoid making severance payments. In late 1996, the government planned to introduce legislation that would decentralize collective bargaining by allowing wage negotiation at the firm rather than at the industry level; remove clauses in existing contracts (the "ultractividad"); and remove the costly system of severance payments by an unemployment insurance system based on individual accounts. But the draft legislation met considerable opposition by unions and Congress, and in March 1998, the Minister of Labor proposed a much diluted version of the reforms. The new legislation, passed in September 1998, postponed the creation of unemployment insurance and, in some respects, actually made the labor market more rigid.

Chapter 8   Exits and Crises

1. Masson (2001), using a Markov transition matrix approach to examine the dynamics of regime changes for alternative three-way classifications, finds little evidence that extreme regimes are "absorbing states"—that is, regimes from which countries, once entered, do not exit. Our results support Masson's finding for the pure floating exchange rate regime, but not for the hard pegs, which—except for Argentina's exit in 2002, which falls outside our sample—appear to have been absorbent states.

2. Classifying countries according to per capita income yields the same trends. Exits from pegged exchange rate regimes in low-income countries (which tend to have capital controls) are about twice as likely to occur as in upper-income countries (which tend to have greater capital mobility). Indeed, exit ratios are uniformly lower for upper-income countries across regimes.

3. The ability of the Bretton Woods system to survive until the early 1970s, despite mounting strains and difficulties, provides a case in point.

4. The very ability to operate under a peg for some time should have positive reputation effects for the monetary authorities. In addition, economic agents will take account of the (perceived) cost-benefit calculus of the monetary authorities, inherently limiting the degree to which any regime is viewed as permanent.

5. While our sample includes no exits from hard pegs, it is worth noting that the exits from the classic colonial currency boards from the 1940s to the 1960s, typically in the context of achieving political independence, were generally quite uneventful, albeit taking place in an environment of extensive capital controls. See Ghosh, Gulde, and Wolf (2000).

6. See, for example, Eichengreen et al. (1998) and Eichengreen et al. (1999).

7. The literature is too large to cite. Studies with a broad country coverage include Eichengreen, Rose, and Wyplosz (1995) and Frankel and Rose (1996), among others.

8. To be consistent with applicable accounting practices, the valuation effect arising from the difference between the market and the accounting exchange rate would be captured in "other items, net."

9. An example makes this clear. Assume that the central bank has US$100 billion of foreign exchange reserves, 100 billion pesos of monetary liabilities, and a one-to-one coverage ratio, and that both the coverage and market exchange rates are one peso per dollar. Now suppose that the market exchange rate depreciates to 2 pesos per dollar. Evaluated at the market exchange rate, the central bank now has excess coverage. But the coverage rule is evaluated at the coverage exchange rate, so the central bank cannot expand domestic credit or sell pesos for dollars (which would tend to depreciate the exchange rate further). To see this, suppose that the central bank were to sell pesos for dollars at the market exchange rate; then for each dollar purchased, the outstanding stock of pesos would increase by two. Thus a US$10 billion purchase by the central bank would increase the outstanding stock of pesos to 120 billion, while the central bank reserves would increase to US$110 billion, lowering the coverage ratio to 0.91 and thereby violating the coverage rule. Therefore, such intervention would not be permissible. The central bank could, however, intervene in the opposite direction, that is, purchase domestic currency for dollars, thereby tending to appreciate the exchange rate. A sale of US$10 billion would reduce the outstanding stock of peso liabilities by 20 billion, thereby improving the coverage ratio to 1.1. By considering the case of an appreciation of the market exchange rate, it is readily established that this rule allows the central bank to intervene in the foreign exchange markets in a manner that tends to return the market exchange rate toward the coverage exchange rate, but not to intervene in a destabilizing manner.

10. By the same token, however, the central bank would only be able to act as lender of last resort or give credit to the government to the extent that it has excess foreign exchange coverage at the coverage exchange rate.

11. Returning to the Turkish case reviewed in chapter 7, during the prepeg period from 1997–1999 the nominal exchange rate plunged by 90 percent, inflation reached 100 percent per year, public sector deficits exceeded 10 percent of GDP, and growth rates plummeted into negative territory. It would be hard to deny that Turkey was in the midst of a crisis. Yet, the collapse of the nominal exchange rate is barely mentioned in most discussions about the 1997–1999 events. During the November 2000 and February 2001 crises, when the fixed exchange rate regime came under attack, attention was squarely focused on the exchange rate regime.

12. Gupta, Mishra, and Sahay (2001), examining output responses to currency crises for a comprehensive set of developing country data, confirm that large exchange rate changes can be associated with a variety of output responses.

13. The literature has grown very rapidly in the last decade; recent contributions include Aizenmann and Hausmann (2000), Burnside, Eichenbaum, and Rebelo (1999), Gavin et al. (1999), Goldfajn and Olivares (2001), and Krugman (1999), among others. For a different view, see Dooley (1997).

14. The dataset contains 93 "occurrences" of a banking crisis; because crises often span multiple years, the "duration" variable has 303 nonzero observations. Data on banking crises are taken from Alexander et al. (1997) and Glick and Hutchinson (2001).

15. Domaç and Martinez Peria (2000) also find banking crises to occur more frequently under flexible regimes but the cost of crises under fixed exchange rate regimes to be higher.

16. Proportion of observations with a banking crisis, in percent.

Chapter 9   Conclusions

1. Ghosh et al. (1997a,b).

References

Aghevli, Bijan B., Mohsin S. Khan, and Peter J. Montiel, eds. 1991. "Exchange Rate Policy in Developing Countries: Some Analytical Issues." IMF Occasional Paper no. 78. Washington, D.C.: International Monetary Fund.

Aghion, Philippe, Philippe Bacchetta, and Abhijit Banerjee. 2000. "Currency Crises and Monetary Policy in an Economy with Credit Constraints." CEPR Working Paper no. 2529, August.

Aizenman, Joshua. 1992. "Exchange Rate Flexibility, Volatility, and Domestic and Foreign Direct Investment." IMF Staff Papers 39 (December): 890–922.

Aizenman, Joshua. 1994. "Monetary and Real Shocks, Productive Capacity and Exchange Rate Regimes." Economica 61 (November): 407–434.

Aizenman, Joshua, and Jacob Frenkel. 1982. "Aspects of the Optimal Management of Exchange Rates." Journal of International Economics 13: 231–256.

Aizenman, Joshua, and Ricardo Hausmann. 2000. "Exchange Rate Regimes and Financial Market Imperfections." NBER Working Paper no. 7738. Cambridge, Mass.

Alesina, Alberto, and Robert Barro, eds. 2001. Currency Unions. Stanford, Calif.: Hoover Institution Press.

Alexander, William E., Jeffrey M. Davies, Liam P. Ebrill, and Carl-Johan Lindgren. 1997. "Systemic Bank Restructuring and Macroeconomic Policy." Washington, D.C.: International Monetary Fund.

Argy, Victor. 1990. "The Choice of Exchange Rate Regime for a Smaller Economy: A Survey of Some Key Issues." In Choosing an Exchange Rate Regime, ed. Victor Argy and Paul De Grauwe, 6–81. Washington, D.C.: International Monetary Fund.

Bacchetta, Phillipe, and Eric van Wincoop. 2000. "Does Exchange-Rate Stability Increase Trade and Welfare?" American Economic Review 90 (December): 1093–1109.

Bailey, Martin, and George Tavlas. 1986. "Exchange Rate Variability and Trade Performance." Weltwirtschaftliches Archiv 122: 466–477.

Ball, Laurence. 1999. "Policy Rules for Open Economies." In Monetary Policy Rules, ed. John B. Taylor. Chicago: University of Chicago Press.

Balogh, Thomas. 1949. The Dollar Crisis. Oxford: Blackwell.

Barro, Robert, and David Gordon. 1983. "Positive Theory of Monetary Policy in a Natural Rate Model." *Journal of Political Economy* 91: 589–610.

Bartolini, Leonardo. 1996. "Are Exchange Rates Excessively Volatile? And What Does Excessively Volatile Mean, Anyway?" *IMF Staff Papers* 43 (March): 72–96.

Baxter, Marianne, and Alan C. Stockman. 1989. "Business Cycles and the Exchange-Rate System: Some International Evidence." *Journal of Monetary Economics* 23: 377–400.

Bayoumi, Tamim, and Barry Eichengreen. 1994. "One Money or Many? Analyzing the Prospects for Monetary Unification in Various Parts of the World." Princeton Studies in International Finance no. 76. Princeton, N.J.: Princeton University International Finance Section.

Bayoumi, Tamim, and Barry Eichengreen. 1995. "The Stability of the Gold Standard and the Evolution of the International Monetary System." In *Modern Perspectives on the Gold Standard*, ed. Tamim Bayoumi, Barry Eichengreen, and Mark Taylor, 165–188. Cambridge: Cambridge University Press.

Bayoumi, Tamim, Barry Eichengreen, and Mark Taylor, eds. 1996. *Modern Perspectives on the Gold Standard*. Cambridge: Cambridge University Press.

Bell, G., and Jose Campa. 1997. "Irreversible Investments and Volatile Markets." *Review of Economics and Statistics* 79: 79–87.

Berg, Andrew, and Eduardo Borensztein. 2000. "Choice of Exchange Rate Regime and Monetary Target in Highly Dollarized Economies." IMF Working Paper no. 29. Washington, D.C.: International Monetary Fund.

Berger, Helge, Henrik Jensen, and Guttorm Schjelderup. 2000. "To Peg or Not to Peg?" Mimeo., University of Munich.

Berger, Helge, Jan-Egbert Sturm, and Jakob de Haan. 2000. "An Empirical Investigation into Exchange Rate Regime Choice and Exchange Rate Volatility." CESifo Working Paper no. 263. Munich.

Bernanke, Ben, and Harold James. 1990. "The Gold Standard, Deflation, and Financial Crisis in the Great Depression." NBER Working Paper no. 3488. Cambridge, Mass.

Bhandari, Jagdeep, Robert Flood, and Jocelyn Horne. 1989. "Evolution of Exchange Rate Regimes." *IMF Staff Papers* 36: 810–835.

Blanchard, Olivier, and Lawrence Katz. 1992. "Regional Evolutions." *Brookings Papers on Economic Activity* 1: 1–75.

Bleaney, Michael. 1999. "The Disappearing Openness-Inflation Relationship." IMF Working Paper no. 161. Washington, D.C.: International Monetary Fund.

Blinder, Alan. 1998. *Central Banking in Theory and Practice*. Cambridge: The MIT Press.

Bloomfield, Arthur. 1959. *Monetary Policy under the International Gold Standard*. New York: Federal Reserve Bank of New York.

Böhm, Hjalmar, and Michael Funke. 2001. "Does the Nominal Exchange Rate Matter for Investment?" CESifo Working Paper no. 578. Munich.

Bordo, Michael. 1993. "The Bretton Woods International Monetary System: A Historical Overview." In *A Retrospective on the Bretton Woods System*, ed. Michael Bordo and Barry Eichengreen, 3–98. Chicago: University of Chicago Press.

Bordo, Michael. 1999. *The Gold Standard and Related Regimes*. Cambridge: Cambridge University Press.

Bordo, Michael, and Barry Eichengreen. 1997. "Implications of the Great Depression for the Development of the International Monetary System." NBER Working Paper no. 5883. Cambridge, Mass.

Bordo, Michael, and Barry Eichengreen, eds. 1993. *A Retrospective on the Bretton Woods System*. Chicago: University of Chicago Press.

Bordo, Michael, Barry Eichengreen, and Jongwoo Kim. 1998. "Was There Really an Earlier Period of International Financial Integration Comparable to Today?" NBER Working Paper no. 6738. Cambridge, Mass.

Bordo, Michael, and Harold James. 2001. "The Adam Klug Memorial Lecture: Haberler versus Nurkse: The case for floating exchange rates as an alternative to Bretton Woods." NBER Working Paper no. 8545. Cambridge, Mass.

Bordo, Michael, and Ronald MacDonald. 1997. "Violations of the 'Rules of the Game' and the Credibility of the Classical Gold Standard 1880–1914." NBER Working Paper no. 6115. Cambridge, Mass.

Bordo, Michael, and Hugh Rockoff. 1996. "The Gold Standard as a Good Housekeeping Seal of Approval." *Journal of Economic History* 56: 389–428.

Bordo, Michael, and Anna J. Schwartz. 1994. "The Specie Standard as a Contingent Rule: Some Evidence for Core and Peripheral Countries, 1880–1990." NBER Working Paper no. 4860. Cambridge, Mass.

Bordo, Michael, and Anna Schwartz. 1996. "Why Clashes Between Internal and External Stability Goals End in Currency Crises, 1797–1994." NBER Working Paper no. 5710. Cambridge, Mass.

Bordo, Michael, and Anna J. Schwartz, eds. 1984. *A Retrospective on the Classical Gold Standard, 1821–1931*. Chicago: University of Chicago Press.

Borensztein, Eduardo, Thomas Philippon, and Jeromin Zettelmeyer. 2001. "Monetary Independence in Emerging Markets: Does the Exchange Rate Regime Make a Difference?" IMF Working Paper no. 1. Washington, D.C.: International Monetary Fund.

Bruno, Michael, Guido DiTella, Rudi Dornbusch, and Stanley Fisher, eds. 1988. *Inflation Stabilization*. Cambridge: The MIT Press.

Burnside, Craig, Martin Eichenbaum, and Sergio Rebelo. 1999. "Hedging and Financial Fragility in Fixed Exchange Rate Regimes." NBER Working Paper no. 7143. Cambridge, Mass.

Caballero, Ricardo. 1991. "On the Sign of the Investment-Uncertainty Relationship." *American Economic Review* 81: 279–288.

Calvo, Guillermo. 1999. "Fixed Versus Flexible Exchange Rates." Mimeo., University of Maryland.

Calvo, Guillermo, and Carmen Reinhart. 1999. "Capital Flow Reversals, the Exchange Rate Debate, and Dollarization." *Finance and Development* 36 (September): 13–15.

Calvo, Guillermo, and Carmen Reinhart. 2000a. "Fear of Floating." NBER Working Paper no. 7993. Cambridge, Mass.

Calvo, Guillermo, and Carmen Reinhart. 2000b."Fixing for Your Life." NBER Working Paper no. 8006. Cambridge, Mass.

Calvo, Guillermo, and Carlos Végh. 1994. "Inflation Stabilization and Nominal Anchors." *Contemporary Economic Policy* 12 (April): 35–45.

Calvo, Guillermo, and Carlos Végh. 1999. "Inflation Stabilization and BOP Crises in Developing Countries." In *Handbook of Macroeconomics*, ed. John Taylor and Michael Woodford. Amsterdam: North-Holland.

Canzoneri, Mathew B., Robert E. Cumby, and Behzad T. Diba. 1998. "Fiscal Discipline and Exchange Rate Regimes." CEPR Discussion Paper no. 1899. London.

Chang, Roberto, and Andres Velasco. 2000. "Exchange Rate Policy for Developing Countries." *American Economic Review Papers and Proceedings* 90: 71–75.

Clarida, Richard, Jordi Gali, and Mark Gertler. 2001. "Optimal Monetary Policy in Open versus Closed Economies." Mimeo., New York University.

Cooper, Richard. 1971. "Currency Devaluation in Developing Countries." Essays in International Finance no. 86. Princeton, N.J.: Princeton University International Finance Section.

Cooper, Richard. 1999. "Exchange Rate Choices." Harvard Institute of Economic Research Discussion Paper no. 1877. Cambridge, Mass.

Corrales, Javier. 1997. "Why Argentines Followed Cavallo: A Technopol Between Democracy and Economic Reform." In *Technolpols: Freeing Politics and Markets in Latin America in the 1990s*, ed. Jorge Dominguez. University Park: Pennsylvania State University Press.

Corsetti, Giancarlo, and Paolo Pesenti. 2001. "Welfare and Macroeconomic Interdependence." *Quarterly Journal of Economics* 116 (May): 421–445.

Cukierman, Alex. 1992. *Central Bank Strategy, Credibility, and Independence*. Cambridge: The MIT Press.

Cukierman, Alex. 1998. "Does a Higher Sacrifice Ratio Mean That Central Bank Independence Is Excessive?" Mimeo., Tel Aviv University.

Cukierman, Alex, Miguel Kiguel, and Nissan Liviatan. 1992. "How much to commit to an exchange rate rule." World Bank Policy Research Working Paper WPS 931, July.

Cukierman, Alex, Pedro Rodriguez, and Steven B. Webb. 1995. "Central Bank Autonomy and Exchange Rate Regimes." Mimeo., Tilburg University.

Cushman, David. 1983. "The Effects of Real Exchange Rate Risk on International Trade." *Journal of International Economics* (August): 45–63.

Darby, J., A. Hughes Hallett, J. Ireland, and L. Piscitelli. 1999. "The Impact of Exchange Rate Uncertainty on the Level of Investment." *Economic Journal* 109: C55–C67.

De Cecco, Marcello. 1974. *Money and Empire: The International Gold Standard*. London: Blackwell.

De Grauwe, Paul. 2000. *Economics of Monetary Union*, 4th ed. Oxford: Oxford University Press.

De Grauwe, Paul, and Bernard Bellefroid. 1987. "Long-Run Exchange Rate Variability and International Trade." In *Real and Financial Linkages among Open Economies*, ed. Sven Arndt and David Richardson, 193–212. Cambridge: The MIT Press.

De Kock, Gabriel, and Vittorio Grilli. 1993. "Fiscal Policies and the Choice of Exchange Rate Regime." *Economic Journal* 103: 347–358.

Devereux, Michael. 2000. "A simple dynamic general equilibrium model of the trade-off between fixed and floating exchange rates." CEPR Working Paper No. 2403, March.

Devereux, Michael, and Charles Engel. 1998. "Fixed Versus Floating Exchange Rates: How Price Setting Affects the Optimal Choice of Exchange Rate Regime." NBER Working Paper Series no. 6867. Cambridge, Mass.

Devereux, Michael, and Charles Engel. 1999. "The Optimal Choice of Exchange Rate Regime." NBER Working Paper Series no. 6992. Cambridge, Mass.

Dooley, Michael. 1997. "A Model of Crisis in Emerging Markets." *Economic Journal* 100: 256–272.

Dornbusch, Rudiger. 1976. "Expectations and Exchange Rate Dynamics." *Journal of Political Economy* 84 (December): 1161–1176.

Dornbusch, Rudiger, Ilan Goldfajn, and Rodrigo Valdes. 1995. "Currency Crises and Collapses." *Brookings Papers on Economic Activity* 2: 219–295.

Dornbusch, Rudiger, Federico Sturzenegger, and Holger Wolf. 1990. "Extreme Inflation." *Brookings Papers on Economic Activity* 2: 1–84.

Dornbusch, Rudiger, and Holger Wolf. 2001. "Curing a Monetary Overhang: Historical Lessons." In *Money, Capital Mobility and Trade*, ed. Guillermo Calvo, Rudi Dornbusch, and Maurice Obstfeld. Cambridge: The MIT Press.

Dulles, Eleanor Lansing. 1929. *The French Franc 1914–1928*. New York: Macmillan.

Dutton, John. 1984. "The Bank of England and the Rules of the Game under the International Gold Standard." In *A Retrospective on the Classical Gold Standard, 1821–1931*, ed. Michael D. Bordo and Anna J. Schwartz, 173–195. Chicago: University of Chicago Press.

Edison, Hali, and Michael Melvin. 1990. "The Determinants and Implications of the Choice of an Exchange Rate System." In *Monetary Policy for a Volatile Global Economy*, ed. William S. Haruf and D. Willett. Washington, D.C.: American Enterprise Institute.

Edwards, Sebastian. 1989. *Real Exchange Rates, Devaluation, and Adjustment*. Cambridge: The MIT Press.

Edwards, Sebastian. 1993a. "Exchange Rates As Nominal Anchors." *Weltwirtschaftliches Archiv* 129, no. 1: 1–32.

Edwards, Sebastian. 1993b. "Openness, Trade Liberalization, and Growth in Developing Countries." *Journal of Economic Literature* 31 (September): 1358–1393.

Edwards, Sebastian. 1996. "The Determinants of the Choice between Fixed and Flexible Exchange-Rate Regimes." NBER Working Paper no. 5756. Cambridge, Mass.

Edwards, Sebastian. 2000. "Exchange Rate Regimes, Capital Flows and Crisis Prevention." Mimeo., NBER, Cambridge, Mass.

Edwards, Sebastian, and Miguel Savastano. 1999. "Exchange Rates in Emerging Economies: What Do We Know? What Do We Need to Know?" NBER Working Paper no. 7228. Cambridge, Mass.

Eichengreen, Barry. 1990. "One Money for Europe? Lessons of the U.S. Currency Union." *Economic Policy* 10: 118–166.

Eichengreen, Barry. 1992a. *Golden Fetters: The Gold Standard and the Great Depression.* New York: Oxford University Press.

Eichengreen, Barry. 1992b. "Should the Maastricht Treaty Be Saved?" *Princeton Studies in International Finance* no. 74. Princeton, N.J.: Princeton University International Finance Section.

Eichengreen, Barry. 1993a. "The Endogeneity of Exchange Rate Regimes." NBER Working Paper no. 4361. Cambridge, Mass.

Eichengreen, Barry. 1993b. "Epilogue: Three Perspectives on the Bretton Woods System." In *A Retrospective on the Bretton Woods System*, ed. Michael Bordo and Barry Eichengreen, 621–658. Chicago: University of Chicago Press.

Eichengreen, Barry. 1993c. *Reconstructing Europe's Trade and Payments.* Ann Arbor: University of Michigan Press.

Eichengreen, Barry. 1994. *International Monetary Arrangements for the 21st Century.* Washington, D.C.: Brookings Institution.

Eichengreen, Barry. 1996. *Globalizing Capital.* Princeton, N.J.: Princeton University Press.

Eichengreen, Barry, Paul Masson, Hugh Bredenkamp, Barry Johnston, Javier Hamann, Estaban Jadresic, and Inci Ötker. 1998. "Exit Strategies: Policy Options for Countries Seeking Greater Exchange Rate Flexibility." IMF Occasional Paper no. 168. Washington, D.C.: International Monetary Fund.

Eichengreen, Barry, Paul Masson, Miguel Savastano and Sunil Sharma. 1999. *Transition Strategies and Nominal Anchors on the Road to Greater Exchange Rate Flexibility.* Essays in International Finance. Princeton, N.J.: Princeton University International Finance Section.

Eichengreen, Barry, Andrew Rose, and Charles Wyplosz. 1995. "Exchange Market Mayhem: The Antecedents and Aftermath of Speculative Attacks." *Economic Policy* 21 (October): 249–312.

Eichengreen, Barry, and Nathan Sussman. 2000. "The International Monetary System in the Very Long Run." In *World Economic Outlook*, 52–85. Washington, D.C.: International Monetary Fund.

Eichengreen, Barry, and Jeffry Frieden, eds. 2001. *The Political Economy of European Monetary Unification.* Boulder: Westview.

Einzig, Paul. 1970. *The Case against Floating Exchanges.* London: Macmillan.

Engel, Charles, and John Rogers. 1996. "How Wide Is the Border?" *American Economic Review* 86: 1112–1125.

Engel, Charles, and John Rogers. 1998. "Regional Patterns in the Law of One Price: The Roles of Geography vs. Currencies." In *The Regionalization of the World Economy*, ed. Jeffrey Frankel, 153–183. Chicago: University of Chicago Press.

Fatás, Antonio, and Andrew Rose. 2001. "Do Monetary Handcuffs Restrain Leviathan?" *IMF Staff Papers* 47 (Special Issue): 40–61.

Fischer, Stanley. 1977. "Stability and Exchange Rate Systems in a Monetarist Model of the Balance of Payments." In *The Political Economy of Monetary Reform*, ed. Robert Aliber, 59–73. New York: Allanheld, Osmun and Co.

Fischer, Stanley. 1993. "Role of Macroeconomic Factors in Growth." *Journal of Monetary Economics* 32 (December): 485–512.

Fischer, Stanley. 2001. "Exchange Rate Regimes: Is the Bipolar View Correct?" *Journal of Economic Perspectives* 15, no. 2: 3–24.

Flanders, June. 1989. *International Monetary Economics 1870–1960*. Cambridge: Cambridge University Press.

Fleming, Marcus. 1962. "Domestic Financial Policies Under Fixed and Floating Exchange Rates." *IMF Staff Papers* 9 (March): 369–380.

Flood, Robert. 1979. "Capital Mobility and the Choice of Exchange Rate Regime." *International Economic Review* 2: 405–416.

Flood, Robert, and Nancy Marion. 1982. "The Transmission of Disturbances under Alternative Exchange Rate Systems with Optimal Indexation." *Quarterly Journal of Economics* 97: 43–68.

Flood, Robert, and Nancy Marion. 1991. "Exchange Rate Regime Choice." IMF Working Paper no. 90. Washington, D.C.: International Monetary Fund.

Flood, Robert, and Nancy Marion. 1994. "Size and Timing of Devaluations in Capital Controlled Developing Economies." NBER Working Paper no. 4957. Cambridge, Mass.

Flood, Robert, and Nancy Marion. 1998. "Perspectives on the Currency Crisis Literature." IMF Working Paper no. 130. Washington, D.C.: International Monetary Fund.

Flood, Robert, and Andrew K. Rose. 1995. "Fixing Exchange Rates: A Virtual Quest for Fundamentals." *Journal of Monetary Economics* 36: 3–37.

Fontagné, Lionel, and Michael Freudenberg. 1999. "Endogenous Symmetry of Shocks in a Monetary Union." *Open Economies Review* 10 (July) 3: 263–287.

Frankel, Jeffrey. 1999. "No Single Currency Regime is Right for All Countries at All Times." Essays in International Finance no. 215. Princeton, N.J.: Princeton University International Finance Section.

Frankel, Jeffrey, and Andrew Rose. 1995. "Empirical Research on Nominal Exchange Rates." In *Handbook of International Economics*, vol. 3, ed. Gene Grossman and Kenneth Rogoff, 1989–1730. Amsterdam: North-Holland.

Frankel, Jeffrey, and Andrew Rose. 1996. "Currency Crashes In Emerging Markets." *Journal of International Economics* 41: 351–366.

Frankel, Jeffrey, and Andrew Rose. 1998. "The Endogeneity of the Optimum Currency Area Criterion." *Economic Journal* 108 (July): 1009–1025.

Frankel, Jeffrey, and Andrew Rose. 1999. "Does Trade Cause Growth?" *American Economic Review* 89 (June): 379–399.

Frankel, Jeffrey, and Andrew Rose. 2001. "An Estimate of the Effect of Common Currencies on Trade and Income." Kennedy School of Government Faculty Research Working Paper RWP01-013, Kennedy School of Government, Harvard University.

Frankel, Jeffrey, Sergio Schmukler, and Luis Servén. 2000a. "Global Transmission of Interest Rates: Monetary Independence and Currency Regime." Mimeo., World Bank (August).

Frankel, Jeffrey, Sergio Schmukler, and Luis Servén. 2000b. "Verifiability and the Vanishing Intermediate Exchange Rate Regime." NBER Working Paper no. 7901. Cambridge, Mass.

Frankel, Jeffrey, and Shang-Jin Wei. 1995. "Emerging Currency Blocs." In *The International Monetary System: Its Institutions and Its Future*, ed. Hans Genberg, 111–143. Berlin: Springer.

Frenkel, Jacob, Morris Goldstein, and Paul Masson. 1991. "Characteristics of a Successful Exchange Rate System." IMF Occasional Paper no. 82. Washington, D.C.: International Monetary Fund.

Friedman, Milton. 1953. "The Case for Flexible Exchange Rates." In *Essays in Positive Economics*, 157–203. Chicago: University of Chicago Press.

Funabashi, Yoichi. 1988. *Managing the Dollar: From the Plaza to the Louvre*. Washington, D.C.: Institute for International Economics.

Gallarotti, Guilio. 1995. *The Anatomy of an International Monetary Regime: The Classical Gold Standard 1880–1914*. New York: Oxford University Press.

Garber, Peter, and Lars Svensson. 1995. "The Operation and Collapse of Fixed Exchange Rate Regimes." In *Handbook of International Economics*, vol. 3, ed. Gene Grossman and Kenneth Rogoff, 1865–1912. Amsterdam: North-Holland.

Gardner, Richard. 1956. *Sterling-Dollar Diplomacy*. Oxford: Clarendon Press. Reprint, New York: McGraw-Hill, 1969.

Gavin, Michael, Ricardo Hausmann, C. Pages-Serra, and E. Stein. 1999. "Financial Turmoil and the Choice of Exchange Rate Regime." IADB Working Paper Series no. 400. Washington, D.C.

Gayer, Arthur. 1937. *The Lessons of Monetary Experience, Festschrift for Irving Fisher's Seventieth Birthday*. New York: Farrar and Rinehart.

Ghosh, Atish. 1998. "International Capital Mobility amongst the Major Industrialized Countries: Too Little or Too Much?" *Economic Journal* 105: 107–128.

Ghosh, Atish. 2002a. "Central Bank Secrecy in the Foreign Exchange Market." *European Economic Review* 46: 253–272.

Ghosh, Atish. 2002b. "The Role of the Currency Board in Argentina's Crisis." Mimeo., International Monetary Fund.

Ghosh, Atish, Anne-Marie Gulde, Jonathan Ostry, and Holger Wolf. 1997a. "Does the Nominal Exchange Rate Regime Matter?" NBER Working Paper no. 5874, January. Cambridge, Mass.

Ghosh, Atish, Anne-Marie Gulde, Jonathan Ostry, and Holger Wolf. 1997b. "Does the Nominal Exchange Rate Regime Matter For Inflation and Growth?" IMF Economic Issues no. 2. Washington, D.C.: International Monetary Fund.

Ghosh, Atish, Anne-Marie Gulde, and Holger Wolf. 2000. "Currency Boards: More than a Quick Fix?" *Economic Policy* 31 (October): 269–335.

Ghosh, Atish, and Paul Masson. 1994. *Economic Cooperation in an Uncertain World.* Cambridge, Mass.: Blackwell Publishers.

Ghosh, Atish, and Paolo Pesenti. 1994. "International Portfolio Diversification, Non-Tradable Human Wealth and Consumption Growth: Some Puzzles and Interpretations." IGIER Working Paper no. 60. University of Bocconi (Italy).

Giavazzi, Francesco, and Alberto Giovannini. 1989. "The Role of Exchange Rate Regime in Disinflation." In *The European Monetary System*, ed. Francesco Giavazzi, S. Micossi, and Marcus Miller. Cambridge: Cambridge University Press.

Glick, Reuven, and Michael Hutchinson. 2001. "Banking and Currency Crises." In *Financial Crises in Emerging Markets*, ed. Reuven Glick, Ramon Moreno, and Mark Spiegel, 35–69. Cambridge: Cambridge University Press.

Glick, Reuven, and Clas Wihlborg. 1997. "Exchange Rate Regimes and International Trade." In *International Trade and Finance: Essays in Honor of Peter B. Kenen*, ed. Benjamin Cohen, 125–156. Cambridge: Cambridge University Press.

Goldberg, Linda. 1993. "Exchange Rates and Investment in the United States Industry." *Review of Economics and Statistics* 75: 575–588.

Goldfajn, Ilan, and Gino Olivares. 2001. "Can Flexible Exchange Rates Still 'Work' in Financially Open Economies." United Nations Conference on Trade and Development, G-24 discussion papers (international) no. 8: 1–21, January.

Goldfajn, Ilan, and Rodrigo Valdés. 1999. "The Aftermath of Appreciations." *Quarterly Journal of Economics* 114 (February): 229–262.

Goldstein, Morris. 1995. "The Exchange Rate System and the IMF." Policy Analyses in International Economics 39, Institute for International Economics.

Gros, Daniel. 1999. "Who Needs an External Anchor." Mimeo., Centre for European Policy Studies, Brussels.

Gulde, Anne-Marie. 1999. "The Role of the Currency Board in Bulgaria's Stabilization." IMF Policy Discussion Paper 3. Washington, D.C.: International Monetary Fund.

Gupta, P., Graciela Kaminsky, and Carmen Reinhart. 2002. "The Twin Crises: Theory and Evidence." In *Essays in International Finance*. Princeton, N.J.: Princeton University International Finance Section.

Gupta, Poonam, Deepak Mishra, and Ratna Sahay. 2000. "Output Responses during Currency Crises." International Monetary Fund Seminar Series no. 2000-25, 1–45, May.

Haberler, Gottfried. 1937. *Prosperity and Depression.* Geneva: League of Nations.

Hahn, Albert. 1964. *Ein Traktat Über Währungsreform.* Tübingen: Kyklos Verlag and J. C. B. Mohr.

Hamann, Javier. 1999. "Exchange-Rate-Based Stabilization." IMF Working Paper no. WP/99/132, October. Washington, D.C.: International Monetary Fund.

Hamann, Javier, and Alessandro Prati. 2001. "Why Do Many Disinflations Fail?" Paper presented at 2nd IMF Annual Research Conference, Washington, D.C., November.

Hanke, Steven, and Kurt Schuler. 2002. "How to Dollarize in Argentina Now." Available online at ⟨www.cato.org⟩.

Hausman, Ricardo, and Andres Velasco. 2002. "The Argentine Collapse: Hard Money's Soft Underbelly." Paper prepared for the Brookings Institution Trade Conference, May.

Hausmann, Ricardo, Ugo Panizza, and Ernesto Stein. 2000. "Why Do Countries Float the Way They Float?" Mimeo., Inter-American Development Bank.

Hawtrey, R. G. 1948. *The Gold Standard in Theory and Practice*. London: Longmans, Green and Co.

Helpman, Elhanan. 1981. "An Exploration in the Theory of Exchange Rate Regimes." *Journal of Political Economy* 89: 865–890.

Herrendorf, Berthold. 1997. "Importing Credibility through Exchange Rate Pegging." *Economic Journal* 107: 687–694.

Hobson, C. K. 1914. *The Export of Capital*. London: Constable and Co.

Holden, Merle, and Paul Holden. 1981. "Policy Objectives, Country Characteristics and Choice of Exchange Rate Regime." *Rivista Internazionale Di Scienze Economiche E Commerciali* 28 (October): 1001–1014.

Hooper, Peter, and Steven W. Kohlhagen. 1978. "The Effect of Exchange Rate Variability on Prices and Volume of International Trade." *Journal of International Economics* 8: 483–511.

Hristov, Kalin. 2002. "Fundamental Equilibrium Exchange Rates and Currency Boards: Evidence from Argentina and Estonia in the '90s."

International Monetary Fund. 1984. "Exchange Rate Volatility and World Trade," IMF Occasional Paper no. 28. Washington, D.C.: International Monetary Fund.

International Monetary Fund. 1997. "Exchange Rate Arrangements and Economic Performance in Developing Countries." *World Economic Outlook* (October), 78–97. Washington, D.C.: International Monetary Fund.

International Monetary Fund. 1998. "Financial Crises: Characteristics and Indicators of Vulnerability," *World Economic Outlook* (May), 74–97. Washington, D.C.: International Monetary Fund.

James, Harold. 1996. *International Monetary Co-operation since Bretton Woods*. Washington, D.C.: International Monetary Fund, and Oxford: Oxford University Press.

Jardresic, Esteban. 1998. "Macroeconomic Performance under Alternative Exchange Rate Regimes: Does Wage Indexation Matter?" IMF Working Paper no. 118. Washington, D.C.: International Monetary Fund.

Johnson, Harry G. 1969. "The Case for Flexible Exchange Rates." *Federal Reserve Bank of St. Louis Review* 51: 12–24.

Kaminsky, Graciela, and Carmen Reinhart. 1999. "The Twin Crisis." *American Economic Review* 89 (June): 473–500.

Kaminsky, Graciela, and Sergio Schmukler. 2001. "Financial Excesses: Do Exchange Rate Regimes Matter?" Mimeo., George Washington University, Washington, D.C.

Kaplan, Jacob, and Günther Schleiminger. 1989. *The European Payments Union.* Oxford: Clarendon Press.

Kemmerer, Edwin. 1935. *Money.* New York: Macmillan.

Kenen, Peter. 1969. "The Theory of Optimum Currency Areas: An Eclectic View." In Robert A. *Monetary Problems of the International Economy*, ed. Robert A. Mundell and Alexandre Swoboda, 41–60. Chicago: University of Chicago Press.

Kenen, Peter. 2000. "Currency Areas, Policy Domains, and the Institutionalization of Fixed Exchange Rates." Mimeo., Princeton University.

Keynes, John Maynard. 1919. *Economic Consequences of the Peace.* London: Macmillan.

Keynes, John Maynard. 1923. *A Tract on Monetary Reform.* London: Macmillan.

Keynes, John Maynard. 1930. *A Treatise on Money*, 2 vols. London: Macmillan.

Kiguel, Miguel, and Nissan Liviatan. 1991. "Lessons from the Heterodox Stabilization Programs." Working Paper 671, Country Economics Department, World Bank.

Kindleberger, Charles. 1950. *The Dollar Shortage.* New York: John Wiley, and Cambridge: The MIT Press.

Kindleberger, Charles. 1984. *A Financial History of Western Europe.* London: Allen and Unwin.

Klein, L. R. 1987. "The Choices among Alternative Exchange-Rate Regimes." *Journal of Policy Modeling* 9, no. 1: 77–18.

Klein, Michael, and Nancy Marion. 1994. "Explaining the Duration of Exchange Rate Pegs." *Journal of Development Economics* 54, no. 2 (December): 387–404.

Kremers, Jeroen. 1990. "Gaining Policy Credibility for a Disinflation". *IMF Staff Papers* 37 (March): 116–145.

Krugman, Paul. 1989. *Exchange Rate Instability.* Cambridge: The MIT Press.

Krugman, Paul. 1999. "Balance Sheets, the Transfer Problem and Financial Crisis." In *International Finance and Financial Crises*, ed. Peter Isard, Assaf Razin, and Andrew Rose. Boston: Kluwer Academic Publishers.

Lahiri, Amartya, and Carlos Végh. 2001. "Living with the Fear of Floating." NBER Working Paper no. 8391. Cambridge, Mass.

Lane, Philip. 1997. "Inflation in Open Economies." *Journal of International Economics* 42 (May): 327–347.

Larrain, Felipe, and Andres Velasco. 1999. "Exchange Rate Policy for Emerging Markets." Occasional Paper no. 60. Washington, D.C., Group of Thirty.

League of Nations. 1946. *The Course and Control of Inflation.* Geneva: League of Nations.

Levy-Yeyati, Eduardo, and Federico Sturzenegger. 1999. "Classifying Exchange Rate Regimes." Mimeo., Universidad Torcuato Di Tella, Buenos Aires.

Levy-Yeyati, Eduardo, and Federico Sturzenegger. 2001a. "To Float or to Trail?" Mimeo., Universidad Torcuato Di Tella, Buenos Aires.

Levy-Yeyati, Eduardo, and Federico Sturzenegger. 2001b. "Exchange Rate Regimes and Economic Performance." *IMF Staff Papers* 47 (Special Issue): 62–98.

Lutz, Friedrich. 1943. "The Keynes and White Proposals." Essays in International Finance no. 1. Princeton, N.J.: Princeton University International Finance Section.

Maddala, G. S. 1989. *Limited Dependent and Qualitative Variables in Econometrics.* Cambridge: Cambridge University Press.

Marston, Richard. 1985. "Stabilization Policies in Open Economies." In *Handbook of International Economics*, vol. 2, ed. Ronald Jones and Peter Kenen, 859–916. Amsterdam: North-Holland.

Masson, Paul. 2001. "Exchange Rate Regime Transitions." *Journal of Development Economics* 6: 571–586.

Masson, Paul, Miguel Savastano, and Sunil Sharma. 1997. "The Scope for Inflation Targeting in Developing Countries." IMF Working Paper no. 130. Washington, D.C.: International Monetary Fund.

McCallum, John. 1995. "National Borders Matter: Canada–U.S. Regional Trade Patterns." *American Economic Review* 85 (June): 615–623.

McKinnon, Ronald. 1963. "Optimum Currency Areas." *American Economic Review* 53: 717–725.

Meltzer, Alan (Chair). 2000. Report of the International Financial Institution Advisory Commission, submitted to the U.S. Congress and U.S. Department of the Treasury, March 8.

Mitchell, Brian. 1991. *International Historical Statistics, Europe 1750–1993.* London: Macmillan Reference, and New York: NY Stockton Press.

Moalla-Fetini, Rakia. 1999. "Turkey Article IV Consultation." Selected Issues Paper. Washington, D.C.: International Monetary Fund.

Mundell, R. 1961. "A Theory of Optimum Currency Areas." *American Economic Review* 51: 657–665.

Mundell, Robert. 1962. "The Appropriate Use of Monetary and Fiscal Policy for Internal and External Balance." *IMF Staff Papers* 29: 70–79.

Mundell, Robert. 1963. "Capital Mobility and Stabilization Policy under Fixed and Flexible Exchange Rates." *Canadian Journal of Economics and Political Science* 29 (November): 475–485.

Mundell, Robert. 1977. "Concluding Remarks." In *The New International Monetary System*, ed. Robert Mundell and Jacques Polak, 237–244. New York: Columbia University Press.

Mussa, Michael. 1986. "Nominal Exchange Rate Regimes and the Behavior of Real Exchange Rates, Evidence and Implications." In *Real Business Cycles, Real Exchange Rates and Actual Policies*, ed. Karl Brunner and Alan Meltzer, 117–214. Amsterdam: North-Holland.

Mussa, Michael, Paul Masson, Alexander Swoboda, Estaban Jadresic, Paolo Mauro, and Andrew Berg. 2000. "Exchange Rate Regimes in an Increasingly Integrated World

Economy." IMF Occasional Paper no. 193. Washington, D.C.: International Monetary Fund.

Nacimento, Jean-Claude. 1987. "Choice of an Optimum Exchange Currency Regime for a Small Economy: An Econometric Analysis." *Journal of Development Economics* 25 (February): 149–165.

Nilsson, Kristian, and Lars Nilsson. 2000. "Exchange Rate Regimes and Export Performance of Developing Countries." *World Economy* 23, no. 3 (March): 331–349.

Nurkse, Ragnar. 1944. *International Currency Experience*. Geneva: League of Nations.

Obstfeld, Maurice. 1985. "Floating Exchange Rates: Experience and Prospects." *Brookings Papers on Economic Activity* 2: 369–450.

Obstfeld, Maurice. 1994. "The Logic of Currency Crisis." *Banque de France, Cahiers Economiques et Monetaires*, no. 34: 189–213.

Obstfeld, Maurice. 1995. "International Currency Experience: New Lessons Relearned." *Brookings Papers on Economic Activity* 1: 119–211.

Obstfeld, Maurice, and Kenneth Rogoff. 1995a. "Exchange Rate Dynamics Redux." *Journal of Political Economy* 103: 624–660.

Obstfeld, Maurice, and Kenneth Rogoff. 1995b. "Mirage of Fixed Exchange Rates." *Journal of Economic Perspectives* 9 (Fall): 73–96.

Obstfeld, Maurice, and Kenneth Rogoff. 2000. "New Directions for Stochastic Economy Models." *Journal of International Economics* (February): 117–154.

Obstfeld, Maurice, and Alan Taylor. 1997. "The Great Depression as a Watershed: International Capital Mobility over the Long Run." In *The Defining Moment: The American Economy in the Twentieth Century*, ed. Michael Bordo, Claudia Goldin, and Eugene White, 353–402. Chicago: University of Chicago Press.

Poirson, Hélène. 2001. "How Do Countries Choose Their Exchange Rate Regime?" IMF Working Paper no. 46. Washington, D.C.: International Monetary Fund.

Posen, Adam. 1998. "Central Bank Independence and Disinflationary Credibility." *Oxford University Papers* 50: 335–359.

Powell, Andrew. 2002. "The Argentine Crisis: Bad Luck, Bad Economics, Bad Politics, Bad Advice?" Paper prepared for the Brookings Institution Trade Conference, May.

Quirk, Peter. 1994. "Fixed or Floating Exchange Regimes: Does It Matter for Inflation?" IMF Working Paper no. 134. Washington, D.C.: International Monetary Fund.

Rebelo, Sergio. 1993. "Inflation in Fixed Exchange Rate Regimes." In *Adjustment and Growth in the European Monetary Union*, ed. F. Torres and F. Giavazzi, 128–149. Cambridge: Cambridge University Press.

Rebelo, Sergio and Carlos Végh. 1996. "Real Effects of Exchange Rate Based Stabilization." In *NBER Macroeconomics Annual*, ed. Ben Bernanke and Julio Rotemberg, 125–174. Cambridge: The MIT Press.

Rist, Charles. 1925. *Die Deflation*. Berlin: Julius Springer.

Rockoff, Hugh. 1990. "'The Wizard of Oz' as a Monetary Allegory." *Journal of Political Economy* 98 (August): 739–760.

Rogoff, Kenneth. 1985. "The Optimal Degree of Commitment to an Intermediate Target." *Quarterly Journal of Economics* 100: 1169–1190.

Romer, David. 1993. "Openness and Inflation: Theory and Evidence." *Quarterly Journal of Economics* 108: 869–903.

Rose, Andrew. 1996. "After the Deluge: Do Fixed Exchange Rates Allow Intertemporal Volatility Tradeoffs?" *International Journal of Finance and Economics* 1 (January): 47–54.

Rose, Andrew. 2000. "One Money, One Market? The Effect of Common Currencies on International Trade." *Economic Policy* 30 (April): 9–45.

Roubini, Nouriel. 1998. "The Case against Currency Boards: Debunking 10 Myths about Benefits of Currency Boards." Available online at ⟨www.stern.nyu.edu/~nroubini⟩.

Russell, Henry. 1898. *International Monetary Conferences*. New York: Harper and Brothers.

Sachs, Jeffrey, and Felipe Larrain. 1999. "Why Dollarization Is More Straightjacket than Salvation." *Foreign Policy* 116 (Fall): 80–93.

Sala-i-Martin, Xavier, and Jeffrey Sachs. 1992. "Fiscal Federalism and Optimum Currency Areas: Evidence for Europe from the United States." In *Establishing a Central Bank: Issues in Europe and Lessons From the U.S.*, ed. Mathew Canzoneri, Vittorio Grilli, and Paul Masson, 195–219. Cambridge: Cambridge University Press.

Savvides, Andreas. 1990. "Real Exchange Rate Variability and the Choice of Exchange Rate Regime by Developing Countries." *Journal of International Money and Finance* 9: 440–454.

Siklos, Pierre. 1994. "Varieties of Monetary Reform." IMF Working Paper no. 57.

Stein, Jerome. 1962. "The Nature and Efficiency of the Foreign Exchange Market." Princeton Essays in International Finance no. 40. Princeton, N.J.: Princeton University International Finance Section.

Stockman, Alan. 1983. "Real Exchange Rates under Alternative Nominal Exchange Rate Systems." *Journal of International Money and Finance* 2: 147–166.

Summers, Lawrence. 2000. "International Financial Crisis." *American Economic Review Papers and Proceedings* 90 (May): 1–16.

Svensson, Lars. 1994. "Fixed Exchange Rates as a Means to Price Stability: What Have We Learned?" *European Economic Review* 38 (May): 447–468.

Svensson, Lars. 2000. "Open-Economy Inflation Targeting." *Journal of International Economics* 50: 155–183.

Thomas, Alun. 2002. "Notes on Argentina's Crisis." Mimeo., International Monetary Fund.

Tornell, Aaron, and Andrés Velasco. 1995. "Fiscal Discipline and the Choice of Exchange Rate Regime." *European Economic Review* 39 (April): 759–770.

Tornell, Aaron, and Andrés Velasco. 2000. "Fixed versus Flexible Exchange Rates: Which Provides More Fiscal Discipline?" *Journal of Monetary Economics* 45 (April): 399–436.

Tower, Edward, and Thomas D. Willet. 1976. "The Theory of Optimal Currency Areas and Exchange Rate Flexibility." Princeton Special Papers in International Economics no. 11. Princeton, N.J.: Princeton University International Finance Section.

Triffin, Robert. 1957. *Europe and the Money Muddle*. New Haven: Yale University Press.

Triffin, Robert. 1960. *Gold and the Dollar Crisis*. New Haven: Yale University Press.

Turnovsky, Stephen. 1976. "The Relative Stability of Alternative Exchange Rate Systems in the Presence of Random Disturbances." *Journal of Money, Credit and Banking* 8, no. 1: 29–50.

Volcker, Paul, and Toyoo Gyohten. 1992. *Changing Fortunes*. New York: Times Books.

Von Glahn, Richard. 1996. *Fountain of Fortune*. Berkeley: University of California Press.

Wei, Shang-Jin. 1999. "Currency Hedging and Goods Trade." *European Economic Review* 43 (June): 1371–1394.

Williamson, John. 1982. "Survey of the Literature on the Optimal Peg." *Journal of Development Economics* 11 (August): 39–61.

Williamson, John. 2000. *Exchange Rate Regimes for Emerging Markets*. Washington, D.C.: Institute for International Economics.

Woodford, Michael. 1994. "Monetary Policy and Price Level Determinacy in a Cash in Advance Economy." *Economic Theory* 4: 345–380.

Yeager, Roland. 1976. *International Monetary Relations*. New York: Harper and Row.

Index